Architecture,
Aesth/Ethics
and
Religion

ARCHITECTURE, AESTH/ETHICS & RELIGION

Sigurd Bergmann
(ed.)

IKO – Verlag für Interkulturelle Kommunikation

Bibliographische Information der Deutschen Bibliothek
Die Deutsche Bibliothek verzeichnet diese Publikation in der Deutschen
Nationalbibliographie; detaillierte bibliographische Daten sind im Internet über
http://dnb.ddb.de abrufbar.

©   IKO-Verlag für Interkulturelle Kommunikation
      Frankfurt am Main • London, 2005

      Frankfurt am Main   London
      Postfach 90 04 21   70 c, Wrentham Avenue
      D - 60444 Frankfurt   London NW10 3HG, UK

      e-mail: info@iko-verlag.de • Internet: www.iko-verlag.de

      ISBN: 3-88939-749-2

Cover photographs:
Trinity Uniting Church, Perth, Western Australia, photo: S. Bergmann.
Housing in Potsdam, photo: S. Bergmann.
The National Museum of Australia, Canberra, photo: S. Bergmann.
Gunilla Bandolin, *Observatory*, 2002, Sickla Udde, Stockholm, photo: G. Bandolin.
The Esplanade, Perth, Western Australia, photo: S. Bergmann.
Cottesloe Beach and the Indiana Tea Room, Cottesloe, Western Australia,
      photo: S. Bergmann.

Form, cover and lay-out: Ingela Bergmann, Trondheim, Norway.
Printed by: Druckerei Hubert & Co, 37079 Göttingen

Contents

7   PREFACE
Sigurd Bergmann

Perspectives

13   BEAUTIFUL, TRUE AND GOOD ARCHITECTURE
An introduction
Birgit Cold

20   ARCHITECTURE AND RELIGION IN SECULARIZED TIMES
Eivind Kasa

39   PLACE IN SCULPTURE
Gunilla Bandolin

45   SPACE AND SPIRIT
Towards a theology of inhabitation
Sigurd Bergmann

104   ETHICS OR AESTHETICS IN ARCHITECTURE
Gernot Böhme

114   HABITABILITY AS A DEEP AESTHETIC VALUE
Pauline von Bonsdorff

131   HOUSING SIX BILLION
A theological plea for the vernacular
Tim Gorringe

Ongoing Research

149   ETHICS, AESTHETICS AND URBAN WELFARE
Tom Nielsen

159   SEA-ING SPIRIT
Ecotheology and a coastal sense of place
Nancy M. Victorin-Vangerud

187   SPIRITUAL EXPERIENCE
Christiane Johannsen

199   CLASSICISM, HISTORICISM AND MODERNISM
Architectural concepts as a gateway to Norwegian cultural debate 1920-30
Per Anders Aas

206   FUSING THE SACRED WITH TECHNOLOGY
The virtual basilica of St. Francis in Assisi
Daniel T. Michaels

220   PRAYERBALLS
Art objects for prayer and meditation in the dialogue between Christianity and Zen-Buddhism
Grete Refsum

227   The Authors

Preface

Are there connections between technology, aesthetics, ethics and religion? How are science and religion related to each other? How do we perceive and depict these interconnections by means of architecture?

How can the significance of aesthetics for the well-being of people in built environments be investigated? How can we improve and deepen the connections between aesthetics, ethics and religion in architecture, technology and science? How can we transform space in technology and science so as to allow life to flourish? What about the spirituality of space and place?

Does the cultural relevance of architecture entail an embodiment of ethical issues? How are religious life-views manifested in the design, building and habitation of houses? How are the buildings of past and future generations connected historically, and what implications does such a connection have with regard to the ethical challenges we confront? Do we really need "less aesthetics, more ethics" (La Biennale di Venezia 2000)?

What is the significance of built space for the experience of the God of the Here-and-Now? How does God act spatially? What are the implications of architecture in the context of global economism for believers who are trying to be faithful to the choice of "God or mammon" and to opt for the God of Life?

What can an intensified cross-disciplinary discourse on architecture, aesthetics, ethics and religion contribute to ongoing practical discourses as well as to social transformations in an age subsequent to late modernity?

Problems such as these have often been neglected in academic discourses and in more practical public debates in both the Natural Sciences and Technology, as well as in Religious Studies and the Humanities. There are many good reasons why we need to close the gap between scientific and the non-scientific cultures, and to break down the compartmentalisation of disciplines.

The human need for built environments is as existential as the need of ecological, moral, spiritual and religious orientation. The "ethical function of architecture" has to be investigated further, especially with regard to late modernity's ecological, intercultural and interreligious challenges, as well as to the increasing gap between the many poor and the few rich of this world.

The one-dimensional focus of the human sciences – favouring time at the expense of space – must be criticised and overcome. Reductionist assumptions and technologically oriented ideologies must be subjected to critical scrutiny. Built spaces encourage us to look for syntheses and varied connections between traditionally separate spheres: aesthetics/ethics, nature/mind, body/soul, God/world, social life in change and in continuity.

The authors of this anthology explore the discursive space of questions such as these. Their contributions invite the reader to share experiences, problems, perspectives, conceptualisations and inventions within and between the interspaces of the theme expressed in our title: architecture, aesthetics, ethics and religion.

In a preliminary section seven many-faceted contributions to the theme are offered from architectural, artistic, philosophical and theological perspectives. Insights into six ongoing research projects of relevance to the interdisciplinary field are proposed in the succeeding second section.

Birgit Cold reconstructs the classical connectedness of the beautiful, the true and the good in architecture. Eivind Kasa interprets significant developments in contemporary architecture in relation to secularisation and the creative expressions of spirituality found in minimalist architecture. The art-works of Gunilla Bandolin present us with sculptures that explore the mystery of place. Sigurd Bergmann invites readers to meander through several areas of the theme, and concludes with a plea for an intensified theology of inhabitation. The relationship of ethics and aesthetics in architecture is considered by Gernot Böhme in a creatively phenomenological contribution that relates architecture to the dramatic arts, and Pauline von Bonsdorff develops the notion of habitability as a central value within fundamental aesthetics. Tim Gorringe concludes by highlighting the ethical challenge to both architects and theologians in a plea for the vernacular in the context of global injustice.

Philosophical perspectives on the problems outlined above are discussed using points of departure provided by Plato, Kierkegaard and Hegel, while architectural insights are formulated in relation to the construction of, movement within, and use of architect-designed buildings. Theological perspectives are developed with regard to the experience of God in the buildings themselves, as well as to the ideology they express. Ethical reflections relate as much to issues of aesthetic design as to problems of social justice in the context of an escalating globalisation that lacks any human or ecological goal. Constructive arguments are developed for a common area of study that includes both architecture and religion, while critical arguments are formulated for the normative evaluation of contemporary architecture. Christian as well as interreligious dimensions are explored. Notions such as "well-being", "spirituality", "atmosphere", "vernacular", "habitability", "inhabitation" and a "critique of the aestheticizing of the economy" become visible as "roofs" for those forthcoming houses that are to be built in the planned transdisciplinary "city" of this book. The reader who expects a study of church or sacred architecture will be disappointed. In the initial stage of our developing co-operation we have decided to concentrate on so-called non-sacred architecture, in order to provide as wide as possible a context, one that also includes theological hermeneutics and aesthetics.

An interesting experience of the symposium out of which this collection springs was that the non-theologians emphasised the importance of the continued study of sacred architecture, while the participating theologians felt a pressing need to maintain open minds, and to leave room for the perception of buildings representative of all kinds of human expression. Is it possible that, as a point of departure for future reflection, we can reach agreement that the sacred has to be sought and built in whatever furthers the flourishing of the living in their diversity and wholeness? Some fruitful reflection might be encouraged in response to the question of what architecture in general can learn from sacred architecture, and what secular architecture might teach the churches. How can the life-giving Spirit become visible in both sacred and secular architecture? Could a theologically enlightened architecture contribute to the spatial transformation of a world system in crisis?

All the contributions in this anthology have their origin in an international symposium with the same title as this book. The symposium took place in Trondheim, Norway, on the 11th and 12th of May 2001, and was jointly arranged by the Department of Religious Studies at the Faculty of Arts, and the Department of Architectural Design at the Faculty of Architecture at the Norwegian University of Science and Technology (NTNU), Trondheim. The symposium was arranged in co-operation with The Center for Theology and the Natural Sciences' (CTNS) Course Program in Europe, and the Norwegian Academy of Technological Sciences (NTVA), Trondheim. 32 participants from 10 countries in Eastern and Western Europe, the United States and Australia and from different academic disciplines including Architecture, Religious and Christian Studies, Philosophy, Visual Arts, and Art History met for two intensive days at Lerchendal Gård, a magnificent manor house dating from 1762. Further discussion took place during an excursion on the Trondheim fjord, and in the Gothic Cathedral in Trondheim.

My acknowledgements are due to all those who participated in discussions that were notable for their display of sensitivity and open-mindedness, and also to those who shared their commitment to the problematic issues under debate by means of an intense and fervent correspondence. Without the encouragement provided by the interaction with my colleagues Birgit Cold and Eivind Kasa, an interaction that became increasingly profound in the course of time, neither the symposium nor the book would have been possible. The Faculty of Architecture has contributed to the book's production by means of a generous subsidy. While Silja König carefully translated Gernot Böhme's contribution, Bjørg and Jeremy Hawthorn and Barbara Lindbak have sensitively transformed the whole manuscript into readable English.

Space is the primary condition of life. I regard it as the Creator's gift to the living. For our spatial life on blue planet Earth we human beings need houses. Built spaces in different places are required for our human artistic capacity to flourish. In order to develop a just well-being, one that allows us to be at peace with one other in natural surroundings, we need good architecture. Architecture as a microcosm of the sciences and the whole culture of knowledge itself needs the resources of both technology and the humanities. Religiosity, faith and spirituality characterise human beings, as do reflexivity, artistic creativity, and practical competence of many kinds. I would like to hand over this anthology to the reader in the hope that the synthetic reflections of its authors may contribute to the healing of some of the damage caused by the all-too-long separation of architecture, aesthetics, ethics and religion.

Sigurd Bergmann, Trondheim, Lent 2002

Perspectives

BEAUTIFUL, TRUE AND GOOD ARCHITECTURE
An introduction

BIRGIT COLD

Being an architect my approach to this multifaceted subject of the symposium is environmental aesthetics-ethics including architecture. My reflections on religion related to these areas of the subject are searching and stem from my curious mind hoping to learn more from you.

When Sigurd Bergmann asked me if I would participate in this dialogue, my first reaction to the subject was that architecture is already an interdisciplinary field including elements of the natural and social sciences, humanities, technology and the fine arts, and following this train of thought: is it really "necessary" to include religion as well?! My next thought was that throughout history architecture has included buildings and places with the purpose of worshipping the Divine or God and the following thought concerned the concept of "the spirit of place" – Genius Loci. Then the total idea behind the subject no longer felt so foreign to me (figure 1).

I would like to follow up the concept of place with the definition of "place identity" by Canter (1977). He describes the identity of place as the interrelation between the physical attributes, the activities and our conceptions of who, how, what and where. This means: who we are going to meet in the place, how it is going to look, what is going to happen there and where the different activities are going to take place. "The spirit of a place", in

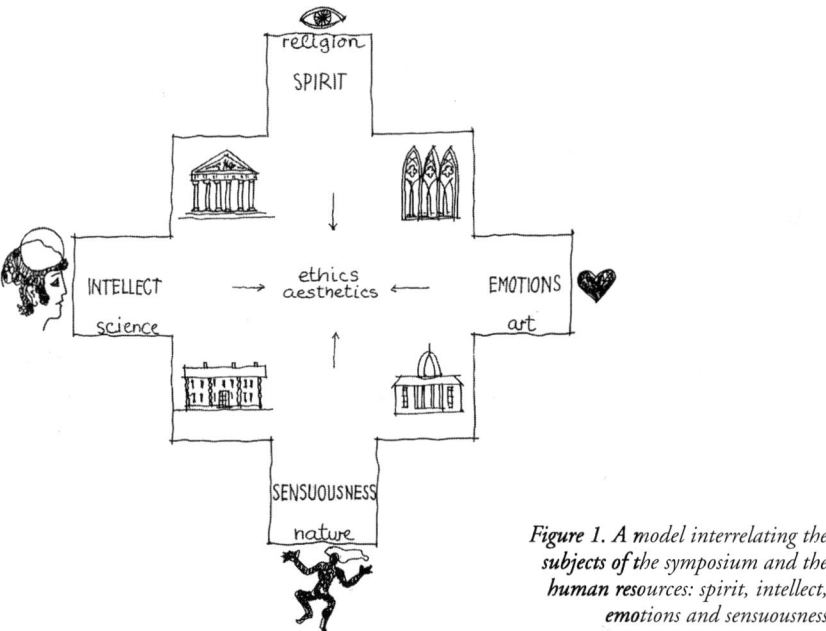

Figure 1. A model interrelating the subjects of the symposium and the human resources: spirit, intellect, emotions and sensuousness

this concept of place identity, is dependent on people's spiritual orientation and sensibility, their conscious and subconscious awareness on activities and behaviour and the architecture and how they interact in both a spiritually stimulating, challenging or harmoniously soothing way.

We have experienced that natural environments, places and architecture offering aesthetic-sensuous experiences in a wide scale may have an indefinable, impressive, spiritual or religious effect on us. Are these then combined with culturally determined ceremonies or dramatic, natural phenomena they may give us a religious effect. The sound of drums, music, singing, thunder or waves, the smell of incense, flowers or the sea, the vision of candle light, moonlight, stars, a ray of sun through darkness, gold and ornaments celebrating the divine, movement with repeated rhythms, colourful processions, and solemn ceremonies, tactile touch or even bodily suffering with symbolic purposes; these aesthetic qualities perceived by our senses and interpreted both on a conscious and subconscious level may be essential for our mental, emotional and spiritual lives.

Throughout history aesthetics has been dressed in different concepts and definitions. Three main areas of aesthetic knowledge can be described:
- knowledge which derives through the senses of things perceivable (the original Greek meaning),
- knowledge of the nature of beauty (aesthetics defined as one of three normative disciplines by Baumgarten, 1750),
- knowledge of theories of criticism within the arts.

This wide definition of the concept aesthetics offers an interesting and wider approach to the interplay between the elements within the subjects of this book, than a pure philosophic-theoretical, artistic or an everyday "nice or ugly, good or bad" assessment.

When trying to grasp the spirit of a place we may ask if it is recognisable in its architecture or if it is in our minds and "disappears" when we leave the place. I believe in a model of interaction, that certain attributes or qualities in the environment and in architecture may communicate in an aesthetically-ethically supportive way with activities of a physical, psychological, social and spiritual nature and vice versa. Meaning that our conceptions of "the spirit of a place" are influenced both by cultural knowledge and individual experience of spiritually impressive environments and architecture.

Within the field of environmental psychology there is a hypothesis, that certain environmental qualities, either real or symbolic, are perceived directly with a minimum of cultural-cognitive or individual-experiential control and thus can be understood as cross-cultural and related to mankind's evolutionary history. In a framework for predictors of preference the American psychologist Steven Kaplan (1987) describes two pairs of main qualities of an environment suitable for survival of early man: coherence and legibility which enabled man immediately to understand and further predict an environmentally adequate behaviour, and complexity and "mystery" which challenged man to explore and learn more about the environment in order to survive.

Can the conception or idea of "the spirit of place" originate from the limitation of the rational and emotional needs to understand and explore the environment? Is spirituality a non-definable abstract human longing of a connecting force between one self, nature and the universe? I imagine that the feeling of being "centre of the world" and at the same time a very small human sand corn in the universe, makes us insecure and afraid, and at the same time curious and deeply moved of the unknown in ourselves and the unknown out there. We may ask if man has found its "relief" in creating spiritually beautiful, true and good places in order to worship the creator of the unknown and the known and thus comfort our souls? In religion the unknown is interpreted as the Divine or God, the creator of everything known as well as unknown.

When studying architectural history and architectural styles in an attempt to characterise the experienced qualities I have sketched models to help me keep the concepts in a time and place dynamics. This model is a way of communicating and discussing the aesthetic-ethic-religious and human resources (figure 2. *Human resources* and figure 3. *Architectural expressions*).

The intention is not to try to convince colleagues and you as scholars, that I have found a key to understanding the complexity of these concepts and their interrelations.

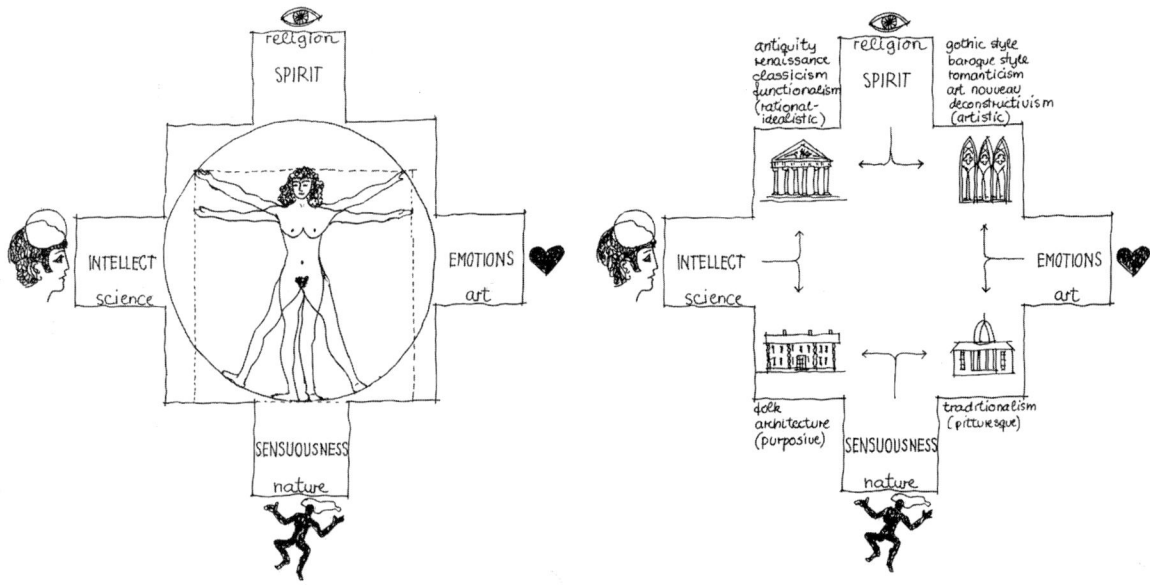

Figure 2. Human resources   *Figure 3. Architectural expressions*

The model contains four qualities essential for experiencing and creating architecture and human environments in a physiological, social, psychological and mental way.

1. *The intellectual force*, reason or rationality helping us to "read", analyse and understand natural and environmental forces and build reasonable and healthy architecture,

2. *The emotional force* enabling us to identify with, to care for, to appreciate and create artistic and pleasurable architecture,

3. *The spiritual force* inspiring our minds to build beautiful architecture and places which rise above the instrumental everyday life and our souls to worship them,

4. *The sensuous-aesthetic ability* making us immediately perceive and cognitively react and act in the environment, and create architecture stimulating our senses, distresses our minds and rebuilding our mental capacity.

These forces could be characterised differently, such as science, art, religion (philosophy), and nature. Other terms are the ancient platonic triad: the Beautiful, the True, the Good, indefinable and indescribable concepts belonging to the "real world of ideas" as Plato put it, and as he also said beauty only exists if it is also true and good (figure 4. *Plato's triad*). The human

BEAUTIFUL, TRUE AND GOOD ARCHITECTURE

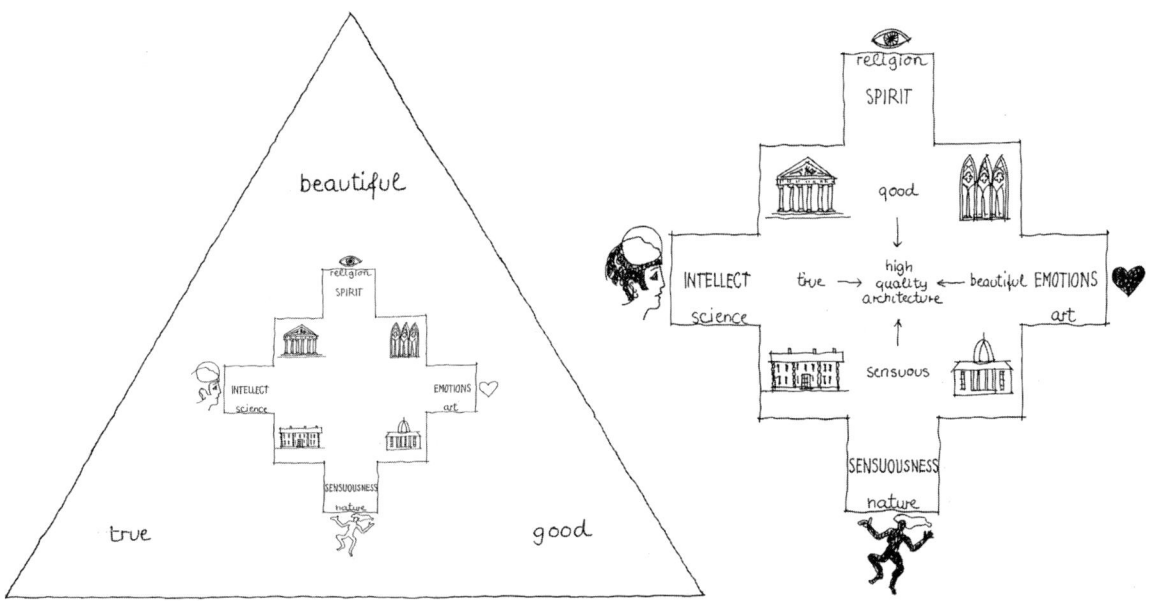

Figure 4. Plato's triad   *Figure 5. High quality architecture*

world, the non-ideal, sensuous-bodily, natural-material and emotional-artistic world was described by Plato as a reflection of the original world of ideas. My intention is not to go further into the platonic ideas. I have, however, reflected on what kind of qualities might characterise "good architecture", and I must admit that Plato has inspired me to realise that my idea of good architecture is close to what I imagine could be characterised and understood as Beautiful, True, and Good architecture. Plato had a different and abstract-ideal meaning of these qualities, whereas mine is more concrete.

When the four qualities or human forces, intellect, emotions, spirit, and sensuousness interact successfully in my model, not necessarily in equal proportions, it is my belief that we have a basis for creating and experiencing architecture of high quality

Beautiful architecture in the meaning of an artistic and culturally conscious architecture giving us sometimes a wonderful feeling of identity, confirming our norms of beauty and sometimes a surprising experience of a sublime, novel artistic expression. In the beautiful-dimension we should realise which aesthetic qualities human beings have perceived and today perceive as spiritual, beautiful and interact positively with, and which, in a narrow meaning, are dominated by trends and fashions and determined by taste. Beauty has, in a spiritual sense, always been the aim of all architecture worshipping The Divine, God or the sovereignty.

True architecture in the sense of a scientific understanding, an honest attitude to creating and using structures and systems, materials and surfaces, dimensions and solutions well suited for human life and with an unmistakable authenticity. The true-dimension should include and take seriously how we interact directly, sensuously and aesthetically with the environment. True means the opposite of false, that is the inauthentic, parroting trends, pretentiously imaging former styles and the unreasonable use of structures, materials and resources.

Good architecture in a spiritual sense includes a respect for the resources of our common earth, an ethical dimension, and a spiritual dimension in the relation between the unknown, people, architecture, place and the natural environment. In the good-dimension I imagine that aesthetics and ethics are in harmony, meaning that what is good for me, you and the environment ecologically, socially, psychologically, spiritually and aesthetically should somehow be "mirrored beautifully" in the architecture-in-place solution.

Spirituality as well as beauty is created or comes to life when the constituents of architecture: – structure and form, form and space, space and light, colours and materials – interact as a piece of art, communicating with the intellect, the emotions, the spirit and the senses. As you see from these descriptions the beautiful, true and good are also interrelated in architecture with the sensuous-aesthetic and vigorous quality.

I imagine that these interrelated beautiful-true-good dimensions, the aesthetic-ethic perspective in architecture and religion are what we are going to discuss at this symposium. If I should look on the gloomy side of these well-meaning concepts I would discuss and try to find contradictions between these positive concepts and include unpleasant questions and "black" ideas and experiences in order to look critically upon the hypothesis and concepts suggested above. For instance, is beautiful architecture an aesthetic delusion, hiding power and elitist aims, causing, at least in former times, the people harm, and bringing them poverty and suppression? Is true architecture a puritan and early/late modern reaction to emotionally cloying, decoratively imitating, unreasonably parvenu manifestations? Is good architecture a romantic illusion in a capitalistic, market-conscious and selfish society? Has religion and spirituality any place or space today?

The following discussions and reflections in this book may give us "a glimmer of truth".

References

Canter, D. (1977) *The Psychology of Place*, London: Architectural Press

Cold, B., Kolstad, A., Larssæther, S. (1998) *Aesthetics, Well-being and Health: Abstracts on theoretical and empirical research within environmental aesthetics,* Oslo: Norsk Form

Cold, B. (ed.) (2001) *Aesthetics, Well-being and Health: Essays within architecture and environmental aesthetics,* Aldershot: Ashgate

Gadamer, H. G. (1986) "The relevance of the beautiful", in *The Relevance of The Beautiful and Other Essays*, (ed. by Bernasconi, R.), Cambridge: Cambridge University Press

Goldman, D. (1995) *Emotional Intelligence*, New York: Bantam Books

Gombrich, E. H. (1968) *Art and Illusion,* London: Phaidon (1956)

Hargittai, I. & M. (1994) *Symmetry: A Unifying Concept*, California: Shelter

Kaplan, S. (1987) "Aesthetics, affect and cognition: Environmental preference from an evolutionary perspective", *Environment and Behaviour* 19/1, pp. 3-32

Lacoste, J. (1997) *Idéen om det skjønne: Trekk fra estetikkens historie,* Stokke: Forsythia, (*L'idée de beau,* Paris 1986)

Pallasmaa, J. (1996) *The Eyes of the Skin: Architecture and the Senses,* Academy Editions, London: Academy Group

Øijord, A. (1992) *Analytisk Estetikk eller Jakten på Skjønnheten,* (Analytic Aesthetics or Hunting the Beautiful), Asker: Tell

1   The place of worship as dominating context: St. Peter's, Rome

ARCHITECTURE AND RELIGION IN SECULARIZED TIMES

EIVIND KASA

Historically, there has been an intimate relationship between architecture and religion; places of worship are often elaborate or even impressive architectural creations. The sanctuaries of the Aztec people, of Buddhism, the mosques as well as the ancient Christian cathedrals are good examples of this. In fact, religious monuments like these are still being built, Gaudí's Sagrada Familia in Barcelona perhaps being the most well known of these today.

Historically, places of worship often enjoy a central position in society, both socially and physically. As such, they have traditionally functioned as context for "life in the world" and the buildings that have made religion manifest in the world have functioned as context for more humble kinds of structures. In this way, religious buildings have joined together different kinds of buildings within a consistent religious worldview.

This is splendidly exemplified by the baroque plan of Trondheim where the main axis stretches out from the cathedral to the island of the monks.

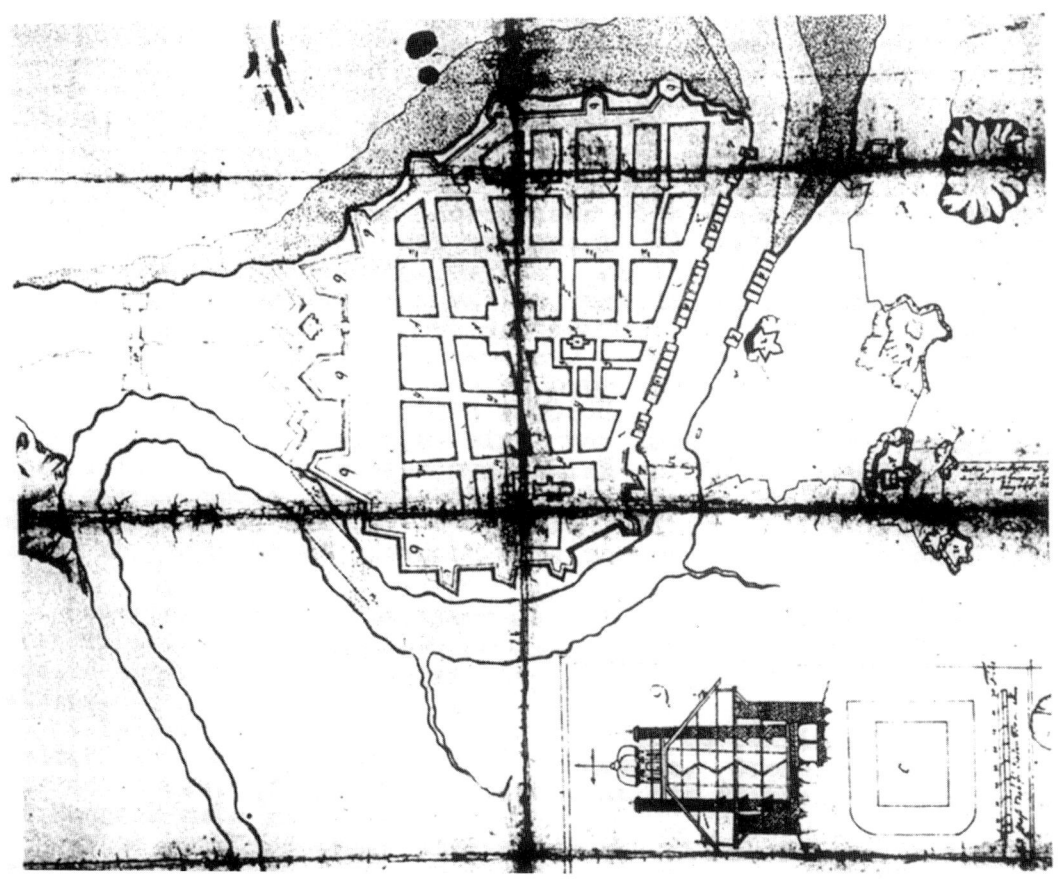

2   *A part of Cicignon's and Coucheron's plan for Trondheim from 1681*

Along this axis the institutions of society – Town Hall, military district command, Cathedral School, and buildings of justice – find their place in a kind of hierarchical order.

However, in our time, this kind of relationship between religion and architecture does not seem to exist anymore. Christianity is weakening, and there seems to be no collective creed that can function any longer as a social glue that unites the whole society. To paraphrase the title of Hans Sedlmayr's book: Contemporary society has lost its "Mitte".

This is concretised by the waning importance of churches in western culture. Even if cities are growing, fewer are being built. There is discussion about how to use empty churches for other purposes. Churches are becoming less important to the urban structure than museums, banks or even cafés. The city itself and the individual buildings no longer seem to be dependent on a religious context – or even any context at all.

Of course this is not new; it has been going on for a long time. However,

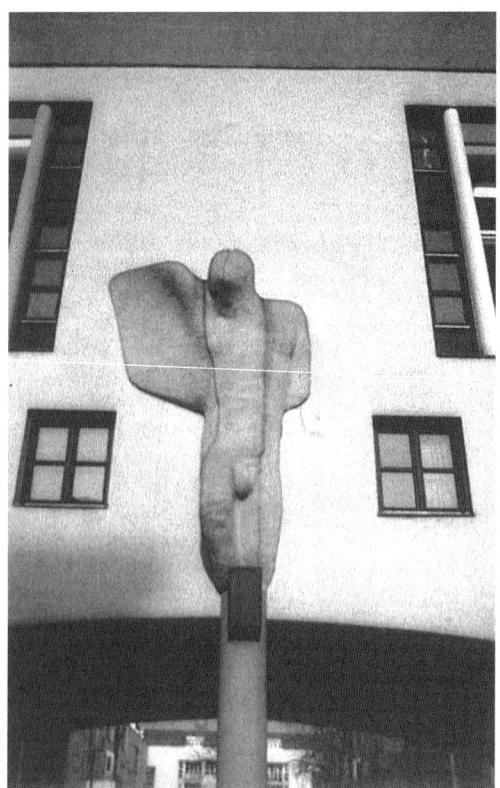

3   Rob Krier: Ritterstraße

4   Iñaki Abelos & Juhan Herreros: Building for the Ministry of the Interior, Madrid, Spain

5   Coop Himmelblau: Café Roter Engel, Vienna

6   Coop Himmelblau: Café Roter Engel

during the 1990s, architecture has entered a phase where it has become increasingly difficult to relate architecture and religion. One illustrative, but perhaps superficial sign of this, is the fact that during the so-called post-modern years of the Seventies and Eighties angels and gods were used – at least as metaphors – in architecture. Examples of this are the *Café Roter Engel* in Vienna designed by the Austrian architect firm Coop Himmelblau, Rob Krier's sculpture above the entrance to the housing in Ritterstraße in Berlin, and Haus-Rucker-

Co's *Nike von Linz*. At the moment phenomena like these have disappeared from architecture. The figurative itself has disappeared and in many ways created an impression of absence and void in more than one sense. This absence regards meaning of every sort, and most clearly any kind of religious meaning.

In this essay, which is an essay in the original meaning of the word as assay or trial, I will try to examine the character of, and reasons for this new situation, for why it seems to be difficult to relate, not historical, but contemporary architecture to religion.

"Secularized times"

From a traditional point of view, this seems to be a result of accelerating secularization. However, in many ways this is an open question. One reason for this is that the concept of secularization itself is open to interpretations, and the way it is specified determines the way one understands contemporary times, as it will determine the course this discussion will be taking. Consequently, the concept of secularization needs clarification.

Encyclopaedia Britannica defines "secularism" as "any movement in society directed away from otherworldliness to life on earth." This is the usual way of viewing the fate of religion in western countries. Modernization leads to the disenchantment of life on earth, and to the disappearance of religion in favor of an interest in life here and now.

However, in certain ways this is a dubious way of viewing the contemporary situation with respect to religion. What has happened is, perhaps, that western societies have moved away from Christianity and the Christian metaphysics. On the other hand, religious thought seems to have experienced a renaissance during recent decades. The growth of New Age-like forms of religion is one good example of this. Thus, even if the worldview of most people may appear secularized in the abovementioned sense, there seems to be a growing part of the population that has faith in a religious worldview, whatever this means.

Consequently, what seems to be taking place is not so much that religion is disappearing, as it is changing character. The religious sensibility of many people is perhaps moving somewhat away from Christianity, but even more it is moving away from the collective religious institutions of Christianity. It is being privatized. Consequently, secularization does not only consist of the disappearance of religion, but perhaps to a greater extent a deinstitutionalization of religious creed and thought.

In the rest of this essay, I will discuss the relationship between contemporary architecture and religion with respect to both of these interpretations of secularization.

After having clarified the concept of secularization to some extent, it is necessary to characterize the contemporary situation in architecture. Of course, this will be done only in broad outline, without any pretence of being exhaustive.

The "second modernity" of contemporary architecture

At the moment, contemporary architecture seems to be going through what has been called a phase of a "second modernity". The concept of a "second modernity" or "Zweite Moderne" to diagnose contemporary society is common to many thinkers such as Werner Hoffmann, Ulrich Beck and Anthony Giddens. It has been particularly linked to the German intellectual debate; one of the first to introduce it to the discussion of architecture was the German architecture critic Heinrich Klotz. Klotz is not just anybody in this debate. He was founder and the first director of Deutsches Architekturmuseum in Frankfurt a. M., and also the first director of Zentrum für Kunst und Medientechnologie in Karlsruhe. It was Klotz who introduced the concept of the post-modern in the German debate. At that time this caused considerable protest. At the end of the 1990s he did the same with the concept of a "second modernity" of art and architecture, and with similar results. Klotz developed his conception through different publications in the Nineties. This produced a vigorous debate, for instance in the German architecture magazine Arch+ in 1998. Klotz' ideas were presented for the last time in *Architektur der Zweiten Moderne: Ein Essay zur Ankündigung des Neuen* in 1999, the year of his death.

Klotz is talking of a "second modernity" firstly, because he wants to separate contemporary architecture from the heroic period of modernism of the Twenties and Thirties, and, secondly, because he wants to describe it as a kind of architecture that stands above, or survives, the rapid change of styles that we have seen in recent decades. One of the most important characteristics of this modern art and architecture is defined by Klotz as "abstraction". In his opinion, the modern abstraction unites old painters like the Fauves, Kandinsky, with Rauschenberg, Newman, Judd, and contemporary art and architecture. It is this abstraction that I am going to take a closer look at.

However, Klotz has been heavily criticised for this, both because he is using abstraction as a kind of demarcation criterion for modern art, as well as the salient feature of contemporary architecture. With respect to architecture, however, the criterion of abstraction has perhaps more ob-

ARCHITECTURE AND RELIGION IN SECULARIZED TIMES

7

Skidmore, Owings and Merill: Inland Steel Company Headquarters Building, Chicago, USA

vious relevance to art. Here it has been both more dominating, for instance being canonised by the so called International Style, and more omnipresent during the first decades after the Second World War, now being linked to what the architecture historians Manfredo Tafuri and Francesco Dal Co have called "the architecture of bureaucracy".

However, very often the architecture of "the second modernity" is created with explicit reference to the avant-garde modernity between the wars, but even more often to this abstract architecture of the 1950s and 60s. Perhaps the most central modern architect in this connection is Ludwig Mies van der Rohe.

The introduction of the concept of a second modernity was followed by the development of other concepts. One of this is "Supermodernism". The concept of the supermodern was introduced by the architecture critic Hans Ibelings in his book *Supermodernism, Architecture in the Age of Globalization*. This was published by The Netherlands Architecture Institute in Rotterdam

EIVIND KASA

8

Office for Metropolitan Architecture (OMA): Villa, Bordeaux

as late as in 1998. In this book Ibelings is consciously creating a new "-ism" in architecture.[1]

While Klotz was focusing upon formal abstraction as a withdrawal from any meaning in the form of symbolic content, Ibelings links this to a kind of abstraction or withdrawal from meaning in the form of the social function of architecture. What he is describing is an architecture that is withdrawing or refraining from the kind of social meaning of post-modern architecture that is contained in the three words place, context and identity. In his theory about "bigness" Rem Koolhaas has formulated this with his famous slogan "Fuck context". What this kind of architecture is interested in is the non-places of contemporary society, for instance the uncontrolled urban sprawl, the linear cities developing along highways with shopping and sports centers, concert hall etc. And perhaps the most typical non-places on the globe are the airports developing into cities of their own, cities that may be more closely linked to each other than to the next city in the country where the airport is situated.

This kind of development is part of a globalization produced by the contemporary version of the techno-economic rationale, realised in our times by electronics, computers, communication technology, the new media and liberalist economics.

The second modernity, and its abstraction is forming contemporary architecture at least in two different ways that have relevance to our investigation. The first appears in Dutch architecture, the second in minimalism. The last one is linked to phenomenology as a third most important trend in contemporary architecture. However, what is relevant to us here shows itself with greatest consequence and perhaps also clarity in minimalism.

The first of these trends, which in many ways is most obviously linked to the first kind of secularization, is the Dutch trend, which without doubt is the one of greatest importance to contemporary architecture.

The leading star of Dutch architecture – and presently even internationally – is Rem Koolhaas and his "Office for Metropolitan Architecture", abbreviated OMA. He has been active for several decades, but started to rise to fame during the Eighties. One important reason for this was the publication of his book *Delirious New York* in 1987. During the Nineties he has become possibly the most important thinker of contemporary architecture, and, somewhat journalistically formulated by "ART, das Kunstmagazin", perhaps the only one left with intellectual credibility. However, Koolhaas is not the only important architect of The Netherlands these days. This country has brought forth an astonishing range of contemporary talent. It may be enough to mention a few offices like Wiel Arets, UN Studio, Mecanoo, and last, but not least, MVRDV.

Dutch architecture of the 20th century was marked by an in many ways unbroken modern tradition. The founding fathers of modernism were

9

Wiel Arets:
Police Station, Cuijk

10   UN Studio van Berkel & Bos: Museum Het Valkhof, Nijmegen

11   Mecanoo: Faculty of Economics and Management Building, Utrecht

12   MVRDV: WoZoCo's, Amsterdam

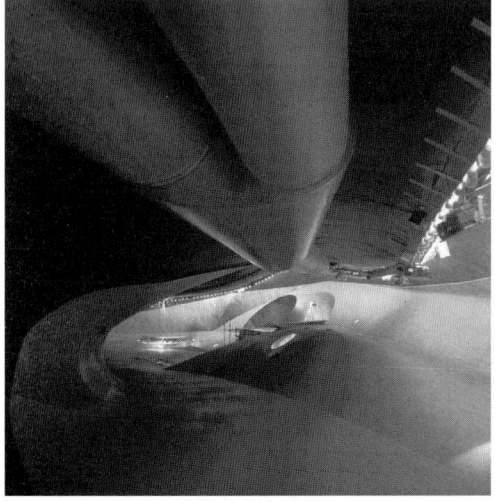

13   NOX: H$_2$O Expo, Neeltje Jans

venerated, and to a certain extent the abstract modern form language survived even post-modernism.

But contemporary Dutch architecture is modern in an even deeper sense than this. It is marked by a great, maybe even radical degree of realism and pragmatism, broadly speaking. The concluding essay of the book *Superdutch, New Architecture in the Netherlands* by Bart Lootsma is called Amnesty for the Real World. This is an emphatic pledge for the immanent. Consequently it is distinctly anti-utopian, and even more anti- or atranscendental or even areligious.

The world to which this architecture is giving amnesty, and towards which is even developing an accepting and playful attitude, is our present world as it is formed, not by "the small discourses" of post-modernism but

14

Housing in Potsdam

by the one and only "great modern discourse" of western techno-economic reason. At the moment this is present, as I said earlier, in the typical form of electronics, information-technology and liberalist economics which are some of the main forces creating globalization.

The Dutch architecture of the second modernity is deeply involved in an effort to develop architecture that accepts and expresses this contemporary situation – even the trivial, chaotic, grim and ugly parts of it. This does not mean that it gives in to it. It is in a less obvious way trying to play a strategic planning game against the forces of globalization. Nonetheless, one should not be surprised by the fact that this radical realism is also creating a sense of spleen or melancholy about the possibilities of creating a human architecture in contemporary society. Sometimes it even creates places of void, emptiness, and even brutality like the one we know from the vulgar functionalism of "the first modernism".

The question is now how the modern, abstract character of contemporary Dutch architecture is to be evaluated in relationship to what has already been said about religion and secularization.

Contemporary Dutch architecture is an emphatic pledge for the immanent. Consequently, it is very reasonable that it also may be experienced as alien to religious experience – at least as something transcendent. But the lack of centre, and consequently of place, context and identity – at least in a postmodern or even traditional – sense, makes it perhaps even more difficult to speak about the holy as something on earth.

15

Juan Bautista Villalpando: In Ezechielem Explanationes (II, 1604), reconstruction of the temple of Solomon

From one perspective, this may be thought of as a consequence of that modernism which according to Horkheimer and Adorno makes an end to gods and qualities. On the other hand, this development may also be viewed as the result of religious processes, more specifically Christian processes. According to Encyclopaedia Britannica, secularization has nowhere happened so spontaneously as in the Christian West. And it has even been alleged that modern secularization is rooted in the Jewish-Christian tradition. In a certain sense, secularization is a consequence of God's absence from this world. God is in heaven, man on earth. Only once have these been united.

This is eminently demonstrated in a way which also has relevance to our discussion, in the understanding of the Jewish temple.

At its consecration, Salomon prayed like this: "But will God in very deed dwell with men on the earth? Behold, heaven and the heaven of heavens cannot contain thee; how much less this house which I have built!" (2. Chron. 6.18) This does not mean that the early Israel did not live in a dynamistic world. It was a world where superhuman powers were at work much in the same way as they were in the surrounding religions. But this did not make place and world something sacred in their own right.

According to the German theologian Gerhard von Rad, this conception of God and his relationship to the holy place is the reason why Israel did not develop a sacred architecture of its own. When Salomon was starting to build his temple, he called upon Phoenician builders. Knowing nothing of Yahweh, they built a sanctuary according to tradition from the times immemorial. So, according to von Rad, they kept to the type of temple common in Syria and Palestine, one which probably derives from Mesopotamia.

This radical difference between Yahweh and his creation is also the reason why Israel was denied the use of images in the cult. Even "gojim" or the heathens knew that their gods were not identical with the images they made of them. But to Israel, even if the presence of Yahweh was radically experienced in this world, the world was not a mode of Yahweh's revelation. He transcended it completely. In late pre-Christian Judaism, the overwhelming presence of Yahweh led, in fact, to the conviction that the pagan gods were sham and ultimately nonexistent (clearest in Deutero-Isaiah). The use of images in the cult was exchanged with the use of God's name, which in its turn was also to become something not to be mentioned. Yahweh's radical difference, and in a way, absence form this world, and the dethronement of all other religious powers, laid the world bare as a pure phenomenon of the creation.

What we have said about Jewish religion also applies to Christianity. Early Christianity knew of religious powers and places where these were present too, for example the tombs of the martyrs and relics. However, this did not lead to a resacralisation of the world. As the temple had been the holy place of a thing – the holy arch – so were these Christian places.

As the Christian congregation grew, it preliminarily solved its spatial needs by adding a few rooms to ordinary private houses. But when congregations became too large to be contained in private homes, they did not choose the established temple as the typology for their assembly buildings. They chose the purely secular basilica. Of course, the importance of the martyr tombs and relics lingered on. But as Christianity grew, most holy places lacked these, without this making them much less appropriate for religious service. Thus, to a great extent Christianity continued the Jewish de-sacralised view upon the world at large.

Different aspects of this understanding of the relationship between God and world are present in Luther's concept of the hidden God or "Deus absconditus", and in the Theology of the Swiss theologian Karl Barth that characterizes God as the totally different or "das ganz Andere". Barth has even written that if he has got any theological "system" at all, it is thinking as clearly as possible what Søren Kierkegaard has called "the infinite qualitative difference" between time and eternity, in its negative and positive sense.

If one accepts this perspective, a theological interpretation of the architecture of the Dutch variant of the second modernity may then be that this is a discourse about the world as a pure creation. It is also about how this world without faith and consequently without a centre falls apart in fragments. Consequently, the emptiness and void of modern industrial buildings like the famous American grain silos or office blocks, as well as the works of the abstract "second modernity", are speaking about the radically absent God of the Jewish-Christian tradition, although they were not consciously created to do this.

16 Post-modern cacophony of meaning: Gaskin & Bezanski: New York, New York Hotel & Casino, Las Vegas

17 John Pawson

However, along with the Dutch variant of the abstraction of our second modernity, there exists another which is much more open to religious interpretation, even within the world of globalization. This is minimalism in architecture. Minimalism represents an even more radical version of the abstraction of the second modernity. It is more characteristic of the second kind of secularization that I have described. Like the Dutch variant, it existed during the post-modern 1980s. But it was during the Nineties it developed into some kind of a popular trend.

Although minimalism represents a continuation of the abstract tradition in modern art and architecture, it developed during the Nineties particular as a reaction against the cacophony of meanings that characterized much of post-modern architecture and thought.

The most important idol also of this variant of the second modernity is Mies van der Rohe, although Louis Kahn is revered by this tradition too. Some of the most important exponents of contemporary architecture are

ARCHITECTURE AND RELIGION IN SECULARIZED TIMES

18   Bruno Silvestrin

19   Kazuyo Sejima. Japan Railway building

Eva Jiricna, John Pawson. David Chipperfield, Bruno Silvestrin, Kazuyo Sejima and Tadao Ando.

The difference between the Dutch tradition and the minimalist, and its particular relevance to our discussion, may be illustrated by looking at a particular work by Mies van der Rohe.

This is Mies' masterplan and individual projects for the campus at Illinois Institute of Technology from 1940, one of his first to be developed in "The New World". This campus contains, among other buildings, a boiler house and a church.

In his well-known book "The Language of Post-Modern Architecture" from 1977, Charles Jencks criticizes Mies because the use of his universal grammar of steel I-beams, beige brick and glass to speak about all the important functions of housing, assembly, classrooms, shops, chapels etc., lead to a serious confusion of meaning, even existential meaning. Jencks discusses how this leads us astray to mistake the boiler house for a cathedral

33

20 Ludwig Mies van der Rohe: masterplan for the Illinois Institute of Technology, Chicago

21 Alberto Campo Baeza, Madrid: Gaspar House

and vice versa. And Ibelings comments somewhat ironically upon Jencks' discussion in this way (p.14): "After claiming that he was unable to discern any appreciable differences between the two buildings, Jencks feigned confusion as to whether this should be interpreted as a devaluation of religion or a revaluation of central heating."

But this reduction of the figurative and separation from literal meaning does not create an impression of void and absence, but of presence. From the almost nothingness of forms emerges some kind of spiritual presence.

This is in a way unqualified, which makes minimalism an ideal kind of architecture for places like cross-confessional chapels at airports. Different concepts have been used to describe this phenomenon in architectural theory. "Genius Loci", "atmosphere" and "aura" characterize this from different angles. Here, I want to discuss it in relationship to the concept "aesthetic transcendence" that Adorno uses in his "Aesthetic Theory." In a way this also illuminates what we have been discussing in relation to the Dutch example.

The concept of aesthetic transcendence is interesting because it unites a religious and aesthetic perspective on art – and we may add: architecture.

ARCHITECTURE AND RELIGION IN SECULARIZED TIMES

22   Ludwig Mies van der Rohe: Illinois Institute of Technology, BoilerHouse

23   Ludwig Mies van der Rohe: Illinois Institute of Technology, Church

According to Adorno, aesthetic transcendence is a recollection of the time when aesthetic phenomena foremost functioned in the cult. At that time they took part in the revelation of the gods. As a result of the disenchantment of the world that enlightenment brought, works of art – and architecture – were liberated from their cultic limitations. But a memory of their former function remained. That is the surplus of aesthetic transcendence. Adorno asserts (p. 50) that all art is secularization of transcendence and as such partakes in enlightenment.

What is interesting in this connection is that minimalism shows how a kind of spiritual experience appears from the abstract forms of the second modernity. And it even shows that this experience may be interpreted as something transcendent or even religious. There are several witnesses of this from the earlier days of modern art. Many of the fathers of modern art expressed a nonconfessional spiritual or religious belief in relation to their art. Malevich, Kandinsky, and others have been discussed in this connection. We also encounter similar attitudes in some of the minimalist architects. Ando has already been mentioned. And, like many others Pawson is impressed and inspired by the architecture of the Shakers. What is interesting as regards our discussion of secularization at the beginning of this essay is that minimalism exemplifies the second variant I sketched earlier. It is an example of how spirituality or even religious experience and thought may take place outside the institutional network of established religion.

However, there is certainly no necessary relationship between the experience that is defined by the concept of aesthetic transcendence and any metaphysics. As Adorno says: "Das von Menschen gemachte Mehr verbürgt an sich nicht den metaphysischen Gehalt von Kunst. Der könnte ganz nichtig sein, und gleichwohl könnten die Kunstwerke jenes Mehr als Erscheinendes setzen." (p. 122)

The appearance of the concept "aesthetic transcendence" is interestingly pointing back to our discussion of the Dutch example. Adorno says in the "Aesthetic Theory" (p. 123) that "Ästhetische Transzendenz und Entzauberung finden zum Unisono im Verstummen" and he uses Beckett's oeuvre as an example of this. In succeeded works of modern art as well as architecture we often experienced a radical kind of withdrawal and even absence which was often related to the concept of the sublime. This was linked to the revolt against atmosphere and aura in art and architecture. Nevertheless, this kind of art and architecture emitted some kind of transcendental quality, even if it was only the quality of suspension of existence. Seen from Adorno's point of view, the difference between Dutch and minimalist architecture may be that the former is more deeply influenced by the process of enlightenment. Perhaps it is not a coincidence that this happens in the reformed Netherlands that is not influenced by the least enlightened variant of Christianity.

Conclusion

It is time to start summing up this effort to understand the religious relevance of some aspects of contemporary architecture. I started by stating that it seems to be difficult to relate contemporary architecture to religion. This, I asserted, was due to secularization. However, an analysis of the concept of secularization, revealed that the concept may have at least two different meanings, one is abandoning the idea of a super sensual world altogether, the other that only the institutionalization of religion is abandoned. Then I went on to discuss how these two kinds of secularization may be related to contemporary architecture. I defined the main trend of contemporary architecture as a second modernity foremost characterised by abstraction. This abstraction was exemplified by Dutch and minimalist architecture. The Dutch was linked to the first kind of secularization, minimalism to the second. The Dutch architecture I asserted, actualised the absence of something transcendent/transcendence, minimalism the presence of it. However, in the end I tried to show how Adorno's conception of aesthetic transcendence was able to account for both.

Note

1. Ibelings is borrowing the name for this from the anthropologist Marc Augé and his book "Non-lieux: Introduction à une anthropologie de la supermodernité" (Non-places: Introduction to an Anthropology of Surmodernity).

Illustrations

1   The place of worship as dominating context: *St. Peter's*, Rome, photo: author.
2   *A part of Cicignon's and Coucheron's plan for Trondheim from 1681*, National Archives of Norway, Trondheim.
3   Rob Krier: *Ritterstraße*, photo: author.
4   Inaki Abelos & Juhan Herreros, *Building for the Ministry of the Interior*, Madrid, Spain, in: Ibelings, p. 103.
5   Coop Himmelblau: *Café Roter Engel*, Vienna, in: Coop Himmelblau, *Architecture is Now: Projects, (Un)buildings, Actions, Statements, Sketches, Commentaries, 1968-1983*, London: Thames & Hudson 1984, p. 83.
6   Coop Himmelblau: *Café Roter Engel*, Vienna, ibid. p. 85.
7   The architecture of bureaucracy: Skidmore, Owings and Merill, *Inland Steel Company Headquarters Building*, Chicago, in: Ibelings, p. 35.
8   Office for Metropolitan Architecture (OMA): *Villa*, Bordeaux, in: Lootsma, p. 197.
9   Wiel Arets, *Police Station*, Cuijk, ibid. p. 46-7.
10 UN Studio van Berkel & Bos, *Museum Het Valkhof*, Nijmegen, ibid. p. 67.
11 Mecanoo, *Faculty of Economics and Management Building*, Utrecht, ibid. p. 108.
12 MVRDV, *WoZoCo's*, Amsterdam, ibid. p. 132-3.
13 NOX: H_2O *Expo, Neeltje Jans*, ibid. p. 164.
14 *Housing in Potsdam*, photo: Sigurd Bergmann
15 Juan Bautista Villalpando, *In Ezechielem Explanationes (II,1604)*, reconstruction of the temple of Solomon, in: Hanno-Walter Krufft, *A History of Architectural Theory from Vitruvius to the Present*, translated by Ronald Tay-

        lor, Elsie Callander and Antony Wood, Zwemmer, Princeton Architectural Press, 1994, ill. 134.
16   Post-modern cacophony of meaning: Gaskin & Bezanski, *New York, New York Hotel & Casino,* Las Vegas, in: Ibelings, p. 74.
17   John Pawson, *Interior in Herbert Ypma: London Minimum*, London: Thames & Hudson 1996, p. 130.
18   Claudio Silvestrin, *Interior*, ibid. p. 152.
19   Kazuyo Sejima, *Japan Railway buildning*, in: *The Japan Architect* no. 35, autumn 1999, p. 107.
20   Ludwig Mies van der Rohe, *Masterplan for the Illinois Institute of Technology*, Chicago, in: Ibelings, p. 46-7.
21   Alberto Campo Baeza, *Gaspar House*, Cadiz, Spain, in: Susan Doubilet and Daralice Boles, *European House Now: Contemporary Architectural Directions*, New York: Universe Publishing 1999, p. 143.
22   Ludwig Mies van der Rohe, *Illinois Institute of Technology, BoilerHouse*, in: Jencks, p. 16.
23   Ludwig Mies van der Rohe, *Illinois Institute of Technology, Church*, in: Jencks, p. 17.

References

Adorno, Theodor (1990) *Ästhetische Theorie*, 5th printing, Frankfurt am Main: Suhrkamp

Augé, Marc (1992) *Non-Lieux: Introduction à une anthropologie de la surmodernité*, Paris: Editions du Seuil

Ibelings, Hans (1998) *Supermodernism: Architecture in the Age of Globalization*, Rotterdam: Nai Publishers

Jencks, Charles (1984) *The Language of Post-Modern Architecture*, 4th revised enlarged edition, London: Academy Editions

Klotz, Heinrich (1999) *Architektur der Zweiten Moderne: Ein Essay zur Ankündigung des Neuen*, Stuttgart: Deutsche Verlags-Anstalt

Lootsma, Bart (2000) *Superdutch: New Architecture in the Netherlands*, London: Thames & Hudson

von Rad, Gerhard (1957) *Theologie des Alten Testaments I: Die Theologie der historischen Überlieferungen Israels*, München: Kaiser

PLACE IN SCULPTURE

GUNILLA BANDOLIN

Sky Park, Östersund

Sky Park is located in the suburb Torvalla in the periphery of the city of Östersund in Sweden.

In 1990 I was asked to create a sculpture for the residential area. The area was still under construction, and when I visited the area it was half finished. The woodland was very prominent and trees surrounded the buildings. However, what caught my attention was the huge heap of waste at the edge of the woods, where soil and waste from the building processes was deposited. The heap had still not yet reached its planned volume.

I proposed a shape for the top of the heap, an oval pit, approx. 20 metres long, 16 metres wide and 2.5 metres deep. The hollow was covered with fieldstones from a nearby boulder ridge and sowed with herbs.

The sculpture is the hike up the approx. 60 metres high mound. The hike starts in the woods. As one ascends above the trees, the view to the scenery

opens – first the lake Storsjön appears and in a distance, majestic mountains. The view from the top of the mound is spectacular. Descending into the hollow of the mound, the panorama disappears, and so does the outside world with the mountains, the lake, the city, and the woods. At the very bottom of the pit one only can see the sky, which there seems to come very close. Sky Park has become a popular site in the area – there are school excursions to the park, people go there to enjoy the panorama view, or to seek solitude.

Solomon's Well, for Frank Lloyd Wright, Queens, New York

In 1994 I was invited to produce a sculpture for the Socrates Sculpture Park in Queens, New York.

The park was originally an old dumpsite for building materials which was transformed into an art park by a group of artists under the leadership of the sculptor Mark di Suvero. The park is located between two black ghettos in Queens in an area with a high crime rate and low income.

The sculpture was funded through a scholarship from the Council of Artists (Konstnärsnämnden) in Stockholm. Companies in New York sponsored me with material (bricks, concrete, iron, etc.). Local companies leased the machinery needed either for free or at a very low cost.

In the spring months of 1994 I built the sculpture with the help of a friend who was an engineer. Several women from the nearby ghettoes were prepared to assist the work for a salary of 10 dollars per hour.

For the local residents, the sculpture, and the art park in general, involved a higher influx of visitors and thus a higher income. Thus the general living conditions were improved and the area became safer place to live. Working in the park also became important for local people's identity and self-esteem in an area where the unemployment was up to nearly 100 per cent, and where people hardly even knew anyone who had a job.

Solomon's Well became a meeting place for people during the two years the piece remained in the park.

Sky Mould, Gothenburg

Sky Mould was located in the park *Kungsparken* in Gothenburg in the summer of 2001 during the international Gothenburg art biennale. It was inaugurated a week before the big European Union summit, which gave rise to violent demonstrations and protests in the streets.

Throughout the entire planning and construction phase for Sky Mould, the city of Gothenburg was preparing for the big summit. The city was in an agitated state, and I believe that this disquiet influenced my work in the shaping of the sculpture.

The sculpture mediates a feeling that the earth arches under our feet. It is completely geometric and its form and construction is inspired by that of a gyrocompass. The sculpture is partially submerged in the ground and partially covered by turf. During the revolts, the piece got some scratches from horseshoes. However, the damage was miniscule and it remained in the park throughout the summer, being a place for recreation and picnics.

The hole in the bottom of the sky, Reykjavik

I built this grass shape with the help of a number of unemployed young people in Reykjavik in 1995 for a Nordic art exhibition in the Nordic House. Between the Nordic House, designed by Alvar Aalto, and the city was a huge, completely flat grass field. The sculpture juts out of the ground – a disc-like shape, with the front facing southwards and the "back" facing northwards. Soon people would gather there to find shelter from the northern winds and to turn their faces to the south. A fairly comfortable microclimate evolved inside the sculpture. In the two years the sculpture was up, it represented a node in the wide, open landscape.

Observatory, 2002, Sickla Udde, Stockholm

All photographs by the author.

SPACE AND SPIRIT

Towards a theology of inhabitation

SIGURD BERGMANN

The Spirituality of Architecture

"Realization of the Godhead"

The quest for the spiritual in architecture does not necessarily have to restrict itself to sacred spaces and holy places that have already been endowed with meaning by religious tradition. The quest for the religious dimension of architecture – a dimension that has been treated as self-evident in premodern worldviews – can also be meaningful with regard to secular buildings, even if these have often lost their capacity to "speak" and have been demoted to the modern function of mere "containers" (H. Klotz).

We do not have to share Hegel's view of the Spirit as the highest shape and dimension of history, nor his thesis that art is dead, in order to follow his argument and to confront questions that are as relevant today in our secularized and post-metaphysical age as they were in his time.

> Architecture is in fact the first pioneer on the highway toward the adequate realization of the Godhead. . . . By this means it levels a space for the God, informs His external

environment, and builds Him His temple, as a fit place for the concentration of the Spirit and for its direction towards the absolute objects of intelligent life. It raises an enclosure for the congregation of those assembled, as a defence against the threating of the tempest, against rain, the hurricane, and savage animals. It in short reveals the will thus to assemble, and although under an external relation, yet in agreement with the principles of art.[1]

Does architecture always incorporate a religious momentum, a movement towards "the adequate realization of the Godhead"? Does it prepare a place for God? Does it create a space for spiritual contemplation? Does it offer us a place in which to congregate where we can find protection from the life-threatening forces of nature?

If we define the concept of "god" to mean "that which is of ultimate concern to humanity",[2] and what "you set your heart on and repose your trust in",[3] then the answer is very simple. How can architecture express our ultimate concerns? What can the planning, construction and use of a building tell us about "that which functions as god"?[4] What is it about a building that tugs at our heart-strings? What religious images and ethical beliefs are displayed in and through architecture? Spatial images are the dreams of society. What do they reveal?

My hypothesis is in fact opposed to Hegel's thesis that (spiritually embodied) art is dead. The claim of this essay is that the spiritual perspective retains a significance for our understanding of secular architecture.

Re-establishing the lost space of sacred architecture

Sacred architecture was possessed of paradigmatic significance for the spiritual, social and ecological lives of the peoples of premodern cultures, and the place of worship was positioned right at the centre of things. The challenge that faces us today, however, is of a different order.[5] Karsten Harries expresses this challenge by means of two questions:

> . . . whether to reoccupy the place once occupied by sacred architecture, and if so how.[6]

Three different types of response can be given to this challenge.

First, we can re-sanctify secular places by a kind of architectural restoration-work designed to re-establish the powers of the ancient church. For instance, conservative forces in the Vatican have called for a so-called re-evangelizing of Europe, one aimed at marginalizing the forces of modernity. In a positive sense, this has led to a liberation of the individual from paternalistic clerical control. Utilizing the potential of anti-modernism to mobilize and manipulate a critique of civilization, the strategy has met with some success, even though it has strengthened rather than curtailed the individual's critical perspective on religion and ideology.

Second, we might rather argue that we should abandon the attempt to recreate the sacred spaces and places of the past. Religion has served its function. Naturally some old buildings need to be protected. Maintaining a link with the past is intrinsically valuable, but it is largely motivated by the interests of cultural history. True, we still design and build churches for those different groups of people which, for some reason or other, want to assemble in them, but church buildings should be conceived of and constructed according to the same criteria of functionality and general aesthetic value as are multi-storey car parks, shopping centres and town halls.

Third, Harries' concept of "place" might be understood metaphorically, allowing us to respond to it in a generally positive manner. We need to reach a critical understanding of the position, function and meaning that older sacred architecture possessed, without necessarily aiming either for its slavish reconstruction or for a pastiche of the past. This does not mean that we should turn a blind eye to the processes of history. Inside us, we will always be able to find an "architecture behind architecture".[7] The Middle Ages are over, and it is hard to imagine that we will ever experience a comparable period of history again. The Renaissance thesis that antiquity could be reborn was based on a fundamental illusion. Accordingly, we are compelled to confront the issue of architecture's religious dimension with open minds and in a wide perspective. How can we reinstate the sacred in the architecture of tomorrow?

The spiritual in architecture

It is interesting to see how artists and architects – in contrast to, for example, natural scientists – never really gave up the struggle for "the spiritual in art" (V. Kandinsky) during the modernist period.[8] Today important architects have recoursed to forms of expression that are both "free" and also linked to traditions of religious discourse in order to express their own creativity.

Peter Eisenman, for example, takes as his starting-point the embeddedness of modern culture in the Jewish religion. He "seeks to go beyond the architecture of the Graeco-Christian Church",[9] that reached its climax in

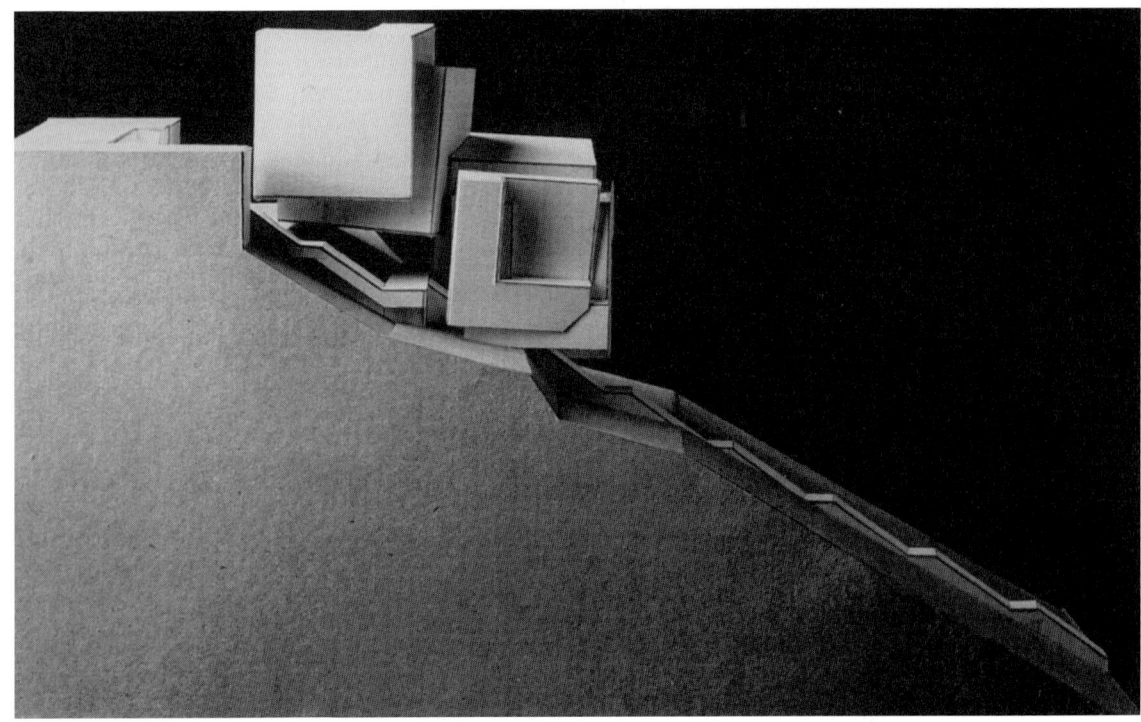

1

Peter Eisenman, Guardiola House, Cádiz, 1988, side view, study model

Hegelian metaphysics, in order to create objects and an architectural theory that are ethically, aesthetically and theologically alive to tradition, and that are autonomous and also individually creative, through a "regenerated ontology"[10] that is clearly based on the traditions, ideas and concepts of Jewish mysticism. Tradition is housed.

The architect makes use of a Jewish form of mysticism to create an empty space of exile beyond Egypt and Greece, one based on the forms of the letter **L** and the Greek letter λ in which a "sliding motion" creates a place for departure, for letting go, for clearing ground.

Tadao Ando typically relates his projects to the mind-sets of different religious traditions. Zen-Buddhist, Shintoist and Christian interpretations of life offer a range of different perspectives, concepts and patterns to which Ando makes free reference, based on a belief in a shared pluralistic and harmonious perspective that is taken from the different religions. In his works the potential for plurality, diversity and interreligious communication is demonstrated by means of an architectonic and multireligious polyvalency. Ando develops this pluralistic vision in both a technical and a spiritual manner, by means of contrasts, lines and surfaces that simultaneously resist and transcend duality.[11]

SPACE AND SPIRIT

2

*Tadao Ando,
Rokko Housing I,
Kobe, 1978-83*

3

*Tadao Ando,
Nariwa Museum,
Okayama, 1992-94*

Ando describes his view of religion in terms of a united vision of a kind of religious essence:

> I feel that the goal of most religions is similar, to make men happier and more at ease with themselves.[12]

We can also interpret Ando's works in the light of this concept of religion. Like religion, they aim to offer the gift of happiness. Ando has designed churches, temples and a special room for meditation for UNESCO, and his other projects designed for non-religious purposes can also be seen from the same spiritual perspective as "shelters and islands for the soul."[13]

SIGURD BERGMANN

4

Tadao Ando, Meditation Space, UNESCO, Paris, 1994-95

To me, one of the most crucial driving forces behind Ando's work is his attempt to allow different identities to relate to one another without renouncing their specificity. As a result, he stands out as a profound and contex-tually aware artist whose works not only display the unresolved inner tensions and conflicts of a globalized world, but that also present themselves as sanctuaries in which peaceful, lasting and mutually loving relationships can flourish, and in which the familiar and the strange can join forces as they progress to a shared but unknown future. Thus Ando's architectural works have been developed in consort with an intensified reflection on the encounter between different religions, a reflection that has contributed to interreligious processes that have as goal the development of an alternative global village – one that is not built merely to be inhabited by the idols of the financial market.

SPACE AND SPIRIT

5

Le Corbusier, Villa Savoye, 1929-31

Le Corbusier famously defines architecture as "a system of spirit":

> un système de l'esprit qui fixe dans un mode matériel le sentiment resultant d'une époque.[14]

In his discussion of the iconoclasms of the Early Church, he aligns himself programmatically with the iconoclasts, so as to offer a counter-force to the worship of graven images that dominates his own time.[15]

To Le Corbusier, architecture is clearly not only the work of human beings, but:

> The spirit of architecture is asserting itself.[16]

Of course, it is not for us to impute a belief in the Holy Spirit to Le Corbusier. In this context it is, however, interesting to see how intent he is on filling the space vacated by earlier sacred architecture by operating with an assumption that there is some inherent and intrinsic essence in architecture: the assumption that the spirit of architecture exists. In his celebrated church, the spirit of architecture is manifested in the place where God's Holy Spirit

51

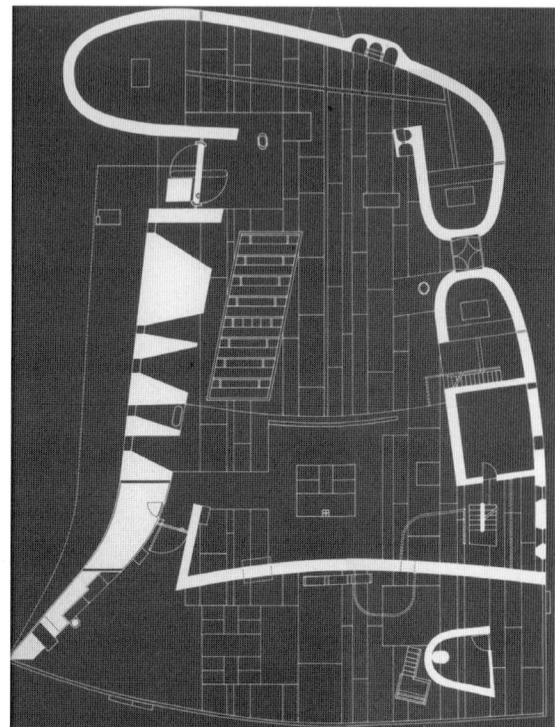

6 *Le Corbusier, The Church at Ronchamp, 1950-54*

7 *Le Corbusier, The Church at Ronchamp, plan*

can become immanent in the communio sanctorum. The architectural body offers a place for God's immanence in the human body.

Thus established religious concepts such as "spirit", "image", "beauty"and "benevolence" function as tools in a process in which architecture is able to become "the necessary prerequisite for human creation."[17] If one thinks of Le Corbusier's strategy of redesigning cities so as to allow for a set of separate zones – something that resulted in a fragmentation of urban environments that is much criticized today – then one can pose the question: how can his conception of a single spirit be reconciled with the fragmentation of human life-worlds?[18]

It seems obvious that the term "spirit" has something new to contribute to our understanding of the sacred nature of the spatial.

The theoretician of architecture Christian Norberg-Schulz has developed a very influential phenomenological line of thought, claiming that every space possesses its own unique spiritual attributes. According to him, the existence of a genius loci should be respected, and every architect should relate to it.[19]

The views of Le Corbusier and of Norberg-Schulz need to be subjected to critical scrutiny. Do they actually believe that there really is a spirit of architecture and place, and, if so, what does this entail? We cannot find any philosophically or theologically acceptable answer in their texts, but it seems clear that they both belong to a long architectural-theoretical tradition that works on the assumption that there is "something" more than just building, technique and form – some kind of metaphysical surplus. This surplus is described by reference to a particular discourse, and this can be the discourse of religiosity (either medieval or of antiquity), or that of aesthetics or rationalism.

In antiquity and in the Middle Ages, God was conceived of as the architect, and architecture was supposed to reflect a divine and eternal (musical) harmony.[20] A Platonic metaphysics of light formed the basis of this view and it was normative for both medieval architectural design and for its underlying theology.[21] Durand was the first to develop a rationalistic theory of architecture and a functionalist aesthetics in which beauty and utility were seen to be related.[22]

In what follows my own contribution aims to explore what a Christian belief in the Holy Spirit and her[23] in-dwelling in Creation can contribute to architectural theory.

Is theology able to contribute to a critical investigation of prevailing concepts of the genius loci and the spirit of architecture? Can it inspire a more profound perception of the sacred nature of that space lying outside holy places? In what ways can a discussion of architecture and space challenge the Christian interpretation of life? What might such a discussion entail with regard to the choice between idols and the God of Life?

To start with, I would like to suggest why we need more interdisciplinary exchange between the disciplines of Architecture and Religious Studies. Following this I will proceed to develop a theological perspective on architectural interpretation by employing terms such as "creation", "Spirit", and "liberation" – seeing such interpretation in the light of the doctrine of the Holy Spirit. Finally, I will discuss in what way a synopsis of aesthetics, ethics and theology can deepen our understanding of the relationship between space and spirit.

8

God, the Architect of the Universe, from a 13th century French Bible moralisée

Why Architecture and Religion?

"Architecture" as an aesthetic and critical act in context

What do we mean by "architecture"? There are very many theoretical definitions of this term, some of which are mutually exclusive.

From a symbolic perspective, architecture is seen as a constellation of symbols, one in which human ideas are brought together and materialized in a building, and according to which architecture is seen to possess intellectual content.[24] The weakness of this definition lies in its distinction between idea and material, form and content.

From a semiotic perspective, architecture is a form of the sign. Buildings are seen as systems of signs whose interrelated significance emerges within a wider process of social communication. The shortcomings of this approach are to be found in the reductionist and universalizing nature of semiotics.[25]

The phenomenological view is to see architecture in the light of the concept of "atmosphere."[26] A building and its surroundings are characterized by specific qualities that have no immediate connection to the human subject or to the constructed physical object. Atmosphere emerges, however, when these two elements meet. A critical objection to the atmosphere theory involves querying whether it really does allow us to link human beings on the one hand and place and space on the other, or whether it fails to escape from anthropocentricity because it makes human awareness the necessary precondition for deciding which particular atmosphere surrounds a given place. Is space "the most fully living of that which surrounds us" (E. Chillida), or is it human spatial existence (Heidegger's "dwelling") that breathes life into atmosphere?

For architectural theorist Finn Werne the architectural project serves a dual function in relation to context and reference. It evolves partly within an extensional context, such as its situatedness in a given world, and partly within an intentional context, such as that of the architect's creative intentions concerning the metaphysical, empirical, ideological, artistic or religious contexts that he or she chooses.[27]

A definition of architecture has to attend to both the subjective and the objective dimension, to both the architect and the building. Architecture is both reality and fiction.

Architecture must focus on the indissoluble connection between the building's physical and conceptual expressions. Furthermore, it must reflect both complex processes of social production, and also historically changing processes of interpretation and use.

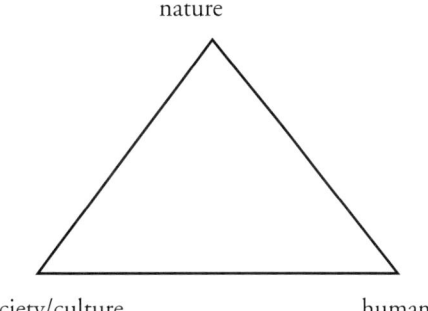

Figure 1 *The human-ecological triangle*

Seen in this way, architecture comes to represent a microcosm of the human, natural and social sciences. Here we find projects that include the individual, nature, society, culture and history. We observe points of intersection between the human being and nature, and we are able to follow processes of human adaptation to given ecological conditions that take place alongside the creative individual transformation of these same conditions.

If we think of the so-called "human-ecological triangle",[28] we can place architecture at the crossroads where humanity, society/culture, and nature all meet. Aesthetic, ethical and religious problems within architecture must be treated in such a way that all three dimensions are taken full account of.

We can distinguish between architecture and the simple building process by envisaging architecture as "a critical act."[29] If we think of architecture as the art of construction, and of art as an autonomous activity whereby human beings can create authentic utopias,[30] then architecture distinguishes itself as a project that is both human-subjective and contextual, creative and critical, nature-embedded and nature-transforming.[31] The specificity of architecture is to be found in the dimension of movement. In contrast to the pictorial arts, spatial constellations are never still, but are connected to those who move in and through them. Architectural design is a dynamic project.

"Religion" – a critical interpretation of the ultimate in context

Religious Studies and architectural theory are both characterized by a multitude of different definitions of "religion."[32] Cognitive theories place emphasis on linguistic and systematic forms of expression. Anthropological theories emphasize the importance of rituals. Psychological theories take the so-called religious experience as their starting-point, and sociological theories are concerned with different courses of action and with empirical phenomena.

There is no consensus on a single definition of religion. We can, however, list the six dimensions of religiosity: a) cognitive and ideological, b) social-ethical, c) ritual, d) institutional, e) aesthetic, and f) psychological. Religious scholars make frequent use of one or more of these dimensions. Religious pragmatics, for instance, defines religious experience as a process of mutual confirmation of worldview and ethos,[33] lying somewhere between the cognitive and the ethical dimension. The Sociology of Religion interprets religion in terms of the social construction of reality.

Historically, religion and religious interpretation have undergone radical changes. The secularization process has led to a looser relationship between religion as such and religious communities. "Religion without God" is as possible as "God without religion." In a wider perspective, religion can comprise individual and social views, ideologies, values and beliefs, without any necessary relation to a given religious institution or tradition. Concepts such as private or personal religion have been pressed into use. In a more restricted sense, religion comprises only that which believers themselves explicitly distinguish from more worldly phenomena.

In consort with the ongoing processes of modernization and globalization that are profoundly affecting today's world, religion and religious concepts are themselves involved in a process of radical transformation. Traditionally, religion competes with modern worldviews such as those of scientism, economism, tribalism and nationalism. New modes of religious expression emerge on a regular basis. The growth of the global media changes the nature of our aesthetic and religious experience. Extensive criticism of religion has failed to weaken its significance, although it has succeeded in altering its contemporary socio-cultural meaning. Religion can, for instance, function as an oppositional spiritual force, one which has much to offer such diverse movements as feminism and ecology.[34] At the same time, it can assume a divisive and destructive function.

Interpretations of life and visions in architecture and religion

We can identify a multitude of theoretical approaches to an interpretation of architecture. From the perspective of the Sociology of Religion, for example, it might be possible to explore the social and religious plausibility of buildings, and to question what a given building project might contribute to our various constructions of reality. A psychological approach to religion might consist of an investigation into how buildings influence our experiences and conceptions of the spiritual. From an aesthetic point of view, we might investigate how buildings help us to perceive particular spheres or pathways to the divine, whether these are developed within traditional ecclesiastical surroundings or in more secular ones. From a theological perspective we might ask which images of God are displayed, and how these interpret God's liberating activity in, through and by means of space and buildings.

If we try to avoid separating Christian belief and theology from the concept of religion then it becomes natural to see theology as a discursive reflection on different aspects of Christian religiosity. I therefore agree with the anthropologist Clifford Geertz's claim that theology is a discursive reflection on God, and on human experience with God, in the space between a worldview and an emancipative ethos. Like architectural theory, theology emerges as a critical activity in which human beings are able to experience, interpret and shape their life-world by means of a dialectics of subjective and contextual influences.[35]

Hence the question of how men and women experience, interpret and express "what tugs at their heart-strings" in architectural projects lies at the centre of a theological interpretation of architecture. What functions as God in the planning, execution and use of the architect-designed building in a given place? The theological quest for God in architecture is part of a much wider problematic in the study of religion: what aspects of religious belief are expressed in the planning, construction and use of a building? What are the Christian views of life that are expressed in architecture?

What can Religious Studies contribute to architecture and architectural theory? Why is architecture of interest to Religious Studies and Theology?

Architectural Studies of religion

In the light of the wider academic notion of religion outlined above, it seems to make sense to interpret not just religious architecture but also so-called secular building-projects in terms of their religious dimensions.

The new functions of traditional religion and of secular interpretations of life are expressed in human buildings. Any architectural theory that fails to take this into account will appear reductionist and imprisoned within a narrow-minded dualistic way of conceiving the borders between the physical and the metaphysical, the bodily and the spiritual, the visible and the invisible.

In architecture, however, it is particularly important to maintain the connection between subject and context, mind and nature, and inner and outer constructions, thus allowing religious interpretations of life to move freely between different elements or levels within a comprehensive model of architectural interpretation.

If we wish to avoid a dualistic understanding of reality that erects a rational distinction between building technology on the one hand, and the life of ideas that supports it on the other, then we can consider setting the aesthetic autonomy of architecture against the deterministic dominance of religion.

If we view architecture as the art of building then it makes sense to see its aesthetic values as superior to its social and religious values. From this perspective, architecture can be seen to belong both to the theory of art and also to the world of applied art, and thus dependent on and subordinate to historically changing ideas of what we define as art.

The question that then follows is this: how are we to apply the claim that modern art and aesthetics represent, or should represent, autonomous spheres, to religion? A reductionist concept of religion, one that characterizes religion as an ideological drug that blocks or counters human enlightenment, and that Kant characterizes as "our release from an undeserved disempowerment",[36] naturally presupposes or entails a conflict between art and religion. But such a conflict is not inevitable.

In view of the varied definitions of religion given above, the challenge is to combine the autonomous and relational dimensions with the intentional and extensional connections, in both our aesthetic and our religious dealings with one another.

As we have seen, religion is also characterized by its alternation between interacting subjective and contextual elements. A contextual perspective makes it possible to relate the critical acts of art criticism (including architecture) and of religion to each other, without being forced to relinquish the autonomy of art.

Peter Eisenman describes the critical goal facing architecture as that of "an architecture without ready-made meaning, an architecture of unmotivated signs."[37] Such an approach requires that the theologian approach space, and God within space, with "emptiness", foreswearing words and the burden of discourse. Emptiness in this context does not mean the negation of content – because space is never really empty[38] – but rather implies an emptying process understood as a positive act that allows the spirituality of space to be recognized.

There are of course systems of belief within which the deity is attributed such superior significance that everything else in the world becomes subordinate, a screen on to which the believer projects an anthropomorphic conception of God. But such an approach is a futile one, indeed, it can be quite destructive for any authentic religious belief. It is for this reason that we can find, for instance, mystic traditions in which resistance to all religious justifications of oppression has the aim of defending a belief in the unapproachability of the divine as S/he is revealed to us.[39]

Without entering into a discussion of the problems involved in the tension between religious belief on the one hand and the autonomy of art on the other, I would like to mention the possibility of reconciling the two, much as Friedrich Schleiermacher has suggested. According to him, divine revelation is in itself an element in the game and the creative freedom of art. Thus the autonomy of art is itself an expression of God's benevolent creation and the intrinsic powers of creation.[40]

Seen from the perspective on aesthetics offered by liberation theology, we might add that the autonomy of art not only reflects the Creator's love for His/Her free creation, but also that the Creator is in a Christian sense the Liberator of all Creation. Art's critical ability to create independent and contrasting images of prevailing concepts in the interests of liberation constitutes an important part of the autonomous concept of art as well as of the existential and religious interpretation of God within liberation theology. The question is: how does God act as a liberator in, through and with art? Ethical reflections on what needs to be done are embedded both in architectural theory and contextual theology.

Kenneth Frampton describes the function of architecture as that of producing a sort of "reality reserve", "a place where man can still find material and spiritual repose." The crucial task of architecture is to create an enclave within which an alternative to the destructive qualities of technological modernity is able to take shape.[41]

The question is whether art, architecture and religion can make contact with one another through the creation of visions that offer all three a critique of existing civilization and also a counter-culture that is life-enhancing.

In addition to the historical arguments against abandoning the religious dimension of the building, we need to take account of the modernist transformation of the meaning of space. Leading theorists of modernity use terms such as "decontextualization"[42] and "despatialization"[43] to characterize the social conditions of our late-modernist era. They thus provide us with a radically new way to perceive space, one that takes account of changes wrought by innovations in global media and transport systems. The rapid exchange of human beings, ideas, goods and money between different parts of the world diminishes our cultural and historical attachments to our immediate surroundings. Our contextual identities become less linked to one place, and world cultures are increasingly "despatialized." At the same time, however, we should not underestimate the importance of the fact that this same development can lead to a drastically renewed search for local attachments, to what we can see as a movement for renewed "spatialization."

This late-modernist dialectic between despatialization and respatialization, in combination with a revaluation of the local within the global, has been very influential within contemporary architecture. The increasing power of a rich minority to participate in the capital and cultural transnationalization of the global village must be set against the exclusion of the poor majority from this same global village. This majority is instead denied the right to move or to remain in freedom, and is unable to retain its human dignity in small-scale contexts. And such a contrast places architecture at the forefront of a radically new ethical challenge. The process of globalization requires that the construction of buildings become "the embodiment of habitable places",[44] especially in the so-called third world. Alongside the need for self-critical reflection on the task of creating an architecture for the poor, ecological problems and issues connected to the environment represent a pressing ethical challenge for contemporary architecture.

Habermas' thesis that systems are used to colonize life-worlds finds a specifically spatial meaning in the projects of architecture.[45] Are such projects part of the colonizing process, or do they participate in that reconstruction of life-worlds that forms part of a resistance to the colonizers?

Critical theology has also concerned itself with both of these ethical problems that have been thrown up by the contemporary globalization process. Its theologians have claimed that the main task facing the interpretation of God is located within the struggle of the poor for survival and in the longing for liberation felt by all living creatures. God reveals Him/Herself in every place where His/Her creatures suffer injustice.[46] How can both religious interpretation and the architectural project each make their own, unique contribution to the struggle to establish habitable places for human beings and other creatures – assuming that we understand "habitable" in an ecological, social and spiritual sense? How can we construct a place within which a flourishing community of living creatures can be established?

Religious Studies of architecture

Why should those involved in Theology and Religious Studies be concerned with the interpretation of architecture?

One reason is that both the hermeneutic tradition of interpreting spoken and written texts in the Western philosophical tradition, and also the tradition of focussing upon social forms of behaviour within the socio-empirical tradition, need to be expanded so as to include other forms of bodily expression that can themselves be understood as forms of faith. Religious Studies has long confined itself to written texts and has maintained a hostility to the iconic. This tradition must now be opposed. The question of the sacred in buildings and in architectural images of God widens the scope of Religious and Christian Studies.

Another reason is that we have as yet failed properly to investigate the significance that space has in the development of a personal existential and religious philosophy. Western concepts of the world have been too preoccupied with the phenomenon of time to have reached further than to a rather feeble philosophical concern with space, something that has also left its mark on Religious Studies.

In contextual theology, it is especially the liberation theologians of the Latin-American Catholic tradition who see the liberation process as a linear temporal phenomenon, set apart from its spatial context. Indigenous theologians, and representatives from other indigenous spiritual beliefs, have steadfastly maintained the importance of the spatial dimension of spirituality.[47]

Within the natural sciences, pre-Einsteinian Physics has led to other, fatal consequences, understanding space from within a philosophy of time, and seeing both space and time as homogeneous entities. Georg Picht has demonstrated how such a reduction of space has significantly contributed to human beings' destructive interaction with nature.[48] Norberg-Schulz claims that our "loss of image" has led us to conceptualize our environment as a mere spatial container.[49]

In ecological theology, which seeks to establish a harmonious connection between human beings and other forms of life, spatial metaphors gain a new and fundamental significance for the critical correction of a Cartesian and anthropocentric worldview. Architecture can allow religious experience and the interpretation of God to regain their complex spatiality. Hence theology is being challenged to reflect upon the way God acts with regard to earth, land, place and environment. How can God act as liberator in, with and through space?

A third reason is that cultural interpretation is an irreplaceable element in both religious scholarship and normative Christian theology. Architecture reflects representative characteristics of contemporary culture, and it is also an independent force in the physical and ideological transformation of this culture. A Christian belief that sees God as the Creator and Liberator of this world needs to seek God in nature as well as in culture. In the same way as

God became man in Jesus and thus entered into a visible, spatial, bodily and gendered relation to a unique context, believers need to question, continuously and with open minds, how, why and where God acts. The Christian God is the God of the Here and Now. Today, the task of interpreting God is inextricably linked to the task of interpreting the space wherein, whereby and whereon God acts. To say that God only acts within religious institutions or within the innermost hearts of believers is hardly in accordance with a classical understanding of the Creation, which maintains that God is "the creator of everything visible and invisible", and thus can and should be sought everywhere between heaven and earth, in constructed as well as in natural places. Faith has to maintain an openness to spatial surprises by means of which God can manifest His/Her presence.

The Inhabitation of the Spirit

Genius loci

> To belong to a place means to have an existential foothold, in a concrete everyday sense.[50]

Thus writes Christian Norberg-Schulz, in development of his well-known thesis that architecture must relate to the "personal spirit of the place."[51] Architecture must concretize the genius loci. Norberg-Schulz interprets works of art as "imago mundi", images of the world, that help man to "dwell". He invokes a biblical reference when he cites God's words to Cain after man had been driven out of paradise: "You shall be a fugitive and a wanderer on the Earth" (Gen. 4,12), which Norberg-Schulz interprets to mean that man's existential purpose is to "regain the lost place".[52] Norberg-Schulz goes on to develop a phenomenology of place, one within which the genius loci becomes "manifest as location, spatial configuration and characterizing articulation".[53] Place bestows identity on the individual, and this identity in turn allows him or her to participate in and contribute to its history.[54] According to Norberg-Schulz, the identity of place is a necessary precondition of human identity.[55] Thus architecture becomes the art of place.

One of the most important contributions of the phenomenology of place is that it attributes intrinsic value to those spatial constellations whose existence is threatened by modern egomania and technological hubris. To me, the notion of the spirit of the place is a plea to stop treating architecture as autocrat, but to allow it to develop in harmony with that environment in which a building is to be erected. Here, the concept of "spirit" points to what is given, to what human beings need to relate to from an ecological and historical perspective. In a similar way, concepts such as mood, character and atmosphere can help us to understand what I will call the intrinsic value of space and its expression. Thus, Norberg-Schulz's theory lays the basis for a potentially valuable critique of a too narrow-minded anthropocentric view of nature and architecture, a critique that can be used constructively to produce a more sensitive attitude to, as well as an improvement of, the relation between architecture and ecology. So far, so good.

My objections to the notion of a genius loci are connected to its underlying ontology. It seems unclear whether Norberg-Schulz sees the spirit exclusively in terms of the definition outlined above, or if he also assumes that the spirit "exists" and that this spirit makes demands on us. It is not especially controversial to maintain that places exist. But what is it that is in, below or above them?[56]

Does the spirit exist within the place independently of human presence, or does it materialize only in the encounter between the human gaze and the returned "look" of the place? Is the human being him/herself a part of the place or is s/he something other, something set radically apart from its natural character? Do the alterations made to a place by earlier generations belong to its history? Or does a place always remain pure; unsullied by human interference?

I am not questioning the importance of Norberg-Schulz's contribution to a more self-critical and ecological conception of architecture. It is, however, difficult to grasp from what precise position he develops his view of the spirit of place.

Perhaps he needs a Hegelian buttress able to transform his notion of the spirit of place into a kind of metaphysics – but the validity of such a metaphysics is hard to defend today. We could, alternatively, interpret his viewpoint in an animistic sense, in which case the earth would appear as a patchwork of places all of which are animated by a limited number of specific spiritual beings. Or we could link his view to the Romantic belief in the spiritual immanence of the elements, such as the spirits of water, earth, and air.[57] Such an approach would also fit into the Jewish-Greek-Christian belief of late antiquity, in which angels reside in particular places.[58] I am certainly not opposed to a rethinking of the animistic view of nature, and I cannot see that this view in itself necessarily conflicts with a Christian belief in Creation, but such a view requires a more comprehensive argumentation than Norberg-Schulz offers.

A third alternative is to see his thesis as a metaphysical foundation-stone for the development of normative claims about what architecture should be, one produced by introducing nature itself as an ethical argument. Those possessed of knowledge about the immanence of place have the competence to decide what is good architecture, or, rather, what constitutes a building style that is in line with the spirit inherent in the place. The question is merely how, and according to what criteria, one should decide what the spirit of the place is and who is competent enough to make such a decision.[59] In this alternative, the idea of the spirit of place completely loses its presumed critical edge. It becomes nothing more than an instrument for the naturalistic execution of power, one in which terms such as "be" and "should" are seen to possess equal force.

The problems in Norberg-Schulz's attempts to come to terms with the importance of the intrinsic value of space and the uniqueness of place uncover an interesting gap in the history of ideas of the West. The anthropological dichotomy of body and soul has made it virtually impossible for us to grasp the link between space and spirit by means of our present-day conceptual terminology. Architectural theory and theology have both become the victims of a violent curtailment of our perception of reality. From a theological perspective the problems of Norberg-Schulz's phenomenology, and, for that matter, of those associated with the interpretation of the concept of atmosphere, lead us to the following question: in what way does the Spirit of God manifest itself? How can we understand the relation between spirituality and space?

Even though biblical accounts and Christian traditions, and, of course, the accounts of other religions, are full of place-embedded interpretations of God's visible and invisible being, and even if spatial metaphors attempt to express different ways of experiencing God in salvation, it is hard to find theologians who have spent much time reflecting on the relationship between space and Spirit.[60]

Spirit and Spirituality

My initial objection to Norberg-Schulz's line of thought is that the spirit of place can under no circumstances be ontologically identified with the Holy Spirit. If this were the case, we would end up with a pantheistic or animistic religion within which Creation would be synonymous with the Godhead. Religions such as Judaism, Christianity and Islam have all been opposed to such a view, and they have resisted any equation of the Creator and the Creation.

This certainly does not entail that the world is no longer experienced as a place of enchantment. Indeed, the opposite is the case: we are forced to question how the Creation, as the work of the Creator, relates to the world as such. The world remains just as sacred if we conceive of it as the book of the Creator, liber naturae, one to be read alongside the biblical book: a surface on which we can read and interpret the traces of God, vestigia Dei, and within which human beings, and life itself, are seen to be in God's image and part of His/Her handiwork. Within a Christian understanding of the Spirit, the concept of a phenomenology of place requires us to question what relation the spirit of place, and the spiritual aspect of architecture, have to the Holy Spirit.

Could we perhaps make use of the terminology of classical theology and talk about the angels of place, and the Spirit, as those who bring life to all creation?

What do we understand by the term "spirit"? The word evokes a large semantic field which proffers many different and overlapping interpretations. The inherent ambivalence of the term is at the same time disturbing and fruitful. "Spirit" can refer to the physical and spiritual characteristics of human beings, or to a cosmological entity which is either metaphysical, such as a world spirit, or an inherent physical principle, such as energy. The spirit can either be a divine celestial being, as in the third person of The Holy Trinity, or the life-giving element in Divinity. "Thou sendest forth thy spirit, they are created; and thou renewest the face of the earth" (Ps. 104, 30).

A formal definition of "spirit" might help us to keep track of its nature, so that neither its diversity nor its uniqueness are lost in its linguistic richness: "spirit" is one's being in or at the other.[61] Spirit is about relations and movement.

Whether spirituality has any influence on architecture is a question that leads us to wonder how one thing can be in or at the other, whether "the other" could include space and places. What does one's being in or at a place involve? How can some invisible presence be in or at a place as well as in an architectural project in such a way that we can sense it with our minds, perceive it with our intuition, and interpret it with our intellect?

From this perspective, the concept of spirit is not at odds with an acceptance of the body. For me, the spirit brings life to the body and causes it to remember and use its mind in intuitive thinking in inner spaces. Thus, the task for a spiritually conscious architecture is to create "places where human bodies filled with memories are able to dwell successfully".[62]

9

After Francesco di Georgio, The human figure in the Latin cross of the church plan

view of religious buildings and places.[65] I am in agreement with the medieval belief that religious buildings manifest Christ, and that the sacrament of communion enables the congregation to become part of this embodiment and to experience the religious building as a material manifestation of the body of God. Where can we find the embodiment of the Human Christ in modern architecture, and how can the shape of the Creator manifest itself in the midst of human society?

If the present renaissance of a functional architecture designed for human needs finds theological support in the Christological approach of a cosmic God who is immanent in the world, in human beings, and in architecture, then manifestations of God as "of this world" may have something to offer us.

The Early Church saw the human body as a space into which God's Spirit could enter, and human bodies themselves were regarded as God's vessels. People were the loci of the sacred.[66]

> The whole building – whether spiritual or material – grew into one holy temple in the Lord. In whom we, too, are taught to be built together for an habitation of God through the Holy Spirit by ourselves in a spiritual way, the more loftily and fitly we strive to build in a material way.[67]

opposed to such a view, and they have resisted any equation of the Creator and the Creation.

This certainly does not entail that the world is no longer experienced as a place of enchantment. Indeed, the opposite is the case: we are forced to question how the Creation, as the work of the Creator, relates to the world as such. The world remains just as sacred if we conceive of it as the book of the Creator, liber naturae, one to be read alongside the biblical book: a surface on which we can read and interpret the traces of God, vestigia Dei, and within which human beings, and life itself, are seen to be in God's image and part of His/Her handiwork. Within a Christian understanding of the Spirit, the concept of a phenomenology of place requires us to question what relation the spirit of place, and the spiritual aspect of architecture, have to the Holy Spirit.

Could we perhaps make use of the terminology of classical theology and talk about the angels of place, and the Spirit, as those who bring life to all creation?

What do we understand by the term "spirit"? The word evokes a large semantic field which proffers many different and overlapping interpretations. The inherent ambivalence of the term is at the same time disturbing and fruitful. "Spirit" can refer to the physical and spiritual characteristics of human beings, or to a cosmological entity which is either metaphysical, such as a world spirit, or an inherent physical principle, such as energy. The spirit can either be a divine celestial being, as in the third person of The Holy Trinity, or the life-giving element in Divinity. "Thou sendest forth thy spirit, they are created; and thou renewest the face of the earth" (Ps. 104, 30).

A formal definition of "spirit" might help us to keep track of its nature, so that neither its diversity nor its uniqueness are lost in its linguistic richness: "spirit" is one's being in or at the other.[61] Spirit is about relations and movement.

Whether spirituality has any influence on architecture is a question that leads us to wonder how one thing can be in or at the other, whether "the other" could include space and places. What does one's being in or at a place involve? How can some invisible presence be in or at a place as well as in an architectural project in such a way that we can sense it with our minds, perceive it with our intuition, and interpret it with our intellect?

From this perspective, the concept of spirit is not at odds with an acceptance of the body. For me, the spirit brings life to the body and causes it to remember and use its mind in intuitive thinking in inner spaces. Thus, the task for a spiritually conscious architecture is to create "places where human bodies filled with memories are able to dwell successfully".[62]

For a start, such a wide definition of the spirit allows us to identify the spiritual in architecture as well as the spiritual in both place and designed space, regardless of creed or religious tradition. Norberg-Schulz's claim that architecture should relate to existing ecological characteristics, and Böhme's insistence that architecture should respect the atmosphere of the place at the same time as it should create new atmospheres, can be expanded with the claim that architecture should contribute to a rendering visible of the invisible at particular places and in particular buildings. It is of little importance whether we use Rudolph Otto's or Mircea Eliade's religious phenomenology of the sacred or the holy, or whether we call it spirituality or genius loci. What is important is that architecture should open up to the prospect of relating to a religious context without having to identify directly with confessional systems of belief. Naturally, various religious traditions offer many worthwhile opportunities to interpret "spirit" in this way. So, how can architecture express the ultimate or conditional concerns of humanity?

Only when we have reached an understanding of this open-ended view of spirituality, one that can become visible even when it is obscured, can we develop a theory of God's creative and life-giving Spirit that can be applied to a theological interpretation of architecture.

If we apply the theory of spirituality directly to the relationship between places and constructed spaces, we run the immediate risk of creating an aesthetic, ethical and theological short-circuit. Believers seek to identify what corresponds to their image of God's spirit in architecture, in order to decide what can be classified as spiritual and non-spiritual architecture. The process is circular and self-confirming.

Such a form of logical self-confirmation threatens to turn both theology and ethics into tools for the unmediated, totalitarian exercise of power. Our faith is stifled if the distinction between a human image of God and God Him/Herself is erased. Mankind turns God into an idol that can be held in the hands. Ethics is stifled when there is no longer room for discursive reflection on what ought to be done in a discussion between parties who are all affected by a moral problem. Aesthetics and architectural design are stifled because they, with all their autonomy and situatedness, can no longer function as a sanctuary within which an experimenting Creator can liberate and surprise us. The creative freedom of aesthetics is a necessary condition, not only for art, but also for a religion which seeks to open up for dynamic evolution, for a God who can maintain His/Her creative freedom to act.

It is of great importance for religious dialogue that this open view of spirituality in architecture is demonstrated in the building construction of the future. Only when different religious traditions are free to recharge, to recognize, to re-interpret and to renew their self-esteem in rooms of their own, only then can we realize the hope of a peaceful pluralistic world in which we live together in transcultural co-existence. In this context, Ando's search for a well-defined pluralistic minimum, one in which houses are designed so as to allow different religious traditions to feel at home, is a step in the right direction.

Such a communion can hardly be a threat to a Christian trinitarian belief in the inhabitation of God's Holy Spirit, unless we maintain the exclusivist doctrine that makes the monistic claim that Christianity offers the sole path leading to God's redemption.

The Spirit as Life-giver to place

Gregory of Nazianz, a theologian of the Eastern Early Church, sees the Spirit as "the liberator of nature". Gregory postulates that God acts in three historical periods. First, during the era of the Father before Incarnation, second, in the time of the Son, and finally in the time of the Spirit after Ascension.[63] According to him, the inhabitation oft the Spirit succeeds incarnation of the Son. God's spirit becomes flesh in Creation, both in the shape of a human being and in those of the many other living creatures. We find an important, radical change in the perception of the Spirit in the writings of Gregory and of other theologians of the Early Church. God is no longer seen as eternal tranquillity and rest, while all change and mobility belong to the lower, physical world. Now the divine has been allowed both bodily feelings and mobility.[64] The Trinitarian Spirit breathes, embodies, dwells and is sensed as both a local and a global revelation of God's immensity.

Incarnation theology with its teaching concerning the mystery of God's embodiment in Christ might have provided us with a different development in Trinitarian architectural theology, a possibility on which I will touch only briefly here.

Just as the iconoclastic movement of the 8th century led to debate as to whether the Deity could be represented, so too the concept of incarnation, or the belief that God became flesh in Christ, may encourage a positive view of our human body-centred experiences and of the structural "bodies" of architecture. The history of the Early Church provides evidence of a clear revaluation of the significance of the suffering body in reaching an understanding of God. This revaluation has in its turn influenced the Christian

9

After Francesco di Georgio, The human figure in the Latin cross of the church plan

view of religious buildings and places.⁶⁵ I am in agreement with the medieval belief that religious buildings manifest Christ, and that the sacrament of communion enables the congregation to become part of this embodiment and to experience the religious building as a material manifestation of the body of God. Where can we find the embodiment of the Human Christ in modern architecture, and how can the shape of the Creator manifest itself in the midst of human society?

If the present renaissance of a functional architecture designed for human needs finds theological support in the Christological approach of a cosmic God who is immanent in the world, in human beings, and in architecture, then manifestations of God as "of this world" may have something to offer us.

The Early Church saw the human body as a space into which God's Spirit could enter, and human bodies themselves were regarded as God's vessels. People were the loci of the sacred.⁶⁶

> The whole building – whether spiritual or material – grew into one holy temple in the Lord. In whom we, too, are taught to be built together for an habitation of God through the Holy Spirit by ourselves in a spiritual way, the more loftily and fitly we strive to build in a material way.⁶⁷

According to this view, the structural body of the building, the physical body of the human being, and the body of Christ as God's manifestation are all intrinsically linked to one another. The doctrine of spiritual immanence combines cosmic, architectural, anthropological and theological dimensions. The Early and Medieval Church's understanding of the human, the worldly and the divine looked upon the human body as its most fundamental metaphor. As Richard Sennett has demonstrated, this notion was the starting-point for all ideology and practice, and for the very fundamentals of urban planning throughout the history of the Western world.

The emergence of a more modern worldview by means of which the natural sciences gained more and more power, technically and otherwise, over nature, and as a result of which human beings have distanced themselves from God and nature, has caused the old concept of spiritual immanence to lose its significance, but there might still be room for a theandric (God-human) theology of architecture in a secularized future. In this essay, however, I have chosen to focus on theories of spirituality, what we refer to as pneumatology.

I agree with Gregory's view of pneumatology as a continuation of the Christological theology of incarnation. The inhabitation of the Spirit unveils the continuing story of God in the world. While the Christological perspective might take us too far into a discussion of church architecture, pneumatology can help us to keep our minds open enough to recognize spiritual presence even in secular buildings.

Classical Christianity is not primarily based on the ontological doctrine of the essence of God, but rather on the soteriological doctrine of God's liberating action. If we seek to reach a traditional theological understanding of architecture, we cannot choose the ontological approach, and it is this that is the flaw in Norberg-Schulz's theory. Arguments such as "Architecture represents the nature of God", which have been common in Western theological and architectural history, need now to be changed to "Architecture shows the act of God in His/Her creation". The question for architectural theology should therefore be: how does God act as liberator in all aspects of architecture?

This question needs to be raised in connection with almost any project, and there is absolutely no need to limit it to religious ones. As long as there are human beings who believe in an acting God, the question will remain important with relation to whether, where and how such a God acts in space and place.

The scholar of Islam John Renard has suggested a method for the comparative study of religious architecture. His method has been constructed with buildings in explicitly religious contexts in mind. But it can also be profitably employed in the study of the spirituality of secular architecture.

Renard establishes his method on the basis of the following four premisses.[68] His method must

a) "take into account both the creative and the expressive dimensions of art",

b) "be aware of the physical, historical and material conditions of its creation",

c) take into account shared "stylistic and formal affinities across religious boundaries", and

d) avoid "postulating any common, universal or ineffable core, either of religious experience or artistic inspiration based on some alleged reservoir of archetypal symbolism."

Renard's method is designed to be used only as "heuristic device" and makes no universalistic claims.

Furthermore, Renard makes us aware of the problem that any interpretation of pictorial art or of construction art does not legitimize self-evident claims about the concepts of belief held by those who created, paid for, or used the objects in question, as artistic creation follows its own aesthetic dynamics.[69] Renard proposes that theology make use of a comparative method which "seeks to interpret the Christian tradition conscientiously in dialogue with the texts and symbols of non-Christian religious traditions."[70]

A pneumatological interpretation of confessional and secular architecture can make use of his method by further developing it so as to be able to investigate the ways in which an architectural project can express a spirituality that has been refined through belief in the Holy Spirit. This Spirit has been characterized as Life-giver and Creator in both the Jewish and the Christian traditions. It has been perceived and described as a liberating force that works by means of the word of truth. The Spirit has also been seen as the guardian of socio-cultural memory, a guardian that enables us to deal with our sufferings, hopes and visions. Inherent in the non-human metaphors of the Spirits of fire and wind is an understanding of the Spirit's immanence in relations and movements. The Spirit blows where s/he wishes, "bloweth where it listeth" (John, 3, 8), it stirs and it moves, it raises the dead, and it is the creator of "life in the world to come." It is not difficult to identify in such traditional terminology the Spirit's topology as "God's Embodied Power" and as the "Intermediator" who is sent to Earth.[71]

Different components out of which a theological interpretation of architecture might thus be formed could include:

10

Nicholas Hawksmoor, Christ Church Spitalfields, west facade from the South, 1715-1729

a) taking the autonomy and the intrinsic value of architectural design into consideration in the search for an identification of its inherent spirituality, i.e. in values such as justice and beauty;
b) consciously developing this interpretation while bearing in mind the importance of context, so that the question of God's acting is not answered in terms of propositional dogmatics, but in terms of a contextual interpretation of specific features of the project's socio-cultural and ecological situatedness;
c) taking into account the specific qualities of visual culture – and in particular those unique artistic aspects of the place – when attempting to develop an independent aesthetic dynamics founded on human body-centred perceptions of inner, remembered and outer spaces;
d) setting to work the question of God's Spirit's life-giving labour in a pluralistic and open horizon, so that other religious and conceptual traditions are neither obscured nor subdued, but can remain in harmony with, or in critical contrast to, the identification of God's Holy Spirit.

How can such a method be made to work?

11   Antoni Gaudí, Casa Milà, Barcelona, 1906-10

Antoni Gaudí's "Casa Milà" – spiritual empowerment of a creative self in nature

Gaudí's apartment building in Barcelona expresses both weight and lightness in a single material "body". The massive darkness of the stone contrasts with the soft, undulating lines of the design. Gaudí's preparation of the stone has caused the façade to reveal a primordial force that leads the onlooker to imagine an ancient, weather-beaten cliff. The balcony railings have been treated in a similar manner so as to make them appear like petrified driftwood. Natural materials have been transformed into powerful images. Humanity thus reveals its power to shape and transform nature. What is unprocessed and raw becomes the material by means of which inner feelings and parabolic images are expressed. Gaudí successfully anticipates the later ethos of Expressionism.[72]

How are we to interpret Gaudí's spirituality? My immediate reaction to Casa Milà was one of surprise. Could a house really look like that? Was this building the product of a civilization, or had it been shaped by nature and then culturally refined and "touched up"? The process of construction had clearly followed the former rather than the latter sequence. Gaudí had begun with a plan and its implementation, and only then could an observer be given a sense of the raw natural force of the material. The historical process of nature becoming culture had been inverted. Culture is used to generate an imagined nature. To use Walter Benjamin's words, the house represents "an emancipated technique, a second nature."[73]

Here, human creative powers are expressed in, as well as by means of, natural materials. The creative human spirit and nature's evolutionary shaping processes of grinding, erosion, and wear-and-tear all work together. The house's obvious allusions to a cave remind us of the old theory that the shape of the cave was the starting-point for all building processes. Gaudí appears to associate himself with those seeking to return to some sort of original state of being, while at the same time we are made strongly aware of the fact that the house is unmistakably a human construction by means of the regularity of the variations of the lines on the façade and by the shapes of the windows.

Gaudí's house conveys a spirituality by visual means inasmuch as its material form communicates to us a range of references to various ideological, ecological and religious realms. It is tempting to regard the house as an object through which a religious worship of nature, as much as a sort of egocentric hubris, are depicted. The house clearly radiates values within which raw natural forces and the architect's creative abilities are seen in balanced relation. The house is an anthropocentric aesthetics of nature constructed of stone! A house like a mountain, in which human beings live as in a cave. A habitation that both contains and represents Gaudí's creative spirit.

What about the inhabitation of the Spirit? In contrast to Gaudí's famous "Familia Sagrada" church, Casa Milà discloses no reference to established religious traditions. Accordingly, theological concepts can be used to interpret the house only if treated as heuristic tools. In this work, we sense the same liberating spiritual power as we do in biblical traditions. The architectural design is so intense and dynamic that the lightness inherent in the otherwise downwards-striving weight of the building is revealed in every nook and corner. Anyone standing on one of the balconies feels completely emancipated from the forces of gravitation and ready to float freely in space.

It is more difficult to recognize a sense of the spirit working to create communion through communication in this house. Its separation from its surroundings, and the plastic mass of the building, are so dynamic in themselves that any sense of respect for place – for the situation of the house – is destroyed. Gaudí wants rather to distinguish himself and his house from its surroundings.

The building seems to have landed accidentally in strange surroundings like a mighty visitor from another planet. It is still an open question whether it can ever form a relationship with its immediate environment. The viewer

12

Antoni Gaudí, Sagrada Familia, Barcelona, 1884 (not yet finished)

feels excluded. The house has the air of a castle or a fortress. Its structure offers our souls an almost impenetrable sanctuary, within which the dark aspects of the city's soul can be hidden away.

The Spirit of liberation may be discovered within the creative force. I sense the Life-giving Spirit in the creative powers that created the house, and not in the house's social and communicative functions. Its symbolic manipulation of light, however, reminds me of a Gothic cathedral, within which a controlled influx of daylight renders it possible to follow movement throughout the day. This is a religious reference with which we are familiar from other works by Gaudì.

I hope that my short interpretation has led to an understanding of how asking questions about the spirituality of architecture, and attempting to answer these questions in a pneumatological key, can throw light on the perception of atmosphere in houses and on the possible meanings of such atmosphere.

The purpose of theological hermeneutics is not to further a confessional dogmatics. Rather, it is one of several interpretative tools made use of to capture the rich imagery in architectural design. What seems to have been closest to the heart of the creator of Casa Milà, and also the ultimate concern of the building itself, are those creative powers that impose form on raw nature and provide it with inner meaning. Such a god does not conflict with my own image of the Holy Spirit, which I see as a liberating, immanent force in this building.

Aesth/Ethics of Inhabitation

An ethos of dwelling?

In his comprehensive study of "the ethical function of architecture", philosopher Karsten Harries develops a critique of the aesthetic approach to architecture. To Harries, this approach consists of a combination of building and decoration, a view that has long been dominant in modernist architecture. He contrasts this with an ethical approach, for which, in his view, the purpose for architecture is:

> . . . to help us find our place and way in an ever more disorienting world.[74]

For Harries, as for Heidegger, ethos is the human "way of dwelling".[75]

Harries makes use of a Heideggerian, anthropological approach to construct his view of the function of architecture. He describes the human existential situation with reference to the metaphor of the Fall, without relating it to its origins in the Jewish Faith and the biblical story.[76] Man/woman is searching for the lost paradise, and the ethical function of architecture is to help him/her find it. Harries calls for critics to treat with suspicion a conventional ethical view of the function of architecture, a view which for him represents the values and interests of those with power. Instead, he sees its function to be to:

> . . . preserve and re-present the inevitable tensions between spirit and nature, community and the individual, private and public, temple and house.[77]

Harries' answer to our introductory question of how to re-establish the space of sacred architecture's position, is that architecture should under no circumstances strive to replace the church or the temple. According to Hegel, this is no longer possible. On the other hand, architecture can, at its best, create "festal qualities of public spaces, squares, streets and parks".[78] Its ethical function is to create the spatial conditions for human fellowship.

I agree with Harries that architectural criticism resembles a decorated shed to the extent that it dissociates the aesthetic from its context. I can also subscribe to his argument that architecture as an act of interpretation, even though his linguistic metaphor of "the language of architecture" complete with texts and messages, threatens to occlude its visual forms of expression.

And finally, I can go along with his claim that architecture contributes to an ethical formulation of and solution to the existential question of how to survive in our contemporary world.

On the other hand, some of his basic arguments seem problematic. Do we have to follow existentialism's pessimistic view of the individual as a fallen, constrained and tragic being? Harries does not argue for his choice of an existential anthropology as the determining factor in his understanding of morality and ethics. From this perspective, morality is the guide pointing the way out of the abyss of our existence. Might not the metaphor of a "paradise lost" allow us to come up with the unlikely premiss that such an ideal, natural condition actually once existed, and that our task is to strive for its resurrection by means of architecture?

In spite of all his post-modernist awareness, Harries seems to remain imprisoned within Rousseau's and Kant's notion of future liberation as a process that closes the historical circle by restoring a natural, ideal state. We may object to such a view from a historical perspective, and ask ourselves when and where such an ideal state could have existed. From a biblical point of view, we may take exception to such an interpretation of Genesis, in which the text has been attributed a meaning that was surely never intended. And finally, from a historical-philosophical and ethical point of view, we might object that it is never specified who will work out and be the judge of the criteria for the creation of such an ideal state, such a perfect human dwelling.

It seems more fruitful to choose a different approach to the ethical consideration of the moral problems of habitation and architecture.

From a phenomenological point of view we are able to ascertain that our whole existence is morally ambiguous. It often remains unclear what is right and wrong, good or evil, and whether our actions, in spite of our intentions and high principles, may lead to consequences which we do not perceive to be proper or desirable. "The good I want to do, I do not, but the evil I do not want to do, that I do", concluded St. Paul (Rom. 7, 19).

An ethical code that strives for a universal morality can also contribute to the undermining of our individual moral responsibility, as the subjective moral impulse will suffocate if we are to rely exclusively on systems to bear all of the moral criteria for our actions.[79] The individual would be freed from all personal responsibility, and immoral activities in the shadow-land between rules and regulations would expand to become what we now call "organized non-responsibility" (U. Beck) in a global, late-capitalist economy of the global casino within which everyone is exempt from personal or collective responsibility. A moral ethics which seeks to confront this development by requiring us to reflect on our personal moral qualities is not, to my mind, very helpful. Only the combination of a social ethics and an ecological ethics of justice, a combination that can embrace our personal as well as our intersubjective responsibilities within a discourse-ethical framework, can serve the purpose here.

Space and justice

I find it hard to see how architecture, by means of an existentialist or moralistic concept of ethics, can help us find a way out of a course of development as a result of which humanity seems to spend most of its time in shopping centres. There is no room in Harries' discourse for raising the question of personal responsibility, or that of how to create a society which encourages such responsibility, instead of handing it over to the machinery of power. Nor does he make any provision for the battle for justice, and values of justice and beauty are contrasted instead of being seen in terms of their interconnections. What we need is a critique of the "aestheticization of economics",[80] as well as a re-examination of the individual's ethical and ecological obligations in and to society.

To Kenneth Frampton, the ethical challenge of architecture is the responsibility to search for enclaves wherein visions of a new kind of relationship between rich and poor can be realized. Zara Hadid accurately sums up architecture's ethical responsibility in her thesis: "No architecture without a social programme."[81] We could adopt Adorno's argument and say that architecture's responsibility is not just to make happiness come true, but also to bring about social and ecological justice. Does this seem unrealistic? Or is it more convenient to stick to a more general kind of ethical discussion which concludes that the duty of architecture is to provide human beings with a place for being and a place for living in this world?

Heidegger's philosophy is hardly the solution, but it is a first step to answering the overall ethical question of how to inhabit the world.

A reflection on the ethical function of architecture must start with an analysis of the world we live in, one that focuses especially on both the negative and the positive aspects of everyday life.[82] Just as liberation theology require of us that we seek God in conflicts in which the living suffer at the hands of violence and evil, so too architecture's ethical function should be seen as a central factor in the threatening conflicts taking place in today's world. Thus architecture's ethical contribution is that of laying the foundation for a positive habitation, one in which equity is the norm for human beings and justice flourishes among human beings and conditions the relations between culture and nature. Architecture must not be reduced to a mere "tool of domination."[83] It must also challenge us to rethink what it is that constitutes a good life. Such a position accords with Eisenman's view of the critical dimension of architecture; architectural design must emerge from areas of violation and despair as a result of the witness borne by places that have not been settled by meanings engendered by obfuscation and reductionism.

Ethical pluralism

In common with those within the field of ecological ethics who have stated the case for pluralism,[84] I do not wish to advocate a single fundamental ethical theory of architecture, but rather to propose a constellation of different models following which such a theory might be constructed. All universalistic theories of ethics have merits and weaknesses which disqualify them as total conceptions. I have chosen a situation-oriented model that allows one to select a combination of different paradigms according to the nature of the moral dilemma, even though the criteria for such a selection cannot always be wholly consistent.

So far as architecture is concerned, this requires an ethics of discourse, one that advocates a practical form of discourse within which everyone involved participates in a process of problem-solving communication. This form is well suited to, for instance, planning processes associated with architectural projects, but it is not at all applicable to the creative building process, for this follows other forms of dynamics.

Utilitarianism has made us aware that specially designed residential areas can have major consequences for future generations, something that should make us sensitive to the need for change and to varied processes of cultural identification. But utilitarians can hardly claim that the aim of architecture is to build as much "happiness" as possible for as many people as possible. Such maxims can easily lead to a world in which the number of parking places constitutes the highest possible measurement of communal happiness and economic success.

A deontological ethics of principle is also significant, as we are in constant need of formal values which are constant in time and space. It seems, for example, meaningful to develop rules and regulations for urban development that are both ethically and aesthetically aware. There are numerous worst-case scenarios that demonstrate what completely uninhibited urban growth can lead to. Discourse ethics could be regarded as a modern way to create a place for an ethics that is in search of sustainable principles for changing times.

I find it more difficult to apply the kind of moralist ethics of virtue that is in vogue at the moment, to architecture, but we can find individual and social virtues even in building design. Older forms of architectural ethics have clearly established a connection between the individual architect and his physical sensibility, the complexity and beauty of the building, and the diversity and splendour of its natural surroundings. The aesthetic and ethical flourishing of the person who designs, the house that is designed, and the ecological contexts to which both belong, must all be seen in their interrelationship.

Questions relating to such things as the ethical theory underpinning architecture, or the claims of pluralism, are complex and belong to another discussion. For the moment I will limit myself to suggesting that it is better to encourage the free investigation of a range of new approaches, than to search – as does Harries – for a single, normative, understanding of "the" ethical function. The time does not seem ripe for such a search.[85]

Ecological Aesthetics

A third critical objection to the case made both by Harries and the 2000 Biennial for "more ethics – less aesthetics" involves the relationship between aesthetics and ethics. It seems problematic to set the two in opposition. Harries' critique is justified in as much as aesthetics cannot serve as the supreme normative planning theory. Aesthetics can never replace ethics, just as reductionist concepts of beauty can never produce a standard measure of what is a good way of life. Contemporary art mercilessly reveals how necessary it is for us to search for what is good and beautiful in amongst all that is ugly and objectionable, rather than seeking for superficial aestheticizing stereotypes. Beauty is just as ambiguous a concept as is benevolence.

Another possible approach to the ethical function of architecture might be that of an ecological aesthetics of nature.[86] Here, the aesthetic approach is completely different from that of Harries or of a superficial aesthetic beautification (Verhübschung) of the world. Gernot Böhme has successfully researched this approach, and he sees aesthetics as a self-aware human reflection on one's living-in-particular-surroundings.

His conclusion is that human beings should no longer maintain a distance from nature, but should rather seek to participate in the natural life cycle that deploys all of their faculties. An ecological aesthetics of nature is as much a subjective self-reflection on human identity as it is a reflection on that which surrounds us – and, in addition, on the difference between humanity and its enveloping environment.

13

*Philibert De L'Orme,
The Bad Architect,
from: Le Premier Tome
De L'Architecture, 1567*

In architectural terms, this model means that atmosphere is both human and physical, subjective and objective. There is no longer any distinction between subject and object, creator/user and building. It is the encounter between them that becomes the focus for meditation. People look at themselves in the mirror of their own, designed spaces,[87] and these in their turn render back a reflection of what is personal and unfamiliar within and around them. Nature, that which is both given and from-the-outside, encounters humanity in a process of procreation. The fruits of such an encounter go on to lead lives of their own. We meet them again in the shape of moods and atmosphere, and in the nature of the place, in ways that allow others to perceive them freely and independently. Here, architecture is seen as an embodiment of spirit: the human spirit and nature's own spirits in harmony. To what degree God's Holy Spirit takes part in and at these encounters between body and spirit is an intriguing theological question that needs to be investigated.

Is this type of aesthetic reflection on architecture also ethically relevant? We might distinguish between ethics and aesthetics, and let the former refer exclusively to a reflection on human sensual encounters and manifestations of their surroundings, while using the latter term to imply a reflection on the moral question of good or evil. Minds do not judge, they just sense,

14

*Philibert De L'Orme,
The Good Architect,
from: Le Premier Tome
De L'Architecture, 1567*

perceive, comprehend and interpret – they are. I find it hard to detect a clear distinction between ethics and aesthetics.

If ethics is defined as a discursive reflection on moral problems, it becomes difficult to exclude people's mental capacities and to separate aesthetic competence from moral competence. The challenge to create aesthetic sensibility in human beings through a specially designed pedagogy of art seems to me to be a very relevant ethical requirement, especially in today's society, and especially if we want to counteract the steadily increasing mystification of the moral problems of our human and non-human neighbours. It takes a sharp mind and the ability to see our neighbour's misery, to answer Cain's question "Lord, am I my brother's keeper?" There are strong forces at work seeking to impose a media-structured reduction on our ability to perceive social and ecological injustice in the world. For this reason aesthetic sensibility is needed in order to create a counterbalance to our contemporary and ongoing superficial aestheticization.[88] We can thus discover an ethical function in aesthetics, both in theory and in practice. Good, beautiful and functional houses cause us to sharpen our senses, to deepen and improve our reasoning and our moral talents in our encounters with the unfamiliar other.

15   Oscar Niemeyer, Cathedral, Brasília, 1950-58

Aesth/Ethics of justice for heterogenity

In his discussion of heterogeneity, Theodor W. Adorno demonstrates that justice and aesthetics are not necessarily far apart. In his book "Ästhetische Theorie", Adorno states:

> Ästhetische Einheit empfängt ihre Dignität durchs Mannigfaltige selbst. Sie läßt dem Heterogenen Gerechtigkeit widerfahren.[89]

Adorno sees no opposition between the autonomy and the social application of art. On the contrary, the autonomous nature of artistic creativity presupposes a special position in society. Art only gains social relevance by being an "antipode to society", and this can only be achieved through autonomy.[90] Art's mere existence provides a special, critical function in society, one which must be allowed to constitute itself independently and without having to submit to the rules and regulations of the instrumentalist forces of specific social interests. Works of art are forms of

16

*Oscar Niemeyer,
Cathedral, Brasília,
1950-58*

In spite of his self-confessed socialism, Niemeyer never actually designed special places for the poor. But his creative intention can be understood as an attempt to open up egalitarian spaces in which all could enter. In order to come into his cathedral in the utopian city of Brasília, we have to dive through a tunnel into the darkness of the earth, before we swim in a sublime movement, up and down and up again, out into a sea of coloured lights under the cathedral crown of God for his Imago Dei et Imago Mundi.

reification which attempt to resist their transformation from matter into commodity.

Adorno suggests that two conditions must be satisfied for art to achieve autonomy. The first of these is the ability to resist submission to the heteronomy of instrumentalization, but instead to proffer self-generated alternatives. The other condition is to possess the ability to visualize that which is heterogenous. This duality, along with "the factual historical status of the inherent heterogeneity of art" is what constitutes the pre-conditions for works of art.[91] According to Adorno, this is how art can help to provide a qualitatively unique dimension to our understanding of justice.

In addition to his concept of aesthetic justice, Adorno is very critical of political-juridical concepts of justice. These are, according to him, incapable of detecting inequalities and differences between individuals and groups of people. The meaning of heterogeneity destroys by means of a formal principle of equality, which actually obscures differences.[92] Unity is constructed on the basis of the levelling-out of differences, rather than by creating a totality based on complexity and diversity.

Only when justice has been guaranteed for the outsider and the stranger can the autonomy of all living beings be fulfilled in a sense of communal belonging. Art can depict in sensuous and meaningful ways how the whole gains its dignity from diversity and the mutual perception and acknowledgement of unequal equals. The more unlike the more equal, the more heteronomous the more autonomous, the more unfamiliar the more recognizably equal. How foreign but yet familiar![93]

Adorno's principle of heterogeneity also applies to architecture, in as much as architecture contributes to a striving for the realization of visions of an alternative life. Architecture should contribute to the sharpening of our senses, so that we may experience injustices in others as well as in ourselves, and so as to create spaces which affect and further our ability to become familiar with the foreign.

To avoid any misunderstanding I must stress that I am not advocating an architectural style of "the just house", but rather that I want to outline a vision of creating houses in which justice can reign. In the ancient Egyptian religion, justice was considered to be a deity: Maàt.[94] A deity does not require a palace, it needs a temple in which believers can perceive his/her existence.

Anyone who has ever been treated unjustly, and anyone who is impoverished through his or her placement within an economic or other structure and thus forcefully prevented from living a decent life, will have experienced how injustice is incorporated in society at large. Such victims see the temples of injustice filled with an atmosphere of evil and meanness. Why not build cathedrals of justice, which was the original idea behind the Gothic cathedrals, buildings in which Christian mercy and human compassion were set against medieval greed, even at the level of urban planning?[95] On the basis of our previous discussion of Harries' ideas of confessional re-sacralization, this vision should lead us not to a temple of justice as the early church saw it, but rather to make us question how we can lay the foundations for justice to reign in all kinds of houses, be they residences, workplaces, or public areas.[96]

Aesthetics should thus not be kept apart from ethics. Aesthetics should precede ethics and set an example for it. It is hard to perceive anything at all of what constitutes a moral problem if we did not have a developed mental ability to succour our physical, intuitive and thus also our rational skills. One might say that good houses develop our abilities to discern moral injustice, and help us to act accordingly. Art can well be both autonomous and ethically and contextually relevant. It is precisely because of its particular, self-governing ability to realize completely different sets of unfettered visions that art can contribute to the widening of our imaginative and creative horizons, so that new perspectives and approaches can be revealed to us. Thus art and aesthetics also provide the space for a greater freedom of ethical discourse.

For Marcuse, the concept of autonomous art is a mirror-image of oppression.[97] With its inherent aesthetic form, art can only contribute in a critical way to the struggle for liberation.[98] In Marcuse's view, art is an inauthentic utopia based on memory.[99] To avoid setting aesthetics apart from ethics, I therefore suggest that the ethical functions of architecture should be worked out not according to an exclusively moral-philosophical discourse, but should be designed as an aesth/ethics for inhabitation.[100] At the core of such an approach lies the question: what do architectural projects express with regard to human self-reflection in the mirror of our natural surroundings? What visions of another life do they express?[101] How can men and women move about, enter and leave, meet and depart, yes, live their lives in a fellowship based on diversity, justice and beauty in places of eco-aesthetic design? From a theological perspective, such places must be seen as spaces in which God's Holy Spirit is present.

In order to avoid a schism between aesthetics and ethics, I would like to suggest that the ethical function of architecture is not exclusively to design an aesth/ethics of inhabitation. The central question in such a postulation is: what can the architectural project tell us about human self-reflection through our natural surroundings? What new visions does it offer for a different way of life, a new way of living?

The aesthetic questions associated with human bodily being, and the task of designing the body of the building in organic nature, must confront the question of humanity's encounter with the environment through architecture. Religious concepts of holiness, invisibility and spirituality, and the theological question of the three-in-one Godhead's liberating power are all embodied in this postulation.

Artists can teach us a lot about the bringing-together of aesthetics, ethics and spirituality in architectural building. In conclusion, I would like to present three visual artists, from very different contexts and backgrounds, in order to illustrate how such a synopsis can come into being, and to discuss what it might mean for an aesth/ethics of inhabitation.

SIGURD BERGMANN

17

Eduardo Chillida, Esertoki III, iron, 1990, collection of the artist

The intrinsic value of space and place for Eduardo Chillida

In order to avoid all the problems of limitation associated with Norberg-Schulz's argument about the spirit of place, I prefer to discuss the intrinsic spiritual value of space. Space is there, regardless of geographical and ecological surface constellation and life-forms. Space is there, in the curved exterior of planets, or in the biosphere which makes the space between heaven and earth habitable. Space is what makes all habitation on earth at all possible. Space is what sets the biosphere in motion with all its natural and cultural atmospheres. Space is like the spirit, says the famous Basque sculptor Eduardo Chillida.

> The space is for me some kind of medium. We are part of it. Space is the most living of all that surrounds us. It is like the spirit. . . . Properly speaking we could not speak of space. This kind of space has to be felt, it has to meet something adequate inside us.[102]

The notion of an intrinsic value of space becomes even more important, if I seek to avoid the obscurity of the notion of atmosphere. Space exists before we experience it with our bodies. I would like to imagine a space for atmosphere, a spatial spiritual reality within which atmospheres can come and go, can be preserved, transformed, and can fade away as in a twilight realm, and then rise again like the dawn.

For the sculptor Eduardo Chillida, his duty as a sculptor is to make this spiritual space visible.

While Chillida's art creates spatial objects in quiet and restful poses, architecture needs to focus too on the dynamics of the moving body and on its need for a designed place in which to move. Humankind and architecture are both on the move. If the spirit in Chillida's spaces were to be applied to architecture, it would be in the form of a blowing, moving, touching spirit which breathes dynamic life into spaces in which human beings are free to move.

Spaces of mythical continuity in the work of Iver Jåks

The indigenous Sami artist Iver Jåks represents another way of depicting the intrinsic value of space.

While Chillida works with powerful designs and with transformations of natural materials, Jåks follows the natural properties of the material as closely as possible. He seeks to find the original expression in the thing itself, which is as far away from the decorative dichotomy between nature and culture of our times as is possible.

In order to find what is characteristic of indigenous art, we must look at the way the materials are treated. Natural and iconic meanings merge as closely as possible. The intrinsic value of nature comes into being precisely in and through its encounter with human creativity. We do not show our respect for nature by distancing ourselves from it, as many urban environmentalist movements do, or by advocating an ideal state of freedom for human beings, but in a peaceful meeting between nature and human creativity. Jåks joins forces with the ancient tradition of a small-scale premodern technology, something that deserves reappraisal in the chaos of our over-aestheticized and hyper-technological world. The aesthetics of economics is here challenged by an aesthetics of the indigenous mythical harmony between culture and nature. It is a challenge that is posed when hands join hands, eyes meet eyes, thoughts, visions and memories are bound to land and to open spaces.

Jåks' use of materials follows the traditions of the older Sami duodji-

18 Iver Jåks, *Lea go, vai ii? Det er, er det?* 1997, wood

culture, artistic handicraft designed to be used in everyday life, but founded on spiritually, religious and culturally inherited traditions. His method is accordingly well-suited to be used as a starting-point for a discussion of how architectural design can utilize building materials as a web from which spaces and visions can be spun.

Aesth/Ethics of transfigured spaces for Kurt Schwitters

Kurt Schwitters, the inimitable Dadaist artist from Hannover who lived in Norway and England during the war, has long dwelt in the shadow-land of art history. Schwitters' artistic expression is effected through architecture. His famous MERZ-buildings could easily be dismissed as eccentric attempts to illustrate the short-lived ideas of contemporary Dadaist ideas. Some critics see Schwitters' pictorial development of the techniques and theory of collage as but a brief episode following Duchamps' earlier breakthrough and Max Ernst's montage programme. To me, Schwitters stands out as a creative artist who anticipated many of our present and future architectural problems, both in his MERZ-art and in his collages. Schwitters developed an aesthetics with ethical significance, an extremely practical way of transforming spaces to fit new concepts of dynamic motion and involving new syntheses. Schwitters converted objects and spaces into artistic abodes for human beings.

Schwitters' main idea behind the MERZ-project was to demonstrate how space changes in accordance with the movements of the human body. Schwitters repudiates Newton's concepts of physics, and devotes himself entirely to the giddying idea that we cannot rely on any notion of the absolute in space. Spaces appear and are transfigured – to use a concept from the Eastern Orthodox Church – in accordance with the position of our bodies. Each individual is a part of space. He/she changes space into place, and place in turn changes him/her by moving his or her body hither and thither. In addition, Schwitters anticipated an insight which has only recently met with acceptance: "Houses can fly." ("Häuser können fliegen.")[103]

Schwitters' MERZ-buildings (most of them now destroyed) thus present us with a complexity which is almost unbearable. It becomes almost impossible to remember in our inner selves what the room that we have just left, looked like. The MERZ-building overloads the recording capacity of our ability to memorize.

From our own position, surrounded by Norwegian landscapes, it feels right to imagine the abundance of nature reflected in the constructed room. The visual complexity of ever-changing shore-lines and hilltops

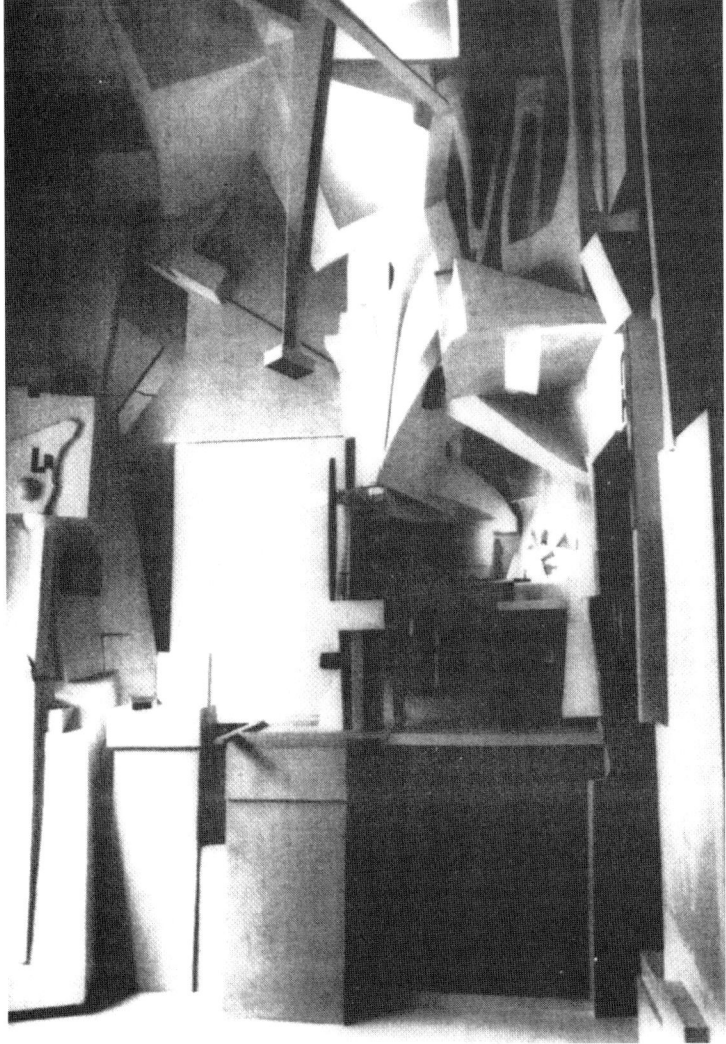

19

Kurt Schwitters, Bewegliche Säule auf Rädern (links) im Merzbau in Hannover, destroyed

21   Kurt Schwitters, Große Merzsäule, 1937-38, Hjertøya, Norway, destroyed

20   Kurt Schwitters, Merz Barn, detail, 1947

makes a wanderer in the Norwegian landscapes of mountain and fjord become almost immediately aware of how important the observer is for the atmosphere of space. You recognize yourself as part of the complexity of space. What does such an aesthetic dimension of the observer's ability to move and change signify for architectural design? From the theology of the Early Church we have already learned that the image of God is the experience and image of a Spirit in motion – in, within, and through a diversity of the changing spaces of life. God's Spirit, along with our human spatial identity, is embedded in the dynamics of a space, both in continuity and in constant change.

The next insight I have obtained from Schwitters' work comes in his extension of montage theory into a theory of collage. While Ernst only allowed a contextual combination of elements to carry any significance for human creativity, Schwitters ascribes the ethical evaluation of the moment vital importance. In his works, the artistic powers of colour come into their own. Objects from the consumer world are incorporated in an artistic frame of reference. They are moved and upgraded, and given new meaning within the frames of the artistic work, at the same time as they are allowed to preserve their original identity as metal boxes, paper-clips, newspaper clippings, etc.

It is easy to misinterpret this as nothing more than an aesthetically creative technique, but Schwitters saw it as something much more profound than that. The method itself implies a completely different form of protest from those of his Dadaist friends. Whereas the Dadaist movement only advocated ways of decoding established norms and conventions in order to formulate its protest, Schwitters went much further. His handling of the idea entailed a refunctionalization of the material. What had seemed to be useless was now the vital ingredient. We remember Jesus' explanation that what is in the way, should not be removed, but granted a new function. The stone that the master builder saw, has now become the cornerstone. His protest did not involve distancing himself, but embracing what is problematic and turning it into a new and liberating configuration. Aesthetic liberation is transfiguration by means of a re- and trans-contextualization.

Schwitters' MERZ-projects did not use protest as a response to the development of his contemporary society; he preferred methods of reappraisal. He upgraded waste material and downgraded demands for utility by using the material as an element in his art. Dada was anti-art; MERZ, on the other hand, was art.[104]

While the Dadaists demolished the validity of objects and sought for a "ruthless destruction of the aura of their appearance" ("eine rücksichtslose Vernichtung der Aura ihrer Hervorbringungen"),[105] Schwitters strove for a transformation and a renaissance of the artistic aura of objects. Once again, objects were to become mystical in open spaces of shapes and colours. They confronted the observer in a completely new atmosphere.[106] Thus objects which have an intrinsic value of their own are able to reposition the human being through an aesthetic experience that can in turn transform his or her view of self in society.

What does such a revaluation mean for architecture?

Re-opening open endings

From a theological perspective, the spiritual aesth/ethics of architecture is an "authentic utopia based on [the] memory" (Marcuse) of God's Holy Spirit who brings life to the world to come.[107]

How can the Spirit, which "bloweth where it listeth", co-operate with men and women in a synergy of architecturally designed places intended for sensitive, just and beautiful forms of communication? How can we re-establish the sacredness of Genesis within a space adequate to the rebirth of a just, beautiful and vibrant life by means of the design, building and transfiguration of our worldly places? How can space be transformed into places where both the spiritual and the temporal can live together in harmony?

Notes

[1] Hegel, *Vorlesungen über die Aesthetik,* 12:125, translation cited in Harries, 352.

[2] Tillich, Volume I, 220.

[3] Luther, *Large Catechism,* first part, first command.

[4] Cf. my monograph on "God in Context", Bergmann (2002b).

[5] Tuan (1974), 141, characterizes the difference between premodern, prescientific and modern ages through "symbolic depth" and the attribution of sacredness to places and landscapes. An interesting function for the sacred space in Japanese geomancy was to mediate between the civilized inside and the wild outside of human surroundings, cf. Kalland, 18. For an extended study of the historical change of views of space and place through Western history se Casey.

[6] Harries, 356.

[7] Cf. Derrida, 572.

[8] Cf. Bergmann (2002a), chapter III.1.2.

[9] Rizzi, 7.

[10] Rizzi, 21.

[11] Cf. Heneghan, 16.

[12] Jodidio, 9.

[13] Jodidio, 31ff. Norberg-Schulz (2000a), 350, obviously misunderstands Ando's religious references by characterizing him as a "nihilist". The "nothing" and the empty space are in the buddhist tradition regarded as the centre of reality which not at all represents the absence but the highest reality of presence.

[14] Le Corbusier, xi.

[15] Le Corbusier, 12.

[16] Le Corbusier, xxv.

[17] Le Corbusier, xxv.

[18] Cf. Sheldrake, 163-167.

[19] Norberg-Schulz (1980), 23.

20 Germann, 32.

21 Cf. Germann, 35ff., and Reuterswärd.

22 Cf. Germann, 238ff.

23 In order to correct the gendered asymmetry of male metaphors for the Divine I prefer to speak of the Holy Spirit as "Sister Spirit" in analogy to "Brother Jesus", God's son. Cf. my essay "Komm, Schwester Geist, befreie das Leben!" in Bergmann (1997b), 11-16.

24 Cf. Werne (1987), 27-32. Not just the act of building but also the act of preserving buildings could be understood in the frame of a "spiritual pattern", Herklint, 269ff. Hoffmann-Axthelm makes the clear statement: "Alte Häuser muss man nicht erhalten. Man kann." (One must not preserve old houses. One can.) The "can" needs a moral argument that has to depart from the insight that we have entered an industrial world that no longer could show any "vordemokratische Anschaulichkeit der Verhältnisse an Gebäuden".

25 Cf. Böhme (1995), 23f.

26 Böhme (1995), 21-48, develops the notion "atmosphere" as a basic category of aesthetics. An extensive discussion of "atmosphere" in architecture is offered by Bonsdorff, 141-150, who investigates the concept in discussion with Merlau-Ponty, Böhme and Levinas. Levinas although wrote on the nakedness of the face of the Other, and I cannot see how filled spaces with unique atmospheres could be related to his universalized ethics. Böhme's grounding of the term seems to be more contextual than Levinas' ethics before ontology. For a critical discussion of Levinas in ethical, theological and aesthetical perspectives see Bergmann (2000). For a discussion of atmosphere in pneumatology see Bergmann (2004).

27 Werne (1998), 13.

28 Steiner, 47ff.

29 Frampton, 7.

30 Marcuse, 74. Böhme (1995), 62-65, criticizes the "aesthetical economics" of the late capitalism, where a specific aesthetic value of the inscenation of a product is emerging, although he does not reflect on the dominance of monetary values and their accumulation in regard to aesthetical value-constructions. The same lack is also found in Welsch's critic of economical aesthetization, 13f.

31 Norberg-Schulz's definition of architecture as "the art of place" (2000a), 11, seems to be all too idealistic in regard to the task of an architecture critics that wants to contribute with its self-critical aesthetical and ethical consciousness to the creation of liberating, sensitive and memorable places. Norberg-Schulz (2000a), 11, characterizes architecture as an "imago mundi" that should mirror "the whole of a presence". But whose presence is this about? If one puts it in Eisenman's terminology Norberg-Schulz seems to be imprisoned in a Greek ontology that tries to understand place as a static location for a single presence while Eisenman regards place as an open text and as a "non-stabile static". The presence of the place implies necessarily its absence of memory and immanence which are designed by Eisenman in his composition of "scaling". Cf. Rizzzi, 80.

Also Christian mystics is familiar with this "nothing", i.e. in the writings of Jacob Böhme who knows that "Gott ist das Nichts, das alles werden will" (according to Sölle, 245).

[32] Cf. McGuire, 14-20, and Auffarth/Mohr.

[33] Geertz (1973).

[34] On the complex relations between nature and religiosity/spirituality cf. the forthcoming *Encyclopedia of Religion and Nature* edited by Bron Taylor, London/New York: Continuum 2005. Cf. also my entry "architecture" in the ERN.

[35] Cf. Sheldrake, 149, who shows in a critical argument against Sennett that Christianity should not be interpreted as a "religion of pilgrimage and dislocation" but allows a much more dialectical and complex perspective on place.

[36] Kant, A 481, p. 53: "Aufklärung ist der Ausgang des Menschen aus seiner selbst verschuldeten Unmündigkeit."

[37] Eisenman, 41: "... eine Architektur ohne vorausinterpretierte Bedeutung, eine Architektur der unmotivierten Zeichen."

[38] Cf. Foucault, 421.

[39] Cf. Sölle, 249f.

[40] On Schleiermacher cf. Jørgensen, 284, and Bergmann (1997a), 65-70.

[41] Frampton, 343.

[42] Giddens, 21-29, uses the term "disembeddedness".

[43] Appadurai, 13.

[44] Frampton, 343.

[45] Habermas, Band II, 293.

[46] Cf. Bergmann (1995), 317ff.

[47] The lutheran Cherokee-theologian George Tinker criticizes the concentration on time and history in Latinamerican liberation theology and promotes a spatial understanding of liberation. Cf. also my ecological topology of the liberating Spirit in: Bergmann (1995), 345ff.

[48] Picht, 33.

[49] Norberg-Schulz (2000b), 122.

[50] Norberg-Schulz (1980), 23.

[51] Norberg-Schulz (2000a), 353.

[52] Norberg-Schulz (1980), 23.

[53] Norberg-Schulz (1980), 180.

[54] Norberg-Schulz (1980), 202.

[55] Norberg-Schulz (1980), 22.

[56] Cf. on the same point also Bonsdorff, 225, who characterizes Norberg-Schulz as an "a-historical and a-political thinker".

[57] Cf. Timm, 35, on the relationship of spirits and the four elements.

58 Bergmann (1995), 171f.

59 Cf. Herklint, 147, who criticizes the idea of the genius loci as a mediating task for the architect and accuses Norberg-Schulz for the "mystification" of a power-relation between the architect and the place.

60 Among the exceptions we find Moltmann, 153-166, and Timm, 165-181.

61 Lessing, 218.

62 Cf. Bloomer/Moore, x. Bloomer/Moore highlight the significance of human bodiness for the imaging and memorizing of spaces. Architecture is demanded to change into a body-centered art. Places have to been constructed with the quality of memorizability. Cf. also Arnheim, 276, and his concise summary: "Thinking is building." Sennett analyzes carefully the historical expression and change of the relationship between the image of the body and the construction of the city.

63 Bergmann (1995), 117.

64 Bergmann (1995), chapter III.2.

65 Cf. Sennett, 170ff.

66 Sheldrake, 37ff.

67 Abbot Suger, *Libellus Alter De Consecratione Ecclesiae Sancti Dionysii*, chapter V., cited in Sheldrake, 55.

68 Renard, 102.

69 Renard, 102.

70 Renard, 104.

71 On the topology of the Liberating Spirit see Bergmann (1995), chapter V.4.

72 Frampton, 66.

73 Benjamin, 444.

74 Harries, 4.

75 Harries, 4.

76 Harries, 365.

77 Harries, 364.

78 Harries, 357.

79 Cf. Bauman, 18-24.

80 Böhme (1995), 62ff.

81 Cited in Norberg-Schulz (2000a), 351.

82 Another aspect worth of further investigation in the ethical dimension is the relationship between architecture and ritual. Cf. Tuan (1993), 242f. and Harries', 365, claim of architecture's highest task "to create festal places".

83 Pérez-Gómez, 6.

84 Cf. Des Jardins, 250ff.

85 On different ways to approach ethical problems in architecture see the antho-

logy of Pelletier/Pérez-Gómez. For an investigation of how a phenomenological approach could be applied to the ethical problems of cultural building preservation see Herklint.

86 For an extensive discussions of concepts in this field see Porteous and Böhme (1989). A collection of several loose ideas on the relationship between ethics and ecology in architecture offers Papanek, who, 49ff., wants to understand the spiritual as the beautiful in design. For a solid study of ecological, ethical and theological problems in urban planning see Kjellberg and Gorringe. Recently Heike Strelow has published an abundant anthology with several important contributions from architects and others deeply connecting aesthetics and ecology. Unfortunately, the findings of her project could not any longer be discussed in this volume.

87 Cf. Böhme (2000), 23ff., who argues for to understand the position of the human being "from the midst of man/woman's relationship to nature".

88 On the contemporary processes of "aesthetization" cf. Welsch, 9ff., and on their relevance for pictorial theology cf. Bergmann (2002a), chapter IV.3. Cold/Kolstad/Larssæther's interdisciplinary project with ethical implications investigates the connections between aesthetics, well-being and health in architecture.

89 Adorno (1995), 285.

90 Adorno (1995), 335.

91 Adorno (1995), 343.

92 Adorno (1984), 304. Kasa, 275, emphasizes Adorno's understanding of the singularity of the artistic object as a criticism of the philosophy of identity.

93 Cf. Bergmann (1998).

94 Cf. Assmann.

95 In distinction from the market's exchange economy the medieval church offered a place for empathy, care and love of the poor. Cf. Sennett, 219ff., 258.

96 Cf. Bergmann (2002c).

97 Marcuse, 74.

98 Marcuse, 17.

99 Marcuse, 74.

100 My invention of the term "Aesth/Ethics" was inspired by Welsch's notion and concept of an "aesthet/hics" (German "Ästhet/hik"), 106-134. While Welsch's term aims at those parts of aesthetics which in themselves imply ethical moments (108), "aesth/ethics" is coined in order to express the aesthetical dimension of moral acting and ethical reflecting. The concept of Aesth/Ethics does not try to transfer ethics in general into a wide aesthetics but it focusses on the embeddedness of moral and ethics in perception, embodied experience and aesthetics.

101 Kipnis, 35, focusses the ethical challenge in the question whether architecture should be regarded from the prespective of an hermeneutics of the sacred or an hermeneutics of suspicion, whether it could be the accumulation of wisdom or the instrument of systematic repression. I would propose that both strategies of

interpretation should be used.

[102] Chillida, 130.

[103] Zara Hadid (citated in Kasa, 276), who departs from the human body as the central place of architecture and characterizes architecture as the movement itself between different places.

[104] Nündel, 36.

[105] Benjamin, 463.

[106] Cf. Weimarck, 4, who argues for some kind of a "phenomenology of things" where both designed objects and sculptures are analyzed by art theory. Things are regarded as both physical materializations and symbolisations of communicative intersubjective relations.

[107] The ecumenical Creed of Constantinople (NC) 381 characterizes the Holy Spirit as the agent of God's coming reign, as "the life of the coming world's age" (ζοηντου μελλοντος αιωνος).

Illustrations

1   Peter Eisenman, *Guardiola House,* Cádiz, 1988, side view, study model, in: Rizzi, 73.

2   Tadao Ando, *Rokko Housing I,* Kobe, 1978-83, in: Jodidio, 56, 57.

3   Tadao Ando, *Nariwa Museum,* Okayama, 1992-94, in: Jodidio, 156.

4   Tadao Ando, *Meditation Space,* UNESCO, Paris, 1994-95, in: Jodidio, 159.

5   Le Corbusier, *Villa Savoye,* 1929-31, in: Bloomer/Moore, 69.

6   Le Corbusier, *The Church at Ronchamp,* in: Petit.

7   Le Corbusier, *The Church at Ronchamp, plan,* in: Petit.

8   *God, the Architect of the Universe,* from a 13th century French Bible moralisée, reproduction in: Wright, figure 1.8., p. 22.

9   Francesco di Georgio, *The human figure in the Latin cross of the church plan,* in: Arnheim, 97.

10 Nicholas Hawksmoor, *Christ Church Spitalfields, west facade from the South,* 1715-1729, in: Du Prey, plate 8.

11 Antoni Gaudí, *Casa Milà,* Barcelona, 1906-10, in: Frampton, 67.

12 Antoni Gaudí, *Sagrada Familia,* Barcelona, 1884 (not yet finished), in: http://web.ics.purdue.edu/~frontera/485gaudi.htm

13 Philibert De L'Orme, *The Bad Architect,* from: Le Premier Tome De L'Architecture, 1567, in: Capelli/Naprstek/Prescott, Frontispiez.

14 Philibert De L'Orme, *The Good Architect,* from: Le Premier Tome De L'Architecture, 1567, in: Capelli/Naprstek/Prescott, Endpiece.

15   Oscar Niemeyer, *Cathedral,* Brasília, 1950-58, in: Norman, 287.
16   Oscar Niemeyer, *Cathedral,* Brasília, 1950-58, in: Niemeyer, 58.
17   Eduardo Chillida, *Esertoki III,* iron, 1990, collection of the artist, in: Mennekes/Röhrig, 133.
18   Iver Jåks, *Lea go, vai ii? Det er, er det?* 1997, wood, in: Jåks, 48f.
19   Kurt Schwitters, *Bewegliche Säule auf Rädern* (links) im Merzbau in Hannover, destroyed, photo: Ernst Schwitters, in: Nündel, 55.
20   Kurt Schwitters, *Merz Barn,* detail, 1947, in: Nündel 126.
21   Kurt Schwitters, *Große Merzsäule,* 1937-38, Hjertøya, Norway, destroyed, in: Stadtmüller, 132.

References

Adorno, Theodor W. (1984) "Negative Dialektik", in *Gesammelte Schriften, Band 6,* 3. ed. Frankfurt am Main: Suhrkamp

---,   (1995) *Ästhetische Theorie,* 13. ed. Frankfurt am Main: Suhrkamp

Altner, Günter/Böhme, Gernot/Ott, Heinrich (eds.) (2000), *Natur erkennen und anerkennen: Über ethikrelevante Wissenszugänge zur Natur,* Zug/Kusterdingen: Die Graue Edition

Appadurai, Arjun *Globale ethnische Räume,* in Beck, pp. 11-40

Arnheim, Rudolf (1980) *Die Dynamik der architektonischen Formen,* Köln: DuMont, (The Dynamics of Architectural Form, 1977)

Assmann, Jan (1990) *Ma'at: Gerechtigkeit und Unsterblichkeit im Alten Ägypten,* München: Beck

Auffarth, Christoph/Mohr, Hubert (2000) Artikel "Religion", in: *Metzler Lexikon Religion, Band 3,* Stuttgart/Weimar: Metzler, pp. 160-172

Bauman, Zygmunt (1995) *Postmodern etik,* Göteborg: Daidalos, (Postmodern Ethics, 1993)

Beck, Ulrich (ed.) (1998) *Perspektiven der Weltgesellschaft,* Frankfurt am Main: Suhrkamp

Benjamin, Walter (1991) "Das Kunstwerk im Zeitalter seiner technischen Reproduzierbarkeit", (Erste Fassung 1935), in *Abhandlungen, Gesammelte Schriften Band I-2,* Frankfurt am Main: Suhrkamp, pp. 431-508

Bergmann, Sigurd (1995) *Geist, der Natur befreit: Die trinitarische Kosmologie Gregors von Nazianz im Horizont einer ökologischen Theologie der Befreiung,* Mainz: Grünewald, (russian edition: Arkhangelsk 1999, revised edition *Creation Set Free: The Spirit as Liberator of Natur,* Grand Rapids: Eerdmans, forthcoming 2005)

---,   (1997a) " 'Die Landschaft ist am Staub zugrunde gegangen' – Die Herausforderung der Theologie durch die bildende Kunst der Moderne", in Bergmann (1997b), pp. 34-70

---, (1997b) *Geist, der lebendig macht: Lavierungen zur ökologischen Befreiungstheologie*, Frankfurt am Main: IKO

---, (1998) "Das Fremde wahrnehmen: Die öko- und ethnologische Herausforderung der Bildkunst und Theologie", in Müller, Wolfgang Erich/Heumann, Jürgen (eds.), *Kunst-Positionen: Kunst als Thema evangelischer und katholischer Theologie*, Stuttgart: Kohlhammer, pp. 96-120

---, (2000) "So fremd das Gleiche: Wie eine interkulturelle Theologie der Befreiung mit dem Fremden über die Alterität hinaus denken kann", in Fritsch-Oppermann, Sybille (ed.), *Das Antlitz des Anderen: Emmanuel Lévinas Philosophie und Hermeneutik als Anfrage an Ethik, Theologie und interreligiösen Dialog*, Loccumer Protokolle 54/99, Loccum, pp. 57-97

---, (2002a) *I begynnelsen är bilden: En befriande bild-konst-kultur-teologi*, Stockholm: Proprius

---, (2002b) *God in Context: A Survey of Contextual Theology*, Aldershot: Ashgate

---, (2002c) "Raum und Gerechtigkeit: Ethische Perspektiven eines großräumigen Umweltschutzes", in Hahlweg, D./Häder, D.-P./Bergmann, S./Seewald, O./Bauer, J./Aßmann, O./Sperling, A., *Großräumiger Umweltschutz*, (Schriftenreihe für Ökologie und Ethologie 28), Wien: Facultas, pp. 33-58

---, (2004) "Ånd" in Busch Nielsen, Kirsten/Grenholm, Cristina (eds.), *Det virker alt den Ånd: Nordiske teologiske tolkninger*, Copenhagen: Anis 2004, pp. 183-216

Bloomer, Kent C. /Moore, Charles W. (1977) *Body, Memory, and Architecture*, New Haven/London: Yale University Press

Böhme, Gernot (1989) *Für eine ökologische Naturästhetik*, Frankfurt am Main: Suhrkamp

---, (1995) *Atmosphäre: Essays zur neuen Ästhetik*, Frankfurt am Main: Suhrkamp

---, (1998) "Atmosphären kirchlicher Räume", in *Kunst und Kirche* 2/1998, pp. 100-103

---, (2000) "Die Stellung des Menschen in der Natur", in Altner/Böhme/Ott, pp. 11-29

---, (2002) *Die Natur vor uns: Naturphilosophie in pragmatischer Hinsicht*, Zug/Kusterdingen: Die Graue Edition

von Bonsdorff, Pauline (1998) *The Human Habitat: Aesthetic and Axiological Perspectives*, Jyväskylä

Capelli, John/Naprstek, Paul/Prescott, Bruce (eds.) (1990) *VIA: Ethics and Architecture*, New York: Rizzoli.

Casey, Edward S. (1997) *The Fate of Place: A Philosophical History*, Berkeley: University of California Press

Chillida, Eduardo (1994) "Eduardo Chillida im Gespräch mit Friedhelm Mennekes", in *Mennekes/Röhrig*, pp. 128-134

Cold, Birgit/Kolstad, Arnulf/Larssæther, Stig (1998) *Aesthetics, Well-being and Health: Abstracts on theoretical and empirical research within environmental aesthetics*, Oslo: Norsk Form

Derrida, Jacques (1986) "Point de folie – Maintenant l'architecture: Essay accompanying the portfolio Bernard Tschumi, La Case Vide: La Villette 1985", London, reprinted in: Hays, K. Michael (ed.), *Architecture Theory since 1968*, Cambridge, Mass./London: MIT 1998, pp. 570-581

Des Jardins, Joseph R. (1997) *Environmental Ethics: An Introduction to Environmental Philosophy*, 2. ed. Belmont: Wadsworth

Du Prey, Pierre De La Ruffinière (2000) *Hawksmoor's London Churches: Architecture and Theology*, Chicago/London: The University of Chicago Press

Eisenbart, Constanze (ed.) (1979) *Humanökologie und Frieden*, Stuttgart: Klett-Cotta

Eisenman, Peter (2001) "Was ist noch kritisch?" (Interview) in *DIE ZEIT*, Nr. 5, 25.1.2001, p. 41

Frampton, Kenneth (1992) *Modern Architecture: A Critical History*, 3. ed. London: Thames & Hudson

Foucault, Michel (1992) "Of Other Spaces: Utopias and Heterotopias", in Ockman, Joan (ed.), *Architecture Culture 1943-1968*, New York: Columbia/Rizzoli

Geertz, Clifford (1973) "Religion as a Cultural System", in *The Interpretation of Cultures*, New York 1973, pp. 87-125

- - -, (1993) "Art as a Cultural System", in *Local Knowledge: Further Essays in Interpretive Anthropology*, London: Fontana pp. 94-120

Germann, Georg (1987) *Einführung in die Geschichte der Architekturtheorie*, 2. ed. Darmstadt: Wissenschaftliche Buchgesellschaft

Giddens, Anthony (1990) *The Consequences of Modernity*, Stanford, reprint Cambridge: Polity Press 1992

Gorringe, Tim (2002) *A Theology of the Built Environment: Justice, Empowerment, Redemption*, Cambridge: Cambridge University Press

Habermas, Jürgen (1981) *Theorie des kommunikativen Handelns*, Erster Band: *Handlungsrationalität und gesellschaftliche Rationalisierung*, Zweiter Band: *Zur Kritik der funktionalistischen Vernunft*, Frankfurt am Main: Suhrkamp 4.ed. 1988

Hallman, David G. (1994) *Ecotheology: Voices from South and North*, Maryknoll/Geneva: Orbis/WCC

Harries, Karsten (1997) *The Ethical Function of Architecture*, Cambridge, Mass.: MIT

Hegel, Georg Wilhelm Friedrich (1964) *Vorlesungen über die Aesthetik*, Erster Band, (Sämtliche Werke hrsg. v. H. Glockner, Band 12), 4. Aufl der Jubiläumsaufl. Stuttgart: Frommann

Heneghan, Tom (2000) "Architektur und Ethik", in Richard Pare, *Tadao Ando: Die Farben des Lichts*, Berlin: Phaidon

Herklint, Evamarie (2000) *Bevarandets etiska funktioner: Relationer mellan människor, platser och hus*, Göteborg: Chalmers

Hoffmann-Axthelm, Dieter, (2000) "Alles bewahren heißt nichts erhalten", in *DIE ZEIT* 22, 25.5.2000, p. 46f

Jodidio, Philip (1997) *Tadao Ando*, Köln: Taschen

Jørgensen, Theodor H. (1977) *Das religionsphilosophische Offenbarungsverständnis des späteren Schleiermacher*, Tübingen: Mohr

Jåks, Iver (1998) *muittasan johtticájáhus/retrospektiv*, exhibition catalogue ed. by Riksutstillinger, Oslo

Kalland, Arne (1996) "Geomancy and Town Planning in a Japanese Community", in *Ethnology* 35, 1, pp. 17-32

Kandinsky, Vasily (1965) *Über das Geistige in der Kunst*, 8. ed. Bern

Kant, Immanuel (1977) "Beantwortung der Frage: Was ist Aufklärung?" in *Werkausgabe* (ed. by Wilhelm Weischedel), Frankfurt am Main

Kasa, Eivind (2000) *Arkitekturen som kunst*, Trondheim: NTNU

Kipnis, Jeffrey (1987) "Architecture: The Sacred and The Suspect", in *Journal of Architectural Education*, 40/2, pp. 33-35

Kjellberg, Seppo (2000) *Urban Ecotheology*, Utrecht: International Books

Klotz, Heinrich (1995) *Geschichte der Architektur: Von der Urhütte zum Wolkenkratzer*, 2. ed. München: Prestel

Le Corbusier (1987) *The Decorative Art of Today*, (translated and introduced by James I. Dunnett), London: The Architectural Press

Lessing, Eckhard (1984) Art. "Geist V. Dogmatisch und ethisch." in *Theologische Realenzyklopädie (TRE) 12*, Berlin/New York, pp. 218-237

Luther, Martin (1979) "Stora katekes", in *Svenska kyrkans bekännelseskrifter*, 4. ed. Stockholm: Verbum, pp. 379-495

Marcuse, Herbert (1980) *Den estetiska dimensionen: Bidrag till kritik av en marxistisk estetik*, Göteborg: Röda bokförlaget, (Die Permanenz der Kunst, München 1977)

McGuire, Meredith B. (1997) *Religion: The Social Context*, 4. ed. London: Wadsworth

Mennekes, Friedhelm/Röhrig, Johannes (1994) *Crucifixus: Das Kreuz in der Kunst unserer Zeit*, Freiburg: Herder

Moltmann, Jürgen (1985) *Gott in der Schöpfung: Ökologische Schöpfungslehre*, München: Kaiser

Niemeyer, Oscar (1982) *Selbstdarstellung, Kritiken, Oeuvre*, ed. by Alexander Fils, Münsterschwarzach: Frölich & Kaufmann

Norberg-Schulz, Christian (1980) *Genius Loci: Towards a Phenomenology of Architecture*, New York: Rizzoli 1984

---, (2000a) *Architecture: Presence, Language and Place,* Milano: Skira

---, (2000b) *Principles of Modern Architecture,* London: Papadakis

Norman, Edward (1990) *The House of God: Church Architecture, Style and History,* London: Thames & Hudson

Nündel, Ernst (1999) *Kurt Schwitters,* 4. ed. Hamburg: Rowohlt

Papanek, Victor (1995) *The Green Imperative: Ecology and Ethics in Design and Architecture,* London: Thames & Hudson

Pelletier, Louise/Pérez-Gómez, Alberto (eds.) (1994) *Architecture, Éthique et Technologie/Architecture, Ethics and Technology,* Montreal: McGill

Pérez-Gómez, Alberto (1994) "Introduction", in *Pelletier/Pérez-Gómez,* pp. 3-14

Petit, Jean (1956) *Chapelle Notre Dame du Haut, Ronchamp: Le Corbusier,* Paris

Picht, Georg (1979) "Ist Humanökologie möglich?" in *Eisenbart,* pp. 14-123

Porteous, J. Douglas (1996) *Environmental Aesthetics: Ideas, politics and planning,* London/New York: Routledge

Renard, John (1996) "A Method for Comparative Studies in Religious Visual Arts: Approaching Architecture" in *Religion and the Arts* 1, 1, pp. 100-123

Reuterswärd, Patrik (1982) "Windows of Divine Light" in *Konsthistorisk Tidskrift,* pp. 95-102, (reprinted in: *The Forgotten Symbols of God,* Acta Universitatis Stockholmiensis 35, Stockholm 1986)

Rizzi, Renato/Eisenman, Peter (1996) *Mystisches Nichts,* Basel: Wiese

Sheldrake, Philip (2001) *Spaces for the Sacred: Place, Memory and Identity,* London: SCM

Sennett, Richard (1995) *Fleisch und Stein: Der Körper und die Stadt in der westlichen Zivilisation,* Berlin, (Flesh and Stone, New York/London 1994)

Sölle, Dorothee (1997) *Mystik und Widerstand: "Du stilles Geschrei",* 3. ed. Hamburg: Hoffmann und Campe

Stadtmüller, Klaus (ed.) (1997) *Schwitters in Norwegen: Arbeiten, Dokumente, Ansichten,* Hannover: Postskriptum

Steiner, Dieter "Human Ecology as Transdisciplinary Science" in Steiner/Nauser, pp. 47-76

Steiner, Dieter/Nauser, Markus (eds.) (1993) *Human Ecology: Fragments of antifragmentary views of the world,* London/New York: Routledge

Strelow, Heike (2004) *Aesthetics of Ecology - Art in Environmental Design: Theory and Practice,* Basel, Berlin, Boston: Birkhäuser

Tillich, Paul (1967) *Systematic Theology, Three volumes in one,* Chicago: The University of Chicago Press

Timm, Hermann (1985) *Das Weltquadrat: Eine religiöse Kosmologie,* Gütersloh: Mohn

Tinker, George (1994) "The Full Circle of Liberation: An American Indian Theology of Place", in *Hallman,* pp. 218-224

Yi-Fu Tuan, (1974) *Topophilia: A Study of Environmental Perception, Attitudes, and Values*, New York: Colombia University Press 1990

---, (1993) *Passing Strange and Wonderful*, New York: Island

Weimarck, Torsten (2001) "Till en teori om design som representationsnivå, som verklighetsnivå", Introduction to "Nordic Conference on Design Theory and Design Research", Lund 16.-17.1.2001, published on: http://www.arthist.lu.se/design/Design.TW.html

Welsch, Wolfgang (1996) *Grenzgänge der Ästhetik*, Stuttgart: Reclam

Werne, Finn (1987) *Den osynliga arkitekturen*, Lund: Vinga

---, (1998) *Arkitekturens ismer*, Stockholm: Arkitektur förlag

Wright, Craig (2001) *The Maze and the Warrior Symbols in Architecture,* Theology and Music, Cambridge Mass.: Harvard University Press

ETHICS OR AESTHETICS IN ARCHITECTURE

GERNOT BÖHME

Recollection of Kierkegaard

When the question of the relation between aesthetics and ethics is raised in the Nordic countries it seems obvious to remind of the well-known book "Enten-Eller" (Either/Or) by Søren Kierkegaard. There is, however, also reason of immediate interest to do so.

A major amount of what is written about ethics in Europe and North America presents itself as *ethics of the good life.* Skilfully the title refers to an Aristotelian phrase, namely his discourse on ευ ζην. In the translations, however, the ευ is transformed from an adverb to an adjective and on the quiet is thus, what was meant as a morally good life, interpreted hedonistically. It is about the *succeeding life*, i.e. about a life where nothing happens to one, where one is secure and successful. This tendency towards hedonistic ethics is supported by the theory of forms of life. With Foucault one understands ethics as self-cultivation, as an aesthetic of forms of life. This is in keeping with the boom of books on the art of life, ahead of all Wilhelm Schmid's "Philosophie der Lebenskunst"[1] (Philosophy of the Art of Life). These ethics are about the wellbeing of the individual and his or her happiness. Wherever there is to be argued morally, the dominant and by almost all accepted way of argumentation is the utilitarian one: Moral questions are decided in view of the optimisation of happiness for all those involved.

In contrast to these trends, the recollection of Søren Kierkegaard signals a distinct stop! He sets a harsh difference between an aesthetic way of life and an ethical way of life. For him it is a matter of phases of life, whereby the ethical way of life is clearly proven by him to be the higher, the more mature and the more complex way of life. The *Either/Or* is primarily a term for this difference: "either a person has to live [a]esthetically or he has to live ethically" (II, 168/II, 152).[2]

The difference of the aesthetic and the ethical life is based on the differentiation of what is pleasant and what is good. *Aesthetic* is thereby – following the Greek sense of the word αισθησις, namely perception – represented as a life with the primacy of sensuality. Its goal is to enjoy life (II, 150/ II, 163). Contrasting to this: "The person who chooses the ethical chooses the good" (II, 169/II, 154). The aesthetic life is mainly a game, a game of life-options – today, we would say: of forms of life. The complete aesthetic is "able to play shuttlecock with all existence"(I, 294/I, 265). For him, life is a masquerade (II, 169/II, 145). He does not commit to any identity. He remains vague for others, a riddle. Nevertheless, even the aesthetic life is not free of choice. Even the aesthete knows an either/or, but it is an indifferent either/or, an "it depends", "one or the other". The choices are manifold, never final, the sheer infinite. What the aesthetic choice lacks is earnestness.

The concept of earnestness is the prototype of a concept of existence. It is elucidated in Kierkegaard's work "On the Concept Anxiety". If one is serious about something, then one is involved in it and is accordingly also on the line in the decision on the case. The earnestness lies exactly in this connection of decision on the case and the decision on what kind of person one is.

Accordingly, one can almost define *moral* questions as questions that are serious, namely with the decision of which one at the same time decides what kind of person one is.[3]

Kierkegaard says that the ethic choice depends on the involvement of him who chooses – even under the risk that he could choose falsely: "Now, if you are to understand me properly, I may very well say that what is important in choosing is not so much to choose the right thing as the energy, the earnestness, and the pathos with which one chooses" (II, 167/ II, 152). That is a risky formulation, but Kierkegaard employs everything in order to make clear that an ethic choice in principle is something different from the aesthetic choice. Strictly speaking, the aesthetic choice is not really a choice because one follows "ones inclination of the heart". The ethic choice, on the contrary, requires a distance, namely the will to want to choose at all.[4] What is therefore actually important about the ethic choice is the constitution of the personality. It is about "the self-determining aspect of the choice" (II, 167/II, 151).

In order to summarise once again: The aesthetic life is about play, about manifold, it is about the moment, about the sensuality, about the enjoyment – hence about happiness. The ethic life, on the other hand, is about earnestness, about clarity, about the constitution of the self, the personality. It is not about being well but being good.

"Here the good is altogether abstract" (II, 169/ II, 154)

Again and again Kierkegaard stresses that ethics have to be abstract and with the good reason that the ethicist cannot take the decision off the individual. It is up to the afflicted individual to give content to the earnestness of life. Nevertheless, Kierkegaard is not entirely vague about what this content could be made of – he names the dimensions of the unfolding of ethical forms of life: They are mainly profession, marriage and with a little less weight: friendship. With professional work and marriage Kierkegaard believes to indicate what all human beings have in common and he believes thus to reproduce the traditional, or rather Kantian identification of the general and the good. For him, to have an occupation, to contract a marriage and to have children means to carry out an essential part of being human. That is why he formulates "It is every person's duty to work for a living"(II, 281/II, 251). Furthermore he lets the ethicist explain "that it is every person's duty to marry" (II, 302/II, 270). As far as the necessity of work is concerned, one has to add that Kierkegaard thinks of professional work and he sees profession in closest relation to calling. Therefore he suggests that one wins oneself in work or, as we would say today, one can realise oneself. As far as marriage is concerned it has to be added that he understands it as a love-relationship that is meant to last. He sees having children as an essential part of marriage. The truth of marriage lies in "becoming himself [i.e. oneself] a moment" (II, 172/II, 156), That means consequently to take ones place in the chain of generations.

These directions of an ethical life may appear strange today. One gets the impression that Kierkegaard, in trying to let the ethics become concrete, reproduces certain basic ideas of bourgeois forms of life. It is quite extraordinary to realise that in the same years in which Marx and Engels formulated the Communist Manifesto – and Marx had already written the Parisian Manuscripts – Kierkegaard so naturally counts on professional work being the choice and development of the self. Since Marx we know that certain social preconditions have to be fulfilled for that, which usually, and that means for most people, are not fulfilled. Today one can say that work, in the strong sense of occupational work, rarely exists. We are a society of job-holders, as Hannah Arendt put it. In addition something like an occupation for life, i.e. identifying oneself with one type of work through education and qualification, is hardly possible today, due to technical innovations and thus the rapid changes in the world of work. People today cannot recognise a concretion of the ethical form of life in their occupational work. Through a manifold of jobs they dissolve, as one says, into multiple identities, different ones in work, leisure and play. Therewith we are dealing with aesthetic forms of life.

The same can be said about the topic of marriage. It seems that marriage as the concretion of an ethical form of life has its social preconditions. Today it is no longer evident to most people that their human nature fulfils itself in marriage. It is not that love has lost weight in human life but wanting to live it as something general, permanent or even connected to duties, is rejected by most people. They prefer living as singles and to engage in love only in individualised and revisable forms. Again we are, according to Kierkegaard, on the way towards an aesthetic form of life. But it is even possible to give ethical reasons for the renunciation of children and thus indirectly for that of marriage.

Does that yet mean that Kierkegaard is outdated and that one has to look at his distinctions as due to conditions of time?

What by all means follows in the light of Kierkegaard's distinctions is the fact that *our* equation of ethics and aesthetics is due to conditions of the time. Here, "due to conditions of the time" means: They equal the state of capital development. We live in the consumer society, we live in the event society and that is why the adequate form of life is the aesthetic one. The aim is to deconstruct Protestant ethics: Saving is dysfunctional, industriousness, i.e. diligence and the will to work are superfluous and burden the labour market. Marriage is dysfunctional because it transforms love into unpaid services and thus withholds the latter from the market. Children, finally, prevent actual consumption, namely luxury-consumption and travelling. In the capitalistic development, Protestant ethics equalled the phase of accumulation. The advanced capitalism in which we live, reveals its real nature, seen by authors like Veblen or Schumpeter and last but not least Battaille: Capitalism does not live on the satisfaction of needs but on waste. After the satisfaction of elementary needs, at least we in the West today have entered into a phase of capitalism which one sensibly should call *aesthetic economy*.[5] It gets the epithet *aesthetic* because the differentiating value, which is produced during this capitalistic phase, is the staging-value. While, according to Marx, the utility value of a product equals its usefulness for certain purposes and the exchange value equals its saleability on the market, the staging value, however, is something else, sort of a product of both: The product gets its value from the contribution it makes to the staging and raising of life. The staging-value has its origins in product aesthetics, i.e. in the special shape, which the product is given, exceeding its utility, in order to make it attractive in trade-context. Special about the staging value is that the aesthetic outfit of the product keeps its value in life-context: Here it serves as outfit for life itself.

Hence, the equation of ethics and aesthetics is up-to-date. It corresponds with the state of affairs, i.e. the state of capitalism. A good life is a comfortable, but most of all an intensified life, a life that is diversely changing that and aesthetically staged. Then what do we need Kierkegaard for? Does not he, by insisting on seriousness, spoil the nice aesthetic game with forms of life, to which contemporary ethics encourage?

Yes, of course. First of all it has to be stated that our social circumstances, which we so nicely circumscribed as the state of the capitalistic development, are only valid for the Western societies. Seen world wide, there still is exploitation, elementary needs are not satisfied and an economy of deficiency, not an economy of affluence is reigning. Furthermore, at a more precise analysis it could turn out that even our developed capitalism is based on underdevelopment elsewhere, i.e. the exploitation of the Third World. Furthermore, the aesthetic economy is by no means already the realm of freedom. Rather, it means exploitation – exploitation on a higher level – also here with us. After the elementary needs are satisfied, capitalism builds on the so-called desires, i.e. such needs that are not appeased by their satisfaction, but are even intensified. They are such needs, as equipment of life, visibility and such. Especially these and just these make possible the boundless extension and a "constant growth of never-ending duration" (J. v. Liebig), as needed by capitalism. But this unfolding of desires leads to new dependencies, to the subjection under the principle of efficiency and, as Marcuse put it, to the colonialism of leisure.

And finally: Even in the consumer- and event-society, one cannot get rid of earnestness. Again and again sickness and death rip us from aesthetic forms of life and with the unavoidable dismay, with which it haunts one, it makes it clear that the game with multiple identities has its limits. And finally Kierkegaard's teaching of desperation looming at the bottom of aesthetic forms of life proves to be true. Behind the funniness of single-life the ghost of loneliness appears. The discretion of changing pleasures reveals itself to be a cover-up of boredom, if not even depression and finally therapy becomes a self-evident part of the so-called good life. So what remains? Is one to stand up against ones own time?

Architecture

When Hegel says philosophy is its time put into thought, then one could accordingly say about architecture that it is its time put into buildings. Even puritan ethics becoming obsolete in train of capital development find their expression in architecture. The harshness and austerity in architecture that is called modern, hence especially Bauhaus-architecture, is obviously in keeping with the phase between wars, i.e. really a period, in which capitalism had to recover after an extensive destruction of capital during the First World War. No wonder that this way of building – functional, disciplined and rational – also ruled the time after the Second World War. All that lies behind us. Capitalism has again fallen into step and has, due to lack of greater wars, entered a phase of productive waste. For architecture that means that to a large extent it is in service of aesthetic economy. That includes the new urbanity, which demands that inner cities become dwelling places, places to stroll, to spend money and for pleasure. That includes the malls and shopping centres, which apparently are not just simply places of product distribution or supply for the people, but on the contrary places where shopping is supposed to become an experience, where reproductive work and pleasure mix; places of local tourism. Furthermore, that includes construction as care for the city-image. Buildings, squares, centres and bridges have to form an arrangement, which gives the city a character not only in order for its inhabitants to be able to identify themselves with their city, but also in order to make the city attractive as a location for new businesses and for city tourism. Finally that includes everything one comprehends as postmodernism, namely, that the appearance of buildings becomes important, it includes the gesture, the diversity, the presence of history in quotation and – last but not least – the return of the ornament.

It would be short sighted to turn up the nose at this development and to do away with it as neo-baroque. This kind of judgement would not do justice to the fact that the New Architecture not only builds in a different way but also has to be evaluated in a different way. In the downgrading judgement as neo-baroque, for instance, it would be looked at under aspects of purpose and form, whereas aesthetically it would be looked at as a product of the visual arts: Buildings as large sculptures. With postmodernism, however, not only a change of style took place but also a change of architecture in general. As architecture was taken in service by aesthetic economy, an element came forward that, in principle, had always been a part of architecture but again and again had been pushed to the background by other factors: Namely the fact that it builds for people. For people who move in its spaces, for people who live in its houses, for people who are exposed to its sight, people who are influenced by the atmospheres it creates. Before all criticism one should state that the new architecture is a new turn towards man, not in an abstract sense, but towards the person who will stay in its rooms. In this new sense, man has become the basic measure for architecture – not as a basic measure for the geometry of the buildings, as with Vitruv, but in a sense as a seismograph for the question, what kind of rooms architecture is creating. How does one feel in a building, in a square, in front of a building, in an underground station, an airport or a museum? According to the new view, architecture is not about large sculptures but about creating atmospheres.

Paradoxically, this tendency has been described by the slogan *Less Aesthetics More Ethics* at the last biennial of architecture in Venice. The reason for it apparently shows in the humanistic tendency – for man! However, according to the differentiation, which we learned from Kierkegaard, we are in fact dealing with the exact opposite: Ethics are swallowed by aesthetics. It is about what is pleasant, not what is good. It is about wellness, a good life and happiness. Man, for whom one builds, is post-modern man, according to the analysis by Zygmunt Bauman, the *flaneur*, the wanderer and global nomad. He is the consumer and participant of the event-society.

It is obvious that architecture has to be in keeping with the needs of its time. But what are these needs? And does not our time have its breaches and contradictions? Is not there a critical architecture that is matching these contradictions? That correspondingly keeps the differentiation between ethics and aesthetics open? It is obvious that architecture has to be in keeping with the needs of the people – but of *what kind* of people? What kind of people are those for whom ethics become the aesthetics of life forms and which people can not keep up? Those are serious questions for architecture. They bundle up to the question: Does architecture become stage design?

The correlation between ethics and aesthetics has to be discussed in architecture as the correlation between architecture and stage designing. Architecture has always looked down a bit on stage designing, sort of as its little brother and imitator. The relations between the two have thereby always been good and since antiquity, with a certain climax in the baroque period and to the present – just think of Mario Botta – architects have worked part-time as stage designers: But there has nevertheless always been a difference between the two – the difference between the good and the pleasant, the difference between earnestness and play, the difference between being and seeming. If today it has to be seen as an achievement of architecture that it relates to participating man and his ability to experience; that it not just satisfies functions and constructs buildings, but creates rooms and atmospheres, then it is obvious that it can learn a lot from its little brother, the stage designer. That is because the profession of the latter has always been to create spaces of certain *climates* by using certain arrangements of props, by light, by sound and insignia to create atmospheres in order to put the audience into the mood of the drama's events. The question is just whether architecture itself should run its profession as stage designing. Architecture as the setting for the great global theatre? The task of the architect: The staging of life?

But life is not just a game – we cannot get rid of earnestness: Werner Durth was therefore quite right when he already in 1977 criticised "the staging of everyday life". Not becoming explicit, his criticism was in line with Walter Benjamin who back in the 30s spoke of an *aestheticising of politics* through which "the masses got their expression but certainly not their right".[6] Werner Durth speaks of the "make-up of a social reality, the breaches and contradictions of which are being covered up with growing effort"[7] and of a making-invisible the world of labour. Eleven years after the first edition, Durth has to realise that his "metaphor of the city as stage" and the "terms of staging and dramaturgy of cities which were put up for discussion with critical intention, were increasingly turned towards the positive and affirmed" (loc. cit., 227). It is thus necessary to take up his criticism again on the current level of development.

Massimiliano Fuksas says in his preface to the catalogue *Città: Less Aesthetics More Ethics:* "What was needed was a rediscovery of the awareness that the quality of architecture and the work is not enough" (loc.cit.12). This sentence is revealing. That is because it implies the possibility of an, in a way, just aesthetic quality of architecture, or respectively states that architecture had been understood in that way over a longer period of time. In fact many architects may have thought this way. With astonishment one also reads in Mario Botta's book "Ethik des Bauens"[8] (The Ethics of Construction) that ethics mainly consists of the architect trying to get the best out of himself.

But at the same time he states that for a long time, architects had punished the weaker parts of society in a double way, namely for one thing by not building for them and secondly by building badly what they did build for them (loc. cit. 41).

On the other hand do many regulations of architecture as a profession name the social responsibility of architecture. In the statute of the Federation of German Architects in the State of Hessen § 2.1, it says for example that its aim is the quality of planning and building in responsibility towards the builder and society. This double responsibility of the architect may be difficult to redeem and the differentiation between builder and society might usually hold a tension if not even a conflict. The builder supplies the money, he invests, and that means in most cases – not if it is a one-family house – that he acts according to maxims of the developed capitalism, which means, according to our analysis: of the aesthetic economy.

Society, however, means all people in principal, but especially those who are affected by the building, once finished. Temporarily they may also be the consuming *flaneurs*, the city-tourists, hungry for events, but most of the time in their life they are not. A very big part of the population cannot even temporarily be counted in. What is rather true for the affected persons is that they are participants in the drama of life and not spectators; that they have to work and not just to consume and that they want to live in their city and do not just want to experience it in a position as tourists.

As far as the greater trends are concerned:

- As to globalization: Regionalisation comes in the way of globalisation. That means for example for the field of living that people who are demanded professional mobility, cling to living in certain places: One wants to belong somewhere and therefore accepts longer hours of travelling to work, even if that leads to doing the splits in marriage and week-splitting.

- In the centre of the consumption- and event-society, the main intention of which it is to raise the desires, the craving for the genuine satisfaction of needs calls in. Just one example is the food market, where in contrast to the shining presentation and diversity on offer, the demand for *real* food produce starts pushing through i.e. for food produce that are healthy, seasonal and nourishing.

- And finally: Not just at the margins but in the centre of the waste-society, shortage becomes evident. Foremost this goes for ecological products, if one can say so, i.e. such that have to be local and cannot be taken from elsewhere in the world by exploitation. The central example for architecture is here the shortage of building land. Here Thomas Sieverts has pointed to a real dilemma, namely to the dilemma between thrifty and gentle management of building land. This dilemma cannot be solved by condensed construction because that leads to a rise of sealing. On the other hand, a gentle management of building land is just not thrifty.[9]

Ethics or aesthetics? Once upon a time there was a beautiful, an aristocratic ideal of the Greeks: The unity of what is beautiful and what is good. This ideal has always had great attraction, if not to say seductive power, on the architect. Of course s/he has to meet both in her/his work, ethics and aesthetics, but s/he would be badly advised to blur their differences in an unreconciled time. In that way s/he would not live up to her/his responsibility for society.

Notes

[1] Wilhelm Schmid, *Philosophie der Lebenskunst: Eine Grundlegung*, Frankfurt/M.: Suhrkamp, 5th ed. 1999.

[2] Quotation according to Søren Kirkegaard, *Either/Or*, ed. and transl. by Howard V. Hong and Edna Hong, Princeton, NJ: Princeton University Press 1987. The numbers refer to the first and second part of *Either/Or* followed by the provided page numbers of the first and second part of *Either/Or* in the Danish complete works.

[3] See my book *Ethik im Kontext: Über den Umgang mit ernsten Fragen*, Frankfurt/M: Suhrkamp 1997, (English edition: *Ethics in Context: On the Art of Dealing with Serious Questions,* Cambridge: Polity Press 2001).

[4] "Therefore, it is not so much a matter of choosing between willing good or willing evil as of choosing to will, but that in turn posits good and evil." II, 169/II, 153f.

[5] See my article "Zur Kritik der ästhetischen Ökonomie" (On Criticism of Aesthetic Economics*)*, English in: Thesis eleven 73, May 2003, 71-82.

[6] Walter Benjamin, *Das Kunstwerk im Zeitalter seiner technischen Reproduzierbarkeit*, Frankfurt/M.: Suhrkamp, 11th ed. 1979, 42.

[7] Werner Durth, *Die Inszenierung der Alltagswelt: Zur Kritik der Stadtgestaltung,* Wiesbaden: Vieweg 1988.

[8] Mario Botta, *Ethik des Bauens*, Basel: Birkhäuser 1966.

[9] Thomas Sieverts, *Zwischenstadt: Zwischen Ort und Welt, Raum und Zeit, Stadt und Land,* Wiesbaden: Vieweg 1998 (*Cities without cities: Between Place and World, Space and Time, Town and Country,* New York: Routledge 2003).

HABITABILITY AS A DEEP AESTHETIC VALUE

PAULINE VON BONSDORFF

An aesthetics of the lifeworld poses many challenges to traditional aesthetic theory. As an object of aesthetic attention, appreciation and experience, the environment differs in many respects from art objects.[1] This is true irrespective of whether there is a fundamental similarity in all aesthetic experience or not. For the purpose of this article, it is enough to note typical differences between listening to a concert or visiting an art show on the one hand and, on the other, enjoying a natural landscape or a streetscape. Especially some works of art are extremely complex and demand perceptive acuity, maturity of thought, openness of mind and a willingness from their audience to draw upon former experiences and let oneself be challenged. An environment might be no less complex, but its complexity is typically of a different kind. It is less intense but also more "on the surface", both in the sense of being immediately perceptible and in the sense of lacking a unified, intentional, historical or expressive meaning.[2] But if aesthetic value is on the surface, is it therefore necessarily shallow? I shall argue that this is not the case. In some cases and contexts, understanding sensuous pleasure and well-being is morally significant.

In this article, I focus upon components and aspects that inform aesthetic environmental quality, or beauty, understood in an everyday sense. What kinds of elements make us, then, experience a place as nice, welcoming, even beautiful? In everyday discourse there is a parallel between the beautiful and the ugly, on the one hand, and the pleasant and the unpleasant, on the other. This parallel is far from the whole truth about beauty, which can indeed be upsetting and difficult.[3] On the other hand we can also find some things, spaces or persons ugly rather than beautiful, yet at the same time interesting and attractive. On the whole, however we prefer the beautiful not so much because it makes us think but because it makes life harmonious and welcoming.[4]

Habitability is a word with rich connotations to everyday life and practices, and I shall use it to explore the beauty of everyday human habitats. Since it applies to different levels of environmental experience from the sensuous to the reflective, it allows me to point out relations between high and low, surface and depth within the aesthetic value of environments. The concept also illuminates connections between beauty and functionality, especially when functionality is understood broadly as providing possibilities for various activities of a practical and impractical – such as social or contemplative – sort. Interpreted as beautiful functionality, habitability is related to ideals of harmony and smoothness, to minimizing aesthetic obstacles such as, for example, colours, sounds or smells that offend our senses. However, it should not be interpreted as implying a minimalist ideal. What is primarily at issue is not the stripping away of unnecessary elements but the opening up of spaces for living in different ways. Similarly, by discussing habitability as one key notion of environmental aesthetics I do not want to replace other theories or concepts, but complement them.

I begin by locating my philosophical points of departure in the phenomenology of the lifeworld developed by Martin Heidegger, Edmund Husserl and Maurice Merleau-Ponty. I argue that the aesthetic appreciation of environments inhabited by humans requires an understanding of human life, which evolves in everyday life. If so, the difference between ordinary and aesthetic experience might not in all cases be very clear. What is lost in conceptual purity is, however, won in aesthetic understanding. In the second part of the article, I discuss relations between pleasure and value in the aesthetic appreciation and judgement of environments. After a presentation of relevant aspects of the cognitivist position and the engagement view, I point out seven ways in which sensuous and moral considerations are interdependent in aesthetic appreciation. These interdependencies appear as a result of reflecting on habitability as an aesthetic value.

Appreciating the lifeworld naively

To approach questions of environmental aesthetics from the perspective of habitability is to adopt a naive view on the issues as compared to a more theoretical one. Naivity is, however, necessary, since habitability is a concept and a quality based in the practices of unreflected, everyday life, where people are not normally concerned with the purification of their views from preconceptions and personality. Such things are, rather, constitutive of the weave of everyday life. However, preconceptions, not to speak of prejudice, as well as the understanding and perspectives that stem from *one's own* situation are often regarded as irrelevant or even harmful for both rational knowledge and aesthetic judgement. In this sense, the idea of habitability goes against the grain of much aesthetic and philosophical thinking and runs the risk of seeming naive, in the sense of lacking insight and reflection. In spite of this, I want to defend naivity as a method or way required by the wish to understand some central aspects of the beauty and attraction of everyday environments.

What points of departure would legitimise naivity as a method? An obvious candidate is the mature phase of phenomenology, where the idea of lifeworld or lived world is discussed by Heidegger, Husserl (in his later thinking) and Merleau-Ponty.[5] A central idea in this thinking is that humanly relevant knowledge about culture, human life and social relations cannnot be obtained if one abstracts from how people live in the world. The concept lifeworld includes both the given, material and immaterial aspects of the world and the relations through which a human being inhabits the world. Culture is therefore central, both as patterns of thought, values and practices and as material artefacts. Further, since various aspects of the lifeworld are interdependent with each other and with particular human beings, they change. Although there are recurrent, existential conditions, such as human finitude, natality and mortality, their interpretation, role and character vary in different cultures and depend on both tradition and interpretation.

A central feature of the lifeworld is that it is socially constituted. The individual is embedded in a "we", surrounded by "them", by the others, or, to translate the term Heidegger uses, *das Man* literally, "one".[6] The "one" stands for general, presupposed and normative expectations about human behaviour: about how one should act, according to which criteria one should judge and how one can expect to be judged by others. Therefore, our embeddedness in the world includes preconceptions and prejudice. Also, freedom and knowledge are possible only from within this situation and therefore relative: freedom is never absolute nor can knowledge about the lifeworld be objective in a strict, scientific sense. The lifeworld itself is likewise fundamentally relational since it exists only in relation to human beings.[7] But in addition to this aspect, I would like to emphasise an implication of Merleau-Ponty's term *monde vécu*, namely that the lifeworld is the world as lived. The world is, then, after all, ontologically different from our views about it. Although the world by necessity *appears* to us indistinguishably from our practices, thought and action, it is *there*, to be explored, and not just *here* with or even within me. That the world is in part unknown is important for the meaning and significance of aesthetic appreciation.

If it is accepted that the human environment is partly constituted by humans, it follows that its aesthetic appreciation should draw upon an understanding of human experience. This argument is parallel to Allen Carlson's view that the correct aesthetic appreciation of nature must be based upon an understanding of nature.[8] But instead of scientific understanding, which Carlson emphasises in the case of nature, understanding the lifeworld is primarily based upon human experience, which is neither scientific nor objective.[9] This does not mean, however, that it fails to offer a basis for understanding and appreciation. Human experience is, for each individual, personal – it is *my* experience – yet personal experience as we (who understand language) know it is inherently intersubjective. Its materials, elements and very structure stem from the shared world of language and social practice. Although our experiences differ, these differences are not a hindrance to interhuman understanding, but are instead among the factors that make the experience of others interesting and understandable to us.

The idea that human experience is necessary for the aesthetic appreciation of human environments and that personal experiences are not beyond the sharable and socially relevant brings us closer to understanding habitability as an aesthetic quality. I suggest, then, that we judge the habitability of an area or a house according to our impressions and imaginings of how people actually live there and of what activities and social patterns are possible or might be typical for the house or area. Even such everyday attitudes and patterns of behaviour as human curiosity and gossiping can be drawn upon. Although our judgements can err and our interests vary – different persons have different tastes – the implicit or explicit understanding of the lifeworld is the general basis on which these judgements rest. The relative stability and reliability of this basis is constituted in intersubjective communication.

It is worth pointing out that by the word judge I do not mean to suggest that we consciously ponder habitability as part of aesthetic judgements. The claim is only that habitability informs aesthetic judgement, which is one face of aesthetic experience and appreciation. Aesthetic judgement is "based" in the feeling of pleasure aroused by our reflective perception of the object.[10] But mostly, the judgement is not the result of a question we pose to ourselves, nor need a judgement be verbally expressed. Mostly we do not ask "is this beautiful?"; aesthetic value, rather, appears as a quality of the world.[11]

If we verbalise the pleasure to someone else or to ourselves, we draw upon our aesthetic vocabulary. We might then characterise a house as beautiful, friendly, peaceful or jolly: aesthetic judgements of which the three last also show our competence in judging the character of the lifeworld. Further, they indicate that habitability is not of one kind but is relative to the function of spaces. The joyful character of a children's daycare centre adds to its aesthetic value but would be inappropriate in a chapel.

As a key word of environmental aesthetics, habitability nevertheless suggests that we appreciate environments aesthetically against a background of ideas about what it would be like to live in a certain place or how it is inhabited. In addition, I suggest that these questions are natural to us: we tend to explore spaces with an interest in how we fit into them or how they fit into human life. However, habitability is relevant also in nature appreciation, for example in contemplating a bird's nest or the sea as the home of other species.[12] Common to every kind of habitability is, however, that its appreciation is based upon our personal experience of being in the world as embodied and social beings in a network of interdependencies with other beings. It is only wise to remember that this world is also the world of non-human creatures and things.

I have suggested that the attitude of daily life is relevant to environmental experience generally including the aesthetic appreciation of environments. But if aesthetic appreciation includes or draws upon our general experience of places, what is the difference between them? Perhaps one cannot draw a definite line here. One difference seems nevertheless to be that aesthetic experience is more reflective and self-reflective: compared to ordinary perception it involves more awareness both of the objects we perceive and contemplate and of ourselves as subjects, or bearers, of experience and judgement.[13] In addition, not all aspects of everyday life are equally relevant or important aesthetically: some stand out. A second difference between aesthetic appreciation and general experience and perception is disinterestedness, which I interpret primarily as "other-directedness".[14] Aesthetic appreciation does not aim at the fulfilment of personal needs and desires or at the cognitive or other control of its object, but much like in (ideal) friendship, the appreciator respects the character and needs of the object, gives it priority and finds satisfaction in appreciating even features that are beyond her grasp.

In the aesthetic mode of perceiving and experiencing, both our openness to and our understanding of the environment are relevant. They also interact. We can be more or less sensitive to the nuances and character of colours, shapes, sounds, smells, textures, and similarly more or less able to perceive what goes on in an environment. It is especially in the latter, narrative dimension that everyday experiences are relevant. The more experienced and knowledgeable we are about certain life forms, the more skilled we are also aesthetically: we can perceive and appreciate.[15] Personal experience can function as a condition of that maturation which Sharpe claimed does not take place with landscapes. Certainly artistic and other modes of representing environments often influence the way we perceive also everyday surroundings, but this influence is often overstated. Especially with places we inhabit in one way or another – areas where we live or work – experience and knowledge from everyday life is more important than the "image" of an area. In a comparison between reality and imagination, reality is richer and feeds imagination more than the other way round.[16] In addition, an important kind of aesthetic value can best be discussed not in terms of contemplation or even appreciation, but in terms of enjoyment.

In addition to the kind of aesthetic appreciation where we reflectively and disinterestedly contemplate an object there are indeed other kinds or levels of aesthetic experience. The aesthetic is not only a separate experience, which constitutes a unit of its own as compared to daily life.[17] There is an aesthetic mode of experiencing and perceiving alongside other activities. We sometimes appreciate things aesthetically when we perform practical tasks, even as part of those tasks. Craftmanship, but also more simple chores such as cleaning, are good examples. It is in reflecting on these other levels of aesthetic experience that the idea of habitability can be helpful, as I will indicate next.

Aesthetic pleasure and value

A discussion of aspects that have hitherto been judged as of little importance for aesthetic value proper is important for understanding habitability, a quality which is often felt rather than discursively explicated. If we were to acknowledge other, more tacit and less reflective levels of aesthetic experience than conscious aesthetic appreciation, these might be described as low-keyed lower or shallow. Playing with the connotations of the vertical, another word that points downward is deep. I would now like to explore how and if the low combines with the deep, or whether it is always shallow. This play with words is a heuristic device where no fundamental significance should be given to the words as such and their semantic relations. Yet words lead and mislead us into patterns of thought that are too easily taken for granted, but which it is good to question, not least because the presuppositions they rest upon and imply might not be valid.

To start with sensuous pleasure for which there is a long tradition of suspicion in aesthetic theory. Also Immanuel Kant, whose importance for modern aesthetics can scarcely be overrated, denies the relevance of merely sensuous pleasure for aesthetic judgement.[18] The reason he gives is not that sensuousness or the passions are dangerous (as Plato thought), but that they are too contingent to provide a basis for the intersubjective validity of aesthetic judgement. In addition, Kant does not grant any significant role for the body[19] in aesthetic judgement but dualistically sees the mind and the flesh as separate to the point of denying any important interaction between them. Kant's presuppositions can, however, be challenged. First, contrary to what Kant's distinction suggests, human beings are basically like each other with respect to the body. Feelings of pleasure and displeasure arising from our sensuous apparatus are not contingent but at most culture-specific and therefore valid intersubjectively (to a large extent they are even universally valid). A universalist but contextual theory of sensuous qualities might, with necessary qualifications, be defensible: there are visual, auditory, olfactory and tactile qualities that in particular contexts disturb people generally and others that add to our well-being. Sounds that are appropriate in a party become noise if we try to take a nap. Second, body and mind are more intricately related than Kant assumed. Instead of drawing a line between feeling and knowledge, it might be more correct to regard also feelings and sensations as forms of cognition.[20] If so, it is important not to reduce feeling to rational knowledge and to observe that cognition undergoes a change when it incorporates the affective dimension.

The denial of cognitive importance to feeling and the separation of mind and body are historical reasons for the neglect and even despisal of sensuous pleasure (and displeasure) in aesthetic theory. The dualism is echoed in Anglo-American environmental aesthetics, where two main positions can be distinguished. On the one hand, there is the cognitivist view defended by Allen Carlson and others, on the other, its criticisms and alternatives, most notably Arnold Berleant's engagement view that emphasise the legitimacy of noncognitive experience in nature appreciation. Both sides support in their own ways, the explorion and illumination of habitability as an overall aesthetic quality.

Carlson's central thesis is that in order to aesthetically appreciate nature correctly, we need to appreciate it as nature, that is, with an understanding of its history and present functioning. This knowledge is provided mainly by the natural sciences, although Carlson grants a secondary role also to cultural knowledge.[21] The suggestion that knowledge deepens aesthetic appreciation by indicating the complexity of its object and affording materials for reflection is promising also for an aesthetics of the human. In that context, as I have argued above, knowledge about the character of the object is, however, gained through experience or by acquaintance. Furthermore, since it is essential to the lifeworld that it is co-constituted by its inhabitants, in order to know a city, suburb, or village in any depth one should not just visit but stay there for some time, or at least approach it from the point of view of an inhabitant.

From the point of view of lifeworld and habitat, a problem with Carlson's approach is his silence on sensuous, experiential, other than more strictly cognitive aspects of environmental experience and appreciation. The qualities we find by inhabiting a space or place, through our bodily situatedness, cannot be separated from the situation of which experiencer and environment are equally fundamental parts.[22] Despite this contribution of ours, to feel the temperature and scents of a space, to attend to its full soundscape, or to sense the scale or atmosphere of a place are no less ways of getting to know it than is scientifically informed perception. There is a clear difference between contributing to the perceived qualities of an environment and projecting meaning upon it. The contribution we make in perception – already by the structure and features of our perceptual and mental apparatus – is not freely chosen by us but, rather, constitutes the world as we know it.

The aesthetics of engagement developed by Arnold Berleant complements cognitivism. For Berleant aesthetic experience, like perceptual experience generally, is essentially characterised by the participation, engagement and even fusion of experiencer and environment.[23] A human being is, according to Berleant, part of his environment, and environment means "a fusion of organic awareness, of meanings both conscious and unaware, of geographical location, of physical presence, personal time, pervasive movement".[24] For the purpose of my discussion, the important implication of the engagement view is that it supports the idea that we can have non-discursive, experientially based environmental knowledge.[25]

Experience has been criticised for being a too subjective concept.[26] In addition to the observation that sensuously gained, experiential knowledge is knowledge about the lifeworld, it is therefore important to discuss in what ways it is subjective and what competence it gives. Here Hans-Georg Gadamer's discussion of the German concepts *Erlebnis* and *Erfahrung*, which are both translated in English as experience, is illuminating.[27] *Erlebnis* points to momentary, vital experience and it seems that for better and worse it has had the upper hand in discussions of aesthetic experience. However, in developing the idea of experiential knowledge, *Erfahrung* might be more important. It implies that humans (and other creatures) can become experienced, as in the maturation of knowledge, worldview and taste that we might admire in people who have had a rich and varied life and also reflected upon it. *Erfahrung* could be referred to as sedimented knowledge. For environmental appreciation, it means an increased ability to understand both sensuous cues and more complicated meanings of human life forms and behavioural patters.[28]

The idea of experiential knowledge and its sedimentation is echoed in the semantic resources of the word habitability. Our ability to move around and act in the world is, like our use of language, based on bodily sedimented behavioural patterns, habits. A habitable place is, on the other hand, a place where one can develop these patterns. A habitable apartment might have, for example, a place to sleep, to eat, to make food, to wash, and in addition to these practical requirements charms such as a window with a view, natural light, enough silence and non-intrusive presence of neighbours. On the other hand, we develop some habits because of the aesthetic resources of an environment: we choose the path through the park rather than a slightly shorter but uglier way, or we frequent the welcoming café.

Granted that habitability has aesthetic relevance in the indicated sense, does it also relate to higher values, such as the good and the beautiful, where beautiful means exceptionally beautiful? On the basis of its intimate connection to an understanding of life forms, it seems at least that habitability is a morally affected aesthetic quality (as perhaps many environmental aesthetic qualities are). There are several connections between habitability as an aesthetic concept and morals or "life values".[29]

First, the aesthetic appreciation of habitability relates to morality in the sense of *mores* or manners. The appreciation of life forms is necessarily an appreciation of how life is lived. We do not perceive simply that an activity takes place: that someone goes fishing, that some play a game, that groceries are sold in a marketplace. At the same time, we perceive how or in what manner this takes place: with grace, or energy, or self-esteem. Manners is a normatively charged word. There are correct and wrong ways of doing things, and the difference is often in the details and nuances.[30]

Second, criteria for the rightness of manners and for the fabrication of artefacts are in part decided on the basis of what is sensuously pleasing. When thoroughly understood, the sensuously pleasing contributes to our wellbeing.[31] At least as soon as we connect this idea to the case of other people or creatures, its relation to moral rightness becomes evident. One could even say that if we do not understand and give due attention to the physical wellbeing of other creatures, we will also be unable to cater for higher, spiritual needs.[32] It is also worth emphasising that in the environment, low-keyed aesthetic qualities can be deeply important precisely as they remain in the background. As examples, think of the texture of a wall or ceiling, or the wind or birdsong in a park. As aesthetic (and morally relevant) qualities, these need not occupy the centre-stage of a visitor's consciousness. Rather, they open a welcoming space for the human being, tune the world so that it appears both receptive and generous.

If an understanding of sensuous qualities is part of an understanding of the good there is also, thirdly, influence in the opposite direction: from morality to the sensuous level. Moral ideas change our perception and appreciation of things and events. To understand that two agents are mating instead of trying to harm each other changes the overall quality of a scene. Passion and violence can have many features in common, but our basic understanding and therefore perception of the situations are different. Similarly, construction and destruction on a building site can look alike to an uninformed perceiver but with information, not to speak of one's own involvement in the process, the perception changes.

Fourth, when contemplating a space we tend to include in our contemplation the awareness of the feel of its sensuous qualities as well as other qualities we have first-hand knowledge of. A picture of a forest is not judged only according to the shape of the trees, but also according to our knowledge of the soft and uneven character of the ground and of silvan smell- and soundscape. Multi-sensuous experience, in other words, informs visual judgement. That the knowledge relevant in aesthetic judgement is in part tacit or knowledge by acquaintance illustrates the need to combine cognitivism and the engagement view. This is also true for how the stories of a place become part of its aesthetic character: they are things we have the competence to perceive, and we have this competence because we are ourselves agents in similar stories. In particular, to feel addressed by a space or its image requires that we can in some sense imagine ourselves as part of it.[33]

An emphasis on the relations between experience and world opens fruitful perspectives for an aesthetics of the lifeworld which emphasises the social dimension. This is a fifth aspect of the links between aesthetics and ethics in habitability. Paths, traces and of course actual human beings in environments are not objects perceived by a distanced perceiver. Rather, they mean company. Even marks and traces indicate the presence of fellow humans or other creatures; in addition, human presence underlies the very existence of cultural landscapes and cities.[34] If the marks of other inhabitants are perceived as their mediated presence, they also demand respectful behaviour from us.

Sixth, the narrative richness of environment is not limited to human life but includes structures, systems, events and agents of sentient and non-sentient nature. As Aldo Leopold and J. Baird Callicott have shown, the idea of community can with good reason be extended to include eco-systems.[35] To aesthetically appreciate the life of other species through the lense of habitability requires, as with humans, some degree of empathy. It is necessary to trust explicitly or implicitly that we have an aesthetically sufficient understanding of the meaning and value of activities such as nurturing and mating for the animals themselves, or of the factors that contribute to the well-being of, for example, a tree.

Aesthetically sufficient understanding does not require that we know exactly how another creature feels. This suspension of exact knowledge is kin to Kant's discussion of beauty, which I shall discuss as a seventh and last moral-aesthetic aspect of habitability. Kant describes beauty as "the expression of aesthetic ideas", where the difference between free and dependent beauty is that in the latter case we have a concept of the object.[36] Now the beauty that habitability contributes to seems to be situated somewhere between free and dependent beauty. It requires more than the perception of "purposiveness without [known] purpose" but perhaps less than a concept of other life forms. However whether we have a concept or not aesthetic judgement is reflective, which means that it does not aim to subsume the perceived under a concept but plays with the relations between the appearance and ideas relevant to it. It is, then, not important that we possess knowledge of the object but, rather that we are open to its ways or manners. Appreciating the life forms of non-human species perhaps shows this more clearly than the more everyday and often taken for granted appreciation (and judgement) of human life forms, activities and manners.[37] But it is wise to remember that our knowledge of other humans, however close to us, is limited. An aesthetic interest in the life of fellow humans might therefore be more respectful to them than a more straightforwardly moral or cognitive interest.

To round off, let me add some reflections on beauty. I am inclined to see beauty and harmony as real features of the world, yet not as independent of humans or human agency. That the beauty of life forms is interdependent with human agency might be evident in the immediate habitat: the atmosphere of our home or of buses or shops we enter are partly dependent on how we treat other people. On a more collective and societal level, our life forms and choices influence the conditions for life also in distant places.

The Western lifestyle, with high rates of consumption, contributes to global warming and many other processes with real effects on human and non-human habitats on the other side of the globe. Second, although beauty is in one sense there for us to perceive, it requires a personal act of appreciation; in other words, what we value and express through the concept of beauty is in the world, but the evaluation is ours. Finally, moral aspects of beauty introduce depth in aesthetic appreciation. Because of the more than narrowly aesthetic relevance of aesthetic and sensuous pleasures a beautiful environment (or the part or aspect of one) can make demands upon us. Features that support the wellbeing of individual inhabitants, groups or species demand to be preserved: their aesthetic and moral perception suggest to us that these features should be preserved, where the word should have moral urgency.

Conclusions

One conclusion of my discussion might be that if we want to promote the good life – good for others and for ourselves – we should make no categorical choice between ethical and aesthetic perspectives. Of course it is important to be sensitive to the differences between these and to the need to check the aesthetic against the ethical, but it is likewise important to check our ideas of the good and right against the aesthetic. The good is perhaps the final arbiter, but a thorough understanding of the good includes reflection upon the pleasant.

I have also argued that the challenge of the everyday requires that we take seriously many aspects of experience that have traditionally been excluded as improper to aesthetic experience. Improper might mean not belonging, which is unconvincing, or impure which, according to traditional standards of aesthetic purity, might be correct. That aesthetic appreciation is pure, and in particular that it can at the same time be pure and reflective is, however, all but evident. In my view rather, aesthetic experience, appreciation and judgement are impure: synthetic, mixed and in many ways open, and for these reasons more appropriate to their objects. This might also make a concept such as habitability useful in mediating between the interests of different groups or species in cases of environmental conflicts. Habitability is not an expert, elitist notion but easily understandable in various contexts. Its impure aspects – that it is sensuously and morally contaminated and dependent rather than free – makes it more accessible in discussions and negotiations. Perhaps habitability is the kind of aesthetic concept needed in environmental management.

Finally, my description of aesthetic experience is in certain respects normative (I describe what aesthetic experience ideally is), yet I also use a realist argumentation (I discuss elements that actually arouse pleasure). My response to this seeming paradox is that aesthetic experience, appreciation and judgement are cultural and axiologically charged concepts, but like other such concepts they are also forms of human, cultural self-understanding. The discussion of such concepts has, in addition to a research aspect, necessarily always a critical (even educational) aspect. By arguing from an intellectual tradition that represents both understanding and forms of life the researcher tries to do better justice to life and at the same time promote understanding.

Notes

[1] The seminal discussion of the characteristics of aesthetic environmental experience in the field of Anglo-American aesthetics is R. W. Hepburn's "Contemporary Aesthetics and the Neglect of Natural Beauty" from 1966. For an overview of contemporary arguments for and against the similarity of art and environmental aesthetic experience, see Carlson (2001).

[2] Some philosophers fail to see anything worth deeper aesthetic reflection in the environment. R. A. Sharpe, 40, for example, thinks that a process of maturation is characteristic of the appreciation of some works of art, but not relevant to landscape. Although environmental aesthetics is a growing research area, many recent introductory books still define aesthetics as the philosophy of art.

[3] See Hickey. One need not go as far as Hickey in order to admit that beauty is not always easy.

[4] On beauty as thought-provoking, see Steiner, i.e. 49-50.

[5] See Heidegger, Husserl, Merleau-Ponty. It would be fruitful to compare both pragmatism and Ludwig Wittgenstein's mature philosophy to these views.

[6] Dreyfus chooses this translation, see 141-162.

[7] The application of the notion of lifeworld to other species than the human would not be acceptable to Heidegger. However, I see no reason to exclude application – *mutatis mutandis* – although humans know little about the worlds of other species.

[8] Carlson (2000). I return to this views in the second part of my article.

[9] On the limits and legitimacy of objectivity and exact science, see Husserl and Merleau-Ponty, "Avant-propus".

[10] See Kant, § 1-22.

11 Also in Kant, there is no indication that judgement (*Urteil*) would have to be preceded by a conscious, "verbalised" inner dialogue of the experiencer.

12 In nature, habitability seems to require that our attitude is one of co-inhabitants rather than outsiders. I return later to this question.

13 I have discussed this difference at length in von Bonsdorff (1998), 60-92, where I emphasise response as a central feature of aesthetic experience. Response, as I understand it in this context, involves a responsibility for the value judgements we make or for how we perceive the situation. Note also that even if the materials we draw upon in aesthetic contemplation stem from reality, reflectivity remains a common denominator of aesthetic experience and the phenomenological *epoché*.

14 This interpretation finds support in discussions by, among others, Shaftesbury, 68-87, Brady and Hepburn (2001), 1-15.

15 See also the discussion of experience in the second part of this article.

16 Compare Merleau-Ponty (1991), 20.

17 John Dewey's idea of art as experience is important in connecting art to everyday life, but I think his structural separation of aesthetic experience from the general weave of experience misses some aesthetically salient aspects. Dewey, 35-57.

18 Kant, §1-5.

19 I use this term (contra Kant) as a shorthand for sensations and feelings which are not primarily deliberate.

20 See Merleau-Ponty (1992) and Böhme (1989) (1995). This line of thought points in a similar direction as the work of such contemporary philosophers and scientists as Mark Johnson and George Lakoff or Antonio Damasio.

21 Carlson (2000), 6, 11-13, 49-52, 54-71.

22 The German word *Befindlichkeit*, "being in" or "finding oneself" in a space, is not easily rendered in English. I have discussed it in "'Nature' in Experience: Body and Environment" (*Nordisk estetisk tidskrift* 1999:19, 111-128), esp. 118-120, drawing upon both Heidegger and Böhme.

23 See Berleant (1991) and (1992).

24 Berleant (1992), 34.

25 See also Abram. Both Berleant and Abram draw partly upon Merleau-Ponty.

26 See, for example, Martin Heidegger's criticism of aesthetics in "Der Ursprung des Kunstwerkes".

27 Gadamer, xxv-xxix, 1-96. For a recent discussion of experience, see Shusterman, 15-34.

28 By suggesting that *Erfahrung* is more important for experiential knowledge I do not want to suggest that *Erlebnis* is irrelevant. Moments of vivid perceptual awareness might indeed become paradigm cases of environmental understanding. Ronald W. Hepburn makes interesting observations on "aesthetic animation" in *The Reach of the Aesthetic*, i.e. 66-67.

[29] Marcia Muelder Eaton and Yrjö Sepänmaa have suggested that there is or can be a connection between the good and the beautiful, so that the beautiful is neither evil nor bad; see Mulder Eaton (1987) (1997), Sepänmaa, esp. 127-136. According to Aarne Kinnunen, it is in the ugly, which is often a morally reprobatory notion, that we find the moral-aesthetic connection rather than in the beautiful. Kinnunen, 317-352.

[30] It might be noted that the sensitivity and awareness of the importance of such things, along with an awareness of the interrelatedness of ethics and aesthetics, seems bigger in Eastern than in Western cultures. In the East, there is also a greater understanding of how bodily and spiritual welfare reinforce rather than compete with each other. The Japanese tea ceremony is a good (although highly formalised) example of the interrelations between beauty and goodness in manners. See Hirota. For a Western contribution to the general topic, see Berleant (1999).

[31] The sensuously pleasing should, for example, be analysed by taking all the senses rather than just the eye into account. For a relevant discussion, see Cranz.

[32] The role of sensuous, bodily pleasure and pain in religious practices might be worth discussion in this context but I can only mention it here.

[33] Is this a reason why one's own travel pictures or those of people one cares about are incomparably more interesting than pictures by people one does not care so much about?

[34] One way to state the difference between a ruin and a house is to say that the ruin is abandoned while the house is still inhabited.

[35] Leopold and Callicott (1989).

[36] Kant, § 51, 175.

[37] See, for example, Callicott (1997).

References

Abram, David (1997) *The Spell of the Sensuous: Perception and Language in a More-Than-Human World*, New York: Vintage Books

von Bonsdorff, Pauline (1998) *The Human Habitat: Aesthetic and Axiological Perspectives* Lahti: International Institute of Applied Aesthetics, pp. 60-92

---, (1999) "'Nature' in Experience: Body and Environment" in *Nordisk estetisk tidskrift* 19, pp. 111-128

Berleant, Arnold (1991) *Art and Engagement,* Philadelphia: Temple University Press

---, (1992) *The Aesthetics of Environment,* Philadelphia: Temple University Press

---, (1999) "On Getting Along Beautifully: Ideas for a Social Aesthetics" in von Bonsdorff, Pauline and Haapala, Arto (eds.), *Aesthetics in the Human Environment,* Lahti: International Institute of Applied Aesthetics, pp. 12-29

Brady, Emily (1998) "Don't Eat the Daisies: Disinterestedness and the Situated Aesthetic" in *Environmental Values* 7:1, pp. 97-114

Böhme, Gernot (1989) *Für eine ökologische Naturästhetik,* Frankfurt am Main: Suhrkamp

---, (1995) *Atmosphäre: Essays zur neuen Ästhetik,* Frankfurt am Main: Suhrkamp

Callicott, J. Baird (1989) *In Defense of the Land Ethic: Essays in Environmental Philosophy* Albany: State University of New York Press

---, (1997) "Whaling in Sand County: The Morality of Norwegian Minke Whale Catching" in Chappell,T. D. J. (ed.), *The Philosophy of the Environment*, Edinburgh: Edinburgh University Press, pp. 156-179

Carlson, Allen (2000) *Aesthetics and the Environment: The Appreciation of Nature, Art and Architecture* London: Routledge

---, (2001) "Environmental Aesthetics" in Gaut, Berysand and McIver Lopes, Dominic (eds.) *The Routledge Companion to Aesthetics*, London: Routledge, pp. 423-436

Cranz, Galen (1998) *The Chair: Rethinking Culture, Body and Design,* New York and London: W.W. Norton & Company

Dewey, John (1980) *Art as Experience,* New York: Berkley (1934)

Dreyfus, Hubert L. (1994) *Being-in-the-World: A Commentary on Heidegger's Being and Time, Division 1,* Cambridge and London: MIT

Gadamer, Hans-Georg (1960) *Wahrheit und Methode: Grundzüge einer philosophischen Hermeneutik*, 2. ed. Tübingen: J.C.B. Mohr

Heidegger, Martin (1949) *Sein und Zeit,* Tübingen: Neomarius (1927)

---, (1972) "Der Ursprung des Kunstwerkes" in *Holzwege,* Frankfurt am Main: Vittorio Klosterman, pp. 7-68

Hepburn, R. W. (1966) "Contemporary Aesthetics and the Neglect of Natural Beauty", reprinted in *"Wonder" and Other Essays: Eight Studies in Aesthetics and Neighbouring Fields*, Edinburgh: Edinburgh University Press 1984, pp. 9-35

---, (2001) *The Reach of the Aesthetic: Collected essays on art and nature,* Aldershot: Ashgate

Hickey, Dave (1999) *The Invisible Dragon: Four Essays on Beauty,* Los Angeles: Art Issues Press (1993)

Hirota, Dennis (ed.) (1995) *Wind in the Pines: Classic Writings on the Way of Tea as a Buddhist Path*, Fremont, California: Asian Humanities Press

Husserl, Edmund (1997) *The Crisis of European Sciences and Transcendental Phenomenology*: *An Introduction to Phenomenological Philosophy*, trans. David Carr Evanston: Northwestern University Press (first German edition 1954)

Kant, Immanuel (1990) *Kritik der Urteilskraft,* Hamburg: Felix Meiner Verlag (1790)

Kinnunen, Aarne (2000) *Estetiikka,* Helsinki: WSOY

Leopold, Aldo (1970) *A Sand County Almanac: With Essays on Conservation from Round River,* New York: Ballantine Books

Merleau-Ponty, Maurice (1992) *Phénoménologie de la perception,* Paris: Gallimard (1945)

---, (1991) *Le visible et l'nvisible,* Paris: Gallimard (1964)

Mulder Eaton, Marcia (1987) *Aesthetics and the Good Life,* London and Toronto: Associated University Presses

---, (1997) "Aesthetics: the Mother of Ethics" in *Journal of Aesthetics and Art Criticism* 55:4, pp. 355-364

Sepänmaa, Yrjö (1993) *The Beauty of Environment: A General Model for Environmental Aesthetics,* 2. ed. Denton: Enviromental Ethics Books

Shaftesbury, Anthony, Earl of (1964) *Characteristics of Men, Manners, Opinions, Times,* John M. Robertson (ed.), Indianapolis and New York: The Bobbs-Merrill Company (first published in 1711)

Sharpe, R. A. (1991) *Contempory Aesthetics,* Aldershot: Gregg Revivals (1984)

Shusterman, Richard (2000) *Performing Live: Aesthetic Alternatives for the Ends of Art,* Ithaca and London: Cornell University Press

Steiner, Wendy (1995) *The Scandal of Pleasure: Art in an Age of Fundamentalism* Chicago and London: University of Chicago Press

HOUSING SIX BILLION
A theological plea for the vernacular[1]

TIM GORRINGE

The Hebrew word for house, beit, is a key word in the Hebrew bible, but almost invariably in its metaphorical sense. Like the Greek oikos, which translates it in the Septuagint, it originally means the structure but comes to do service for both house and family, and then for a whole people. This is the fundamental sense, and there is a sharp critique of putting physical structure, especially if it is pretentious, before concern for the people of Israel in the story in 2 Samuel 7. According to this theology YHWH never dwelt in a house, but lived in a tent, and moved with the people. The very idea of a "house" implies much too static a picture of one who is a "wayfaring God." Judaeo Christian culture, comments Richard Sennett, is at its very roots about spiritual dislocation and homelessness. "Our faith began at odds with place, because our gods themselves were disposed to wander."[2] This means that there is, to say the least, an ambivalence about settlement and dwelling in Judaism and Christianity which there may not be in cosmically oriented cultures. Throughout the writings of the great prophets luxury housing is the target of some of the fiercest prophetic invective, and Ecclesiastes later considers the building of great houses to be "vanity."[3]

In the New Testament this relativization of the importance of the house is radicalised. Jesus, according to Luke, was born in an outhouse and, according to Matthew, became a refugee immediately after his birth. The nineteenth century artists liked to depict Jesus "at home" learning the carpenter's trade, but Jesus seems to have aligned himself with the rootless and homeless:

Foxes have holes and the birds of the air have nests, but the Human one has nowhere to lay his head. (Lk 9.58)

When this tradition is interpreted through the Christian idea of incarnation it means that God takes God's place alongside those who have no home, who lack, perhaps, even shelter. The apocryphal Acts of Thomas contain a nice story about Thomas landing in India and extracting huge sums of money from the king on the promise of building him a house. No house materializes. When he is arrested for fraud he reveals that all the money has been given to the poor in order to build the king a "house in heaven."[4] Like Nathan, Thomas directs attention to the needs of the poor, and away from pharonic building projects. This is not to deny the need for shelter. On the contrary, God is the one who "shelters you under his wings" (Ps 61.4), who provides shelter and water for Hagar, cast out into the desert, or for Jonah overlooking Nineveh. The editor of the Book of Hosea includes an oracle which promises that they shall "again live beneath my shade (tsel), they shall flourish as a garden" (Hos 14.7). The biblical tradition, whilst critical of the housing of the rich, is not hostile to the establishing of homes as such. Rather, it offers a vision for the refugee:

They shall build houses and inhabit them; they shall plant vineyards and eat their fruit. They shall not build and another inhabit; they shall not plant and another eat; for like the days of a tree shall the days of my people be, and my chosen shall long enjoy the work of their hands (Is 65.21).

Likewise in the gospels there is no puritan condemnation of the security of the house. In Mark, for example, the house is a "safe" site for the discipleship community. There Jesus dines with the outcast (2.15; 14.3) and attends to the crowds (1.32; 3.20); it is the locus for private instruction (7.17, 9.33; 10.10) and healing. Only once is the house a site of conflict (3.20ff), and this is explained by the fact that this episode narrates the rejection of Jesus by his own family.[5] This helps us to understand why the house becomes the centre for early Christian worship after the resurrection. What is challenged, however, is possession and exclusive use. In the story commonly known as the "rich young ruler" we find a vision of a radical re-distribution of property. The story of the rich young man turns, Ched Myers argues, on the fact that he possesses many ktemata – lands. These are the properties he has acquired through the debt default of others, against the prophetic injunctions and the clear commands of Torah.[6] Jesus points out that if Torah is followed there will be plenty for everyone:

Jesus said, Truly I tell you, There is no one who has left house, or brothers or sisters or mother or father, or children, or lands, for my sake and for the gospel's sake, but they will receive a hundredfold now in this time, houses and brethren and sisters and mothers and children and lands, with persecutions. (Mk 10. 29-30)

In the light of this biblical scepticism, can we proceed to a theology of the domestic dwelling? I think we both can and have to. We can, in virtue of what the gospel has to say about the importance of bodies. If bodies are temples of the Spirit, as Paul claims (1 Cor 6), then it is not just what we do with them, but how we care for them and sustain them which is a matter of theological concern – food, fashion, shelter. We have to, for what we do with bodies raises the question of justice, as the entire Judaeo-Christian tradition from the prophet Nathan onwards has seen. That some live in shanties and others in palaces is as much a moral issue as the fact that, to use Paul's phrase, "some eat whilst others go hungry." Further, houses are important not simply for shelter but because, as the architect Christopher Day puts it, we do not look at buildings, but rather breathe them in. Buildings, and especially the houses we live in, form the third human skin.[7] Houses express, and are intended to express, a moral order. Twentieth century domestic architecture in Europe and the United States is a mapping of changing ways of understanding family and gender relationships.[8] In reflecting on this moral order we can begin with the most obvious contrast, between "the great house" on the one hand, and vernacular houses on the other.

The vernacular and the monumental

Christopher Day argues that we have two traditions of architecture, high and low:

One concerns itself with cosmic rules – proportion, geometry and classically-differentiated elements representing material principles: relation to the earth, to the vault of the heavens, to the vertical boundaries of free stretching space ... this is the stream of great architecture – temples, cathedrals, sometimes palaces and civic buildings. In scale and commitment to a singular idea such buildings often dominate the surroundings.

The other stream is the vernacular. Its keynote is response to climate, materials, social form and tradition. It concerns itself very much with textures, meetings of materials and tends to be rich for the senses. Almost without fail, the resulting landscape or townscape warms the soul ... The high architecture stream is inspired by cosmic ideas, the vernacular stream is rooted in daily reality – one is learnt by prolonged esoteric study, the other by making, doing and building, by mud, dirt and wood shavings. Both are artistic but neither is complete or balanced without the other: they need to be brought into conversation.[9]

Day's twofold distinction corresponds to the Sri Lankan theologian Aloysius Pieris' distinction between cosmic and metacosmic religions: high and literate traditions on the one hand, with their great scriptures, buildings, works of art and great music, and folk religion on the other, with its small local shrines, folk dances and folk music.[10] Like Day he believes neither tradition can be dispensed with. The American architectural critic J.B. Jackson likewise speaks of a twofold tradition, between houses built to last and those with a life expectancy of a generation or less, "dwellings" and "mansions." A dwelling, he argues, is a makeshift place, more or less thrown together, often moveable and not of much consequence if destroyed. The words "manor" and "mansion" however come from a root meaning lasting, enduring. In the sixteenth and seventeenth centuries in Europe there was, he argues, an architectural revolution in which wood and mud was replaced by stone.[11]

The word "vernacular" comes from the Latin verna, meaning a slave born in the household, and by extension the life of one confined to a village or estate. Thus a vernacular culture implies "a way of life ruled by tradition and custom, entirely remote from the larger world of politics and law; a way of life where identity derived not from permanent possession of land but from membership in a group or super-family."[12] This dominance of tradition means that vernacular building "displays very few devices not found in primitive buildings." Adolf Loos spoke of peasant houses as "shaped by the hand of God."[13] What he means by this is the way in which vernacular architecture responds so subtly to its region that it seems to be a "natural" creation. Think of the igloo, with its L shaped tunnel, to trap the wind, its raised sleeping platform, its ventilation louvres, its rounded shape to deflect fierce winds. It is a masterpiece of engineering. Rapoport speaks of the "amazing skill" shown by primitive and peasant builders in dealing with climatic problems and their ability to use minimum resources for maximum comfort. "The Eskimo has only snow and ice, fur and bone, and some driftwood; the Sudanese have mud, reeds and some palm logs … the marsh dwellers of Iraq have only reeds. While this scarcity does not determine form, it does make some solutions impossible and reduces the choice to an extent, depending on the severity of the limitations."[14] "It is perhaps symptomatic of professional blindness", says Jeffrey Cook, "that the often amazing comfort and environmental performances of vernacular architecture continue to be largely ignored by professional designers of the built environment".[15]

The vernacular has been defined as "a common sense approach built out of necessity." Ecologically there are many advantages in making a virtue out of necessity. "Traditionally we built according to our limits. Today, however, there are no apparent limits. Building form is defined by our technology, by global markets and by consumer taste. Traditionally, resources had to be used wisely, because their scarcity and the effort needed to manufacture them were automatically understood. We now use more and more of them, and bring them further and further away."[16] The vernacular tradition responded to local climate conditions, and also embodied a deep knowledge of, and respect for, its materials: it understood the difference between beech, oak and pine, the capacities and limitations of granite or limestone, of slate or marl, and it adapted design accordingly. The vernacular, however, represents not just response to climate and materials, but to social form and tradition. "The folk tradition", says Rapoport, "is the direct and unselfconscious translation into physical form of a culture, its needs and values – as well as the desires, dreams and passions of a people."[17] Vernacular architecture manifested no "libido dominandi", none of the desire to dominate which Augustine believed characterized the earthly city and which was so marked a feature of all modernist architecture.[18]

We must not romanticise the buildings of the past which, where they survive, are now often sold as "dream houses". In a country where most vernacular architecture has disappeared, like Britain, what survives are the houses of the better off artisans. Much vernacular building was undoubtedly wretched and often condemned in the early twentieth century as rural slums.[19] On the other hand, as we have seen, it also had great virtues. Unselfconsciousness, lack of pretension or desire to impress, direct response to a way of life, climate and technology, use of the "model and variations" method of building, the attitude towards nature and landscape, all play a part in the beauty, simplicity and effectiveness of vernacular architecture.[20] But is it not essentially rural, and does it have any place in a world which is now more than half urban? Could a new vernacular meet the needs of sustainability? In one sense it certainly could, for "Vernacular buildings waste nothing: they hate to destroy a structure, and will adapt the most unlikely buildings for new purposes."[21] By "vernacular" here I do not mean the neo-vernacular of contemporary architect designed houses, "volks vernacular", but the emergence of a genuine vernacular, which is to say, of the people of a distinct region. In Britain it seems extraordinary that between a third and a half of the world's population still build their own homes, and that self help accounts for 40% of domestic building in Belgium, West Germany, Austria, Italy, France, Norway, Finland, and Ireland. In Britain it is well under 10 per cent.[22] This is due in part to the professionalisation of knowledge which, as Ivan Illich argued, "makes people dependent on having their knowledge produced for them and leads to a paralysis of the moral and political imagination."[23] Not just of the moral and political, but of the practical imagination. Creativity is supposed to be for the gifted few and the rest of us are compelled to live in environments constructed by them. Building upon this lie, says Simon Nicholson, the dominant cultural elite tell us that the planning, design and building of any part of the environment is so difficult and so special that only those with degrees and certificates in planning, engineering, architecture, art, education, behavioural psychology and so on – can properly solve environmental problems. The result is that the vast majority of people are not allowed (and worse – feel that they are incompetent) to experiment with the components of building. The majority of the community has been deprived of a crucial part of their lives and lifestyle.[24]

At the opposite end of the scale to vernacular building is the monumental, buildings designed either to overawe the populace, or to impress the owner's peer group by their demonstration of wealth and good taste. As we see from the stories about Solomon, the great house represents an ancient tradition. From the European Renaissance on, this tradition has littered the countryside with its products, aspiring, as Henry Crawford puts it in Jane Austen's Mansfield Park, to turn "a house" into "a place". Today such "places" constitute the bulk of our "heritage." Raymond Williams offers a trenchant and necessary comment on this tradition:

> People still pass from village to village, guidebook in hand, to see the next and yet the next example, to look at the stones and the furniture. But stand at any point and look at the land. Look at those fields, those streams, those woods even today produce. Think it through as labour and see how long and systematic the exploitation and seizure must have been, to rear that many houses, on that scale. See, by contrast, what any ancient isolated farm, in uncounted generations of labour, has managed to become, by the efforts of any single real family ... And then turn and look at what these other "families", these systematic owners, have accumulated and arrogantly declared. It isn't only that you know, looking at the land and then at the house, how much robbery and fraud there must have been, for so long, to produce that degree of disparity, that barbarous disproportion of scale. The working farms and cottages are so small beside them ... What these "great" houses do is to break the scale, by an act of will corresponding to their real and systematic exploitation of others.
>
> To stand in that shadow, even today, is to know what

many generations of countrymen bitterly learned and were consciously taught: that these were the families, this the shape of society. And will you then think of community?[25]

Williams echoes the scathing critiques of Isaiah or Jeremiah and raises for us the question of historical memory. If "heritage" is largely the great house does this serve to glorify or perpetuate the social relationships which produced it Is it sufficient to wander around the great houses remembering, with Walter Benjamin, that every monument of culture is at the same time a monument of barbarism? These are questions which ought to be discussed by the community of faith, but on which there has never been consensus, as we could see by comparing, say, Eusebius of Caesarea, the panegyrist of Constantine and his building programme, and John Chrysostom, the scourge of the rich in fourth century Constantinople.

Modern mass housing

Both vernacular and monumental building have been with us since the dawn of history, but with the industrial revolution two new forms of domestic building arose to cope with the enormous rise in population, and especially with the rise of unprecedently large cities. These were mass housing and the new suburbs.

Mass housing was not the invention of the nineteenth century, but it was in this century that it spread across both Europe, the "new world" and on into the colonised world. The sudden rise in population (from an estimated 2 million to 11 million in Britain between 1700 and 1800, for example, and then to 33 million by 1901), and the growth of great cities at the same time, usually led to the "throwing up" of thousands of houses on the cheap. The same period witnessed the advent of mass production, which was antithetical to the local trades and traditions which had produced the vernacular. "Man is regressing to the cave dwelling" wrote Marx in 1845, "but in an alienated malignant form."

The savage in his cave (a natural element which is freely offered for his use and protection) does not feel himself a stranger; on the contrary he feels as much at home as a fish in water. But the cellar dwelling of the poor man is a hostile dwelling, "an alien, constricting power which only surrenders itself to him in exchange for blood and sweat." He cannot regard it as his home, as a place where he might at last say, "here I am at home." Instead, he finds himself in another person's house, the house of a stranger who lies in wait for him every day and evicts him if he does not pay the rent.[26]

Here what Marx has in mind is not so much the actual physical conditions of the house, but the fact that the poor had no control over it and could be evicted at will. More than a century later John Turner agreed with him, finding the "hideousness of characteristic modern housing" to be but a reflection of "the defilement of personal relations and the desecration of life, as well as the dirtying of the environment." In fact, however, this housing was often a great achievement, as Mumford pointed out. "People slept on a different floor than they ate; the smell of urine and faeces no longer pervaded the interior."[27] In continental Europe and North America the apartment block offered a mediating form between mass housing and suburbia providing, chiefly for the middle class, accommodation which was popular and often elegant, as well as being built according to human scale and avoiding urban sprawl.

In an effort to provide decent housing for all countries with socialist governments stepped in to build houses on a large scale. The principle behind this building programme was excellent: the provision of decent, affordable, and secure housing for all. To vest it in local government or the state also meant that it was not subject to the "discipline of the market", where poorer tenants could be priced out, but that standards and rents were democratically accountable. These principles remain important, but there was a crucial factor missing in the provision of mass housing, namely, the involvement of the people who had to live in the houses. It was conceived and executed "top down". In particular the tower blocks which appeared all over the world from the 1950s on were not created by people in the community, for themselves, but either by "experts" or by councils looking for cheap housing solutions. "Rarely were people asked whether they wanted to move into a box in the sky", comments Herbert Girardet.[28] "The inhabitants of a Mass Housing town cannot possess their town", wrote the Dutch architect Nicholas Habraken. "They remain lodged in an environment which is no part of themselves what happens to day is nothing but the production of perfected barracks."[29] Following the Habitat Conference of 1976 Social Regeneration budgets came to require community consultation for their awarding, but we are still light years away from what John Turner called "building by people".

In the nineteenth century a new mode of housing made its appearance, neither elite nor vernacular – suburban. Suburbs in themselves were not new, but the rise of a new middle class brought with it the demand for a new type of housing. The very first of these houses, in the 1820s, were a continuation of elite building, but the process of cultural seepage had already produced pattern books for the salaried classes by 1835. This housing was architect designed, and from the start the emphasis was on difference.

As cultural seepage continued so the element of difference became more and more attenuated. In Britain nearly three million suburban homes were designed by unqualified assistants or from pattern books between the wars.[30] In the United States the Levitts built 17000 homes for 82,000 people using prefabricated materials and standardized designs after World War II. Mumford described theses suburbs as "a multitude of uniform, unidentifiable houses, lined up inflexibly, at uniform distances, on uniform roads, in a treeless communal waste, inhabited by people of the same class, the same income, the same age group ... Thus the ultimate effect of the suburban escape in our time is, ironically, a low grade uniform environment from which escape is impossible."[31] Herbert Gans, who conducted his field work by living in Levittown, replied to this that it represented a thinly veiled attack on the culture of working and lower middle class people, implying that mass produced housing leads to mass produced lives. Only the rich can afford custom built housing, he pointed out, and these charges were not levelled against the upper class terraces of the eighteenth and nineteenth centuries.[32] Others point out that even Levittown has softened over the years, and because suburban dwellers continually make little changes to both house and garden there is a great deal of difference on the micro scale. Gans insisted that it was a good place to live, and its popularity has held.[33]

The need for a new vernacular

At the millennium world population stands at more than six billion, the last billion added in just twelve years. Current estimates are 9 billion by 2050, but this may well be an underestimate. We are familiar with the question of how they are to be fed and watered, but the question of how they are to be housed is also urgent, given the fact that the majority of the world's population live in poverty. Rapoport argues that four objectives need to be borne in mind for successful housing: it should have social and cultural validity; it should be sufficiently economical to ensure that the greatest number can afford it;[34] it should ensure the maintenance of the health of the occupants;[35] and finally, there should be a minimum of maintenance over the life of a building.[36]

The need for social and cultural validity raises the obvious question of what constitutes validity. Colin Ward points out that in the new city of Milton Keynes the houses that are most disliked are those designed by the most prestigious architects, whilst the most sought after are those which most resemble the traditional image of house-and-home, with a pitched roof and a chimney on top, and a front porch with roses round the door.[37] Part of the reason for this is, of course, lay disenchantment with contemporary art in general. It is also, however, to do with a pattern of alienation in the built environment which echoes the analysis of the early Marx. The architect, says Papanek, is commissioned by a speculator, himself acting for an investor. The person who lives in the house stands in no direct relationship to the chain of talent, speculation, greed, know how and craft which produces the house. "The end user's only contribution seems to lie in passively adapting to land rights, market forces, existing structures and decisions made for and about him or her."[38] For this reason Habraken calls for individual involvement "to break the bonds of Mass Housing". Mass Housing, he argues, was an emergency measure which became generalised, and which we need to abandon.[39] His solution is for "supports" concrete frameworks, with mains services connected, which people can then fashion to their own design.[40] For many years John Turner and Colin Ward have argued a similar position.[41] What Rapoport calls cultural validity Turner speaks of in terms of dweller control:

> When dwellers control the major decisions and are free to make their own contributions in the design, construction, or management of their housing, both this process and the environment produced stimulate individual and social wellbeing. When people have no control over nor responsibility for key decisions in the housing process, on the other hand, dwelling environments may instead becomes a barrier to personal fulfilment and a burden on the economy.[42]

It is dweller control which is the key. Saunders argues that ownership contributes to our sense of self and identity, and this would a fortiori be the case with self build.[43] Although Turner insists that self-build can produce good housing on any criteria over a period of years, he does not want a situation where people are compelled to build their own houses, nor does he reject all high technology. Rather, he argues that planning should be proscriptive, warding off bad practice, rather than prescriptive, and that central government's major role is in providing infrastructure.

These aims demand, as some Green thinkers have argued, a search for a new vernacular. The vernacular is the language of ordinary people. According to Rapoport it is the sharing of a world view and other image and value systems, which makes possible the process of vernacular building.[44] In many cases traditional buildings, which used wood or stone, are now too costly to build, but also the common shared value system and image of the world which they expressed has been lost.[45] Victor Papanek has shown that there is no need for contemporary vernacular building to take the form of a nostalgic throw back to the past. New materials can be used, new functions designed for, but the principles of the vernacular can still be honoured.[46] In the older industrialized world, however, it is the loss of shared value systems which is the key problem. This is the reason that, as Gillian Darley points out, the "neo vernacular" of postmodernism is as alienated in its way as the modernism it succeeds.[47] A new vernacular must be precisely that: genuinely of the people. It is this which Turner was asking for in his three principles of self government in local affairs and the freedom to build; the use of the least necessary power, weight and size of tools for the job; and the confinement of planning to an essentially legislative role, and separating it clearly from design.[48]

Put theologically these demands for new housing can be translated into a threefold, or trinitarian, form. In virtue of the theology of creation the theologian is concerned for an ecologically sustainable mode of building; in virtue of the concern for justice we need to affirm, with the post second world war US government, the right of everyone "to a decent house in a suitable living environment";[49] in virtue of belief in the Spirit at work in all that makes for life, we are concerned with houses which speak to the human soul.

To bring this together, I have been arguing, we need the principle of Numbers 11, that all the Lord's people should be prophets, a principle which brings empowerment and education together, which is not populist precisely in insisting on education. Christopher Day articulates this concern in insisting that aesthetics are not irrelevant to the conditions of social justice. Rows of rectangular buildings, he believes, oppress the freedom of the individual and, we can add, depress the spirit. In his own buildings he tries not to make one window the same as another:

> The verterbrae of the spine each carry a slightly different load and accept a slightly different movement. They are not identical. Each window likewise has an individual set of requirements to fulfil – unless we are just providing containers for people, albeit elaborate ones. It may be ridiculous to make every window different just for the sake of being different, but it is even more so to make every one the same just for the sake of being the same, or to shape them just to impose an elevational pattern.[50]

Building for six or nine billion will not make sense without this recovery of the sacred in the broadest sense. This involves the ability of our senses to tell us what is good or bad for us. Polyurethane coated wood, for example, feels hard, smooth and cold and does not breathe. It looks like wood but it is a lie and is bad food for the human spirit. "If you want to bring children up to be honest it is not going to help if their environment is full of lies."[51] Harmony in our surroundings, Day argues, is no mere luxury. Our surroundings are the framework which subtly confine, organize and colour our daily lives. Harmonious surroundings provide support for outer social and inner personal harmony. Harmony can be achieved by rules – but rules lack life. Or it can arise as an inevitable but life-filled consequence of listening conversation.[52]

That reference to conversation takes us back to the dialogue both Day and Harries ask for between high and low traditions. In the world of casino capitalism whilst buying an old property is often a status symbol, new palaces are still being created, embodying all the gadgetry of Information technology. In relation to that we face yet another conundrum. There is no doubt at all that the biblical emphasis is on the stakeholder economy, seeing "every family under its vine and fig tree." Furthermore, the demand for participatory building takes us back to Blake's citation of Numbers: "Would that all the Lord's people were prophets." Homes for nine billion can only possibly be provided when this is the priority. On the other hand some, though by no means all of those great houses which we wander around "guide book in hand" are undeniably beautiful and do express a vision of grace filled life which we cannot but honour. And this, of course, is a standard argument for a class society: the rich function as patrons of the arts and lead the way in architecture. To set against this we have the example of classical Athens, where the entire population lived in extremely modest dwellings, but produced the Parthenon for their communal worship. Perhaps the same might be said for medieval Norwich or even Paris. It is true that "surplus" is needed to provide the freedom for great architecture to which not all can aspire. Karsten Harries argues that the "pedigreed" tradition of architecture takes us out of the everyday and sends us back to it with fresh eyes. Perhaps so, but pedigreed buildings which focus the community's values are one thing and those which simply make status claims for the rich are quite another. What we certainly do not need is a situation where the vast majority – including the world's burgeoning middle class – are condemned to live in soul deadening and unimaginative buildings. Human beings are spiritual creatures. The DIY movement – one of the biggest money spinners in the European economy – is a testimony to the need people feel to shape their own environment. Unfortunately, as our northern rubbish tips show, this often involves the superimposition of mass produced "trim". In building as in every other area in life we get nowhere without education ñ a process by no means to be identified, of course, with what happens in school and university. All the Lord's people need to be prophets in the shaping of their dwellings from the ground up. We need a new vernacular. But this requires, in turn, education and spiritual discipline if Jane Jacobs' "great blight of dullness" is to be replaced. And this is an agenda we have scarcely begun to face.

Notes

[1] This chapter is a drastically shortened version of a chapter in *A Theology of the Built Environment*.
[2] Sennett (1990), 6.
[3] For example, Amos 3.15,5.11; Isaiah 3.14-5,5.7ff; Jer 22.13ff; Eccle 2. 4-7.
[4] *The Apocryphal New Testament,* tr M. R. James, Oxford 1923, 364ff. The story is a neat inversion of the usual burden of "pie in the sky when you die".
[5] Myers (1988), 151.
[6] Myers (1994).
[7] Day, 10, 42.
[8] Spain, 127-135.
[9] Day, 28.
[10] Pieris (1988), 69-85.
[11] Jackson, 91ff.
[12] Jackson, 149.
[13] "May I take you to the shores of a mountain lake? The sky is blue, the water is green and everything is at peace. The mountains and clouds are reflected in the lake, as are the houses, farms and chapels. They do not seem man made, but more like the product of God's workshop, like the mountains and trees, the clouds and the blue sky. And everything breathes beauty and tranquillity." *Architecture, 1910* in *The Architecture of Adolf Loos: An Arts Council Exhibition,* Arts Council, London 1985.
[14] Rapoport, 105.
[15] Cook, 143.
[16] Smith, Whiteleg, Williams, 63.
[17] Rapoport, 2. Cf. Vance: "Self conscious architecture withers without public adulation, so only the vernacular form can live in the crowded area of organic growth." Vance, 50.
[18] Rudofsky, cited by Harries, 271.
[19] Mingay.
[20] Rapoport, 77.

21. Ward, (1996), 13.
22. It is still, however, 12000 homes a year. Fairlie, 94. This difference between Britain and Continental Europe is one of many which follow from the fact that Britain was the first country to industrialise, and eradicated its peasantry more effectively, and earlier, than any other. Saunders, 13.
23. Cited in Ward (1996), 20.
24. Cited in Ward (1996), 23.
25. Williams, 105/6.
26. Marx, 118.
27. Sennett, (1994), 334. So also Saunders, 149, pointing out the huge fall in numbers of people sharing a room between 1951 and 1976, and citing the view that "The poor live in what would have been thought of in the pre-capitalist period as ill-maintained castles."
28. Girardet, 80.
29. Habraken, 13.
30. Hall, 76.
31. Mumford, 553.
32. Gans (1967).
33. Gans (1968), 140.
34. In primitive and vernacular contexts, Rapoport notes, most, if not all, people have houses, as opposed to the situation under any form of capitalism.
35. In relation to climate, he says, traditional housing succeeds, in relation to sanitation and parasites it usually fails.
36. Rapoport, 129.
37. Ward (1985), 88.
38. Papanek, 127.
39. Habraken, 24.
40. Habraken described supports as "constructions which are not in themselves dwellings – but which contain individual dwellings as a bookcase contains books – a construction which allows the provision of dwellings which can be built, altered and taken down, independently of others." Habraken, 59/60.
41. Turner; Ward (1976).
42. Turner and Fichter, 241.
43. Saunders, 80.
44. Rapoport, 48.
45. Rapoport, 6.
46. Papanek, 137. He remarks that the Hopi Indians are building motels with souvenir shops "without sacrificing their own vernacular approach to space and place."

47 Darley. She writes: "Superficial neo-traditionalism has gone a long way towards destroying and devaluing precisely the traditional qualities that professionals and the lay public alike believe that they are safeguarding." Harries likewise talks of re-building in post war Germany which borrowed certain aspects of the vernacular "without preserving the former's life". Harries, 272.

48 Turner, 155.

49 Harvey, 394.

50 Day, 90.

51 Day, 51.

52 Day, 70.

References

Cook, J. (1994) "Environmentally benign architecture" in Samuels, R. and Prasad, D. (eds.), *Global Warming and the Built Environment,* London: Spon

Darley, G. (1993) "Local Distinctiveness: An Architectural Conundrum" in Clifford, S., King, A. (eds.) *Local Distinctiveness: Place, Particularity and Identity, Common Ground,* London: Common Ground

Day, C. (1990) *Places of the Soul,* London: Harper Collins

Fairlie, S. (1996) *Low Impact Development,* Charlbury: Jon Carpenter

Gans, H. (1967) *The Levittowners,* London: Allen Lane

---, (1968) *People and Plans,* New York: Basic Books

Gorringe, Tim (2002) *A Theology of the Built Environment,* Cambridge: Cambridge University Press

Girardet, H. (1996) *The Gaia Atlas of Cities,* revised edition London: Gaia

Habraken, N. (1972) *Supports: An Alternative to Mass Housing,* London: The Architectural Press

Hall, P. (1988) *Cities of Tomorrow,* Oxford: Blackwell

Harries, K. (1998) *The Ethical Function of Architecture,* Cambridge Massachusetts: MIT

Harvey, D. (1996) *Justice, Nature and the Geography of Difference,* Oxford: Blackwell

Jackson, J. B. (1984) *Discovering the Vernacular Landscape*, New Haven and London: Yale University Press

Marx, K. (1974) *Economic and Philosophical Manuscripts,* Moscow: Progress

Mingay, G. "The rural slum" in S. M. Gaskell (ed.), *Slums,* Leicester: Leicester University Press, pp. 92-143

Mumford, L. (1991) *The City in History,* Harmondsworth: Penguin (orig 1961)

Myers, C. (1988) *Binding the Strong Man,* Maryknoll: Orbis
---,   (1994) *Who Will Roll Away the Stone?* Maryknoll: Orbis
Rapoport, A. (1969) *House, Form and Culture,* New Jersey: Prentice Hall
Papanek, V. (1995) *The Green Imperative,* London: Thames & Hudson
Pieris, A. (1988) *An Asian Theology of Liberation,* Edinburgh: T & T Clark
Saunders, P. (1990) *A Nation of Home Owners,* London: Unwin Hyman
Sennett, R. (1990) *The Conscience of the Eye,* New York: Norton
---,   (1994) *Flesh and Stone,* London: Faber
Smith, M., Whiteleg, J. and Williams, N. (1998) *Greening the Built Environment,* London: Earthscan
Spain, D. (1992) *Gendered Spaces,* Chapel Hill: University of North Carolina Press
Turner, J. F. C. (1972) "Housing by People" in Turner, J. F. C. and Fichter, R. *Freedom to Build: Dweller Control of the Housing Process,* London: Macmillan
Vance Jnr., J. E. (1990) *The Continuing City,* Baltimore: John Hopkins
Ward, C. (1976) *Housing: An Anarchist Approach,* London: Freeman
---,   (1985) *When We Build Again,* London: Pluto
---,   (1996) *Talking to Architects,* London: Freedom
Williams, R. (1985) *The Country and the City,* London: Hogarth

Ongoing Research

ETHICS, AESTHETICS AND URBAN WELFARE

TOM NIELSEN

The research project "Ethics, Aesthetics and Urban Welfare" is a part of an inter-institutional research project – "The Welfare City" – running from 1997 to 2002. The two year project "Ethics, Aesthetics and Urban Welfare" was completed at the end of 2002.

This text presents the general problems and discussions I worked on, and particularly the main points I developed during the final years of work.

Further information about the research project, the author, as well as links to publications, can be obtained at the Welfare City-homepage at: http://www.a-aarhus.dk/welfarecity .

Consumer society and the aesthetics of self-creation

During the last part of the 20th century, what has been called welfare societies have developed – in Denmark as well as in other countries. This label describes a society that is the consequence of early welfare state politics, and the economic safety and spare-time that it has resulted in for a great majority of people. Whereas people in pre-2nd World War industrial societies identified with their occupational and "class status", people living in the welfare society (which also in a broader context has been called the consumer society), tend to identify with what they do in the time spent outside the workplace, and with the products they buy. According to Bocock "People now work, not just to stay alive, but in order to be able to afford to buy consumer products." (Bocock 1995: 49)

As we know from the investigations of, for instance, Thorstein Veblen and Pierre Bourdieu, consumer products and their consumption are identity-constructing. Products and consumption practices hold a symbolic capital, and the individual itself can be concerned about the "construction of its life as a work of art" – free from the burdens of having to work for survival. Thereby "the good life" becomes "the beautiful life", and as Gernot Böhme pointed to in his contribution: "A major amount of what is written about ethics in Europe and North America presents itself as 'ethics of the good life'."

That can be seen, for instance, in the increased interest in the body; in how it looks and presents itself in the collective space.

One of the consequences of the individualism, or even narcissism of the consumer can therefore also be understood as a recognition of, and interest in, other people and the collective space.

This, then, becomes very relevant for the development of contemporary architecture and collective spaces in urban areas. The growing interest in, and market for, leisure activities and sites, which seems to infiltrate everywhere and everyplace, obviously has consequences for the way cities develop. They, too, have to construct identity, to serve the people living in and using them. They have to have physical space for the consumption of time and money, the activities that are the logical and unsurprising consequence of the economic security and spare time ensured by welfare state politics within the capitalist economy.

At the same time there is no, or only very little, tradition and "given ways" in the practices of architecture and urbanism that makes them ready for this shift. The discussions of the proper response to these societal developments have covered a wide field: From rejection and resistance through design and regulation to their happy embrace, as a basis for the development of new forms of collective spaces for a leisure-based, "aesthetisized" urban life.

During this current period of professional wavering, questions concerning ethics, as well as questions of the relationship between ethics and aesthetics, are often brought up.

The aesthetization of cities and the collapse of distinctions between public and private

At the present moment it already seems a long time since the historic city centre were transformed into monofunctional leisure- and entertainment zones with shopping facilities, cafés, cinemas etc. Any "proper" city has been "revitalised". Historic districts have been reconstructed into a seemingly authentic, early modern commercial centre, with pedestrians, speciality shops and street musicians.

The collective urban space is territorialized, by producers of products and events that are used by consumers to construct their identity, and by the consumers as a stage for the "presentation of the self" (Goffman). One reason for the success and significance ascribed to these new urban spaces, therefore, is that they are based on pedestrians, which makes them perfect scenes for the construction of personal identity through the bodily presence in the collective space.

The citizen of the industrial society (and Jürgen Habermas) is replaced with the consumer of the welfare society, and accordingly the role of the "shopping-centre" shifts from a place where the worker buys necessities at a reasonable price as quickly and conveniently as possible in order to go home and relax, to a symbolic place of exchange on several levels.

This process has been understood as an aesthetization process, where the primary concern of urban planners and developers is about image and atmosphere, rather than content. Historic buildings are mixed with new cultural centres and granite-paved squares with new street furniture into an urban scenography. A stage for both the tourist and the modern urban dweller to see, and be seen. Subsequently urban design and architecture have been ascribed a new important symbolic function. New monumental architecture points to the idea that a certain city is worth visiting, clean and on its way "up." (The Bilbao-model)

This "nursing" of the local atmosphere in the city centre, which can be recognized both "live" and on postcards as a lively authentic place, in Denmark is the basis of a national prohibition against the construction of new shopping-centres, enforced since 1996. This prohibitive law exemplifies some of the difficulties and resulting paradoxes that are consequential of the current unclear situation, and of the lack of knowledge of the "aesthetization" phenomena.

In many aspects this law is a result of classic welfare policy. The weak individual (and shop owner) is to be protected against the large commercial actors and their economic interests. The attempt to stop the expansion of the large retail shops and shopping centres is thought of as a protection of weak citizens living in the city (weak in this context means those that can't buy a car), and of the environment. Paradoxically it is the same welfare politics that has created the need for new leisure zones. Furthermore, stopping the development of shopping centres just accelerates the process that transforms historic districts into the, up to now, most successful version of the shopping-centre, and distances them further from the desired authentic mixed-use urban situation. The process transforms urban centres into tourist attractions, to compete with other cities, theme parks and shopping centres. This is one of the reasons that most of the "weak" people without a car, as opposed to those living before the welfare state and politics, live outside historic centres, where prices are considerably lower.

In such a city, where the centres are slowly rebuilt to become sites of advanced symbolic and monetary exchange, the private actors and the companies behind the lifestyle-producing products and brands naturally become important actors.

That means that the socialization and other activities that have been known as "public" now clearly take place within environments staged for consumption. A phenomenon that has been called "the erosion of the public".

Services that earlier were administered by public institutions are now being organized privately. Law, and certainly order, is being kept by private guards, just like hospitals, kindergartens, and all kinds of welfare functions are being offered by private companies and institutions.

Simultaneously, the idea of welfare has taken an "ethical" turn. It is no longer just a matter of economic safety and survival, but also of more "soft" human values as, for instance, the feeling of belonging somewhere. The community idea has become part of the contemporary welfare programme. To a great extent these "values" are being delivered by non-state, civic society groups. All this means that the opposition and distinction between public and private, no longer seem to be a very operational tool (neither strategically nor analytically) in a world of the evermore hybrid partnering produced by the welfare society of late capitalism.

The prohibition of new shopping centres is an illustration. It is a law based on a rather rigid distinction between public and private space and interests, and on an antiquated idea of the city. Therefore, it misses its goal. (During the prohibition, the historic centres have been transformed into shopping centres as described, and developers have succeeded in getting a couple of centres built.)

The fact that large commercial companies nowadays are organised as global network actors makes it very hard to confront them in a simple and powerful way as this law tries to. The way that so called public and private interests are mixed makes the organising of retail on a national scale a matter that is complex beyond control.

Although public and private interests have always been mixed, what is new seems to be that the global network economies make it impossible for the nation state to maintain control of the way they are mixed, which again leads to the loss of the state's planning monopoly.

Therefore the distinction between interests and the organisational idea of the state (as an actor stepping between the market and the individual that has been defining for welfare-state politics), and the law against shopping centres, is impossible to maintain without paradoxical consequences.

The problem of planning

Through the exaggeration of local order and difference, cities have transformed into formless urban regions outside the control of existing national and regional planning authorities. Rem Koolhaas, one of the keenest observers of this condition described it like this: "The professionals of the city are like chess players who lose to computers. A perverse automatic pilot constantly outwits all attempts at capturing the city, exhausts all ambitions of its definition, ridicules the most passionate assertions of its present failure and future impossibility, steers it implacably on its flight forward." (Koolhaas & Mau 1995: 962-3)

Even when planning authorities with extensive legislated authority, as is the case in Denmark, seek to maintain maximal control, the result is not very much different from urban areas with hardly any regulation. (As examples of this, see the comparisons between Shenzen, China and Berlin (Koolhaas/Obrist 1998), between Houston and Randstad (Driessen 1998) or between Las Vegas and Aarhus (Nielsen 2001).)

This is due to the speed of the transformation, the relatively limited investments (nobody is able or willing to tear the entire city down to start again), the desire for total control, formally as well as organisational (and sometimes socially), which results in the development of cities as a network of finished and closed enclaves that together makes up a heterogeneous urban field (Nielsen 2001).

The need for every city to attract investments, taxes and jobs has resulted in a practice where local development plans, are now made after a potential developer has shown interest in building something.

If the market demands lots of a certain size, situated in a certain setting, then normally only preservation laws or the National Planning Act will stand in the way. And even that can be "bent" and negotiated by putting the right pressure on the right places in the network of different partners, coalitions and authorities. In reality the number, the size and the organisation of the different actors and their goals render centrally controlled planning impossible.

Private companies have economies the size of cities, some even the size of countries like Denmark. People do not only live in, and depend on, the city and nation-state they live in, but also the companies whose products they spent a great part of their resources to get, and with which they identify. People also, live in the "nations without territory" of IKEA, Ford, and Greenpeace etc.

The construction of identity that contemporary individuals seems to depend on cannot unfold in a "pure" public space. Common national or local values cannot work as total identification models for the contemporary individual, who also depends on the different and "partial" identities that different brands, different quarters and different cities can offer.

Just as the consumer that inhabits the welfare society depends on specifically programmed localities to consume excessive time, and on designed events and products to consume excessive money, he/she is dependent of the differences that only the market is able to generate.

The planning of a more or less homogeneous order, which is the object of traditional urban spatial planning (expressed more or less rigid), seems to be equally impossible and unattractive.

This problem on the level of urban design and spatial planning is currently met by many different strategies and possible "answers" that roughly and by way of introduction can be described under two "labels": The idea of "the good city", and that which could be called the pragmatic approach. Resistance or opportunism.

Resistance: The good city

The strategies that can be roughly characterised as "Models for the good city", depart from a critique of the formlessness and uncontrolled growth that since the 2nd World War, increasingly and worldwide, have characterised the cities and their development.

Recent urban development models like New Rationalism, New Urbanism or the revised modernist ideals in schemes like "Towards an Urban

Renaissance" of the British Urban Task Force follow the critique of modernist planning put forward in the beginning of the 1960s, with Jane Jacobs, Kevin Lynch and Gordon Cullen as the most important contributors.

This critique became a declaration of love to urban forms dominant up until the 2d World War. The critics pointed towards traditional urban features, and especially the quality of the "space between the buildings."

Whereas Jacobs and the New Rationalists see the early-modern metropolis as the lost ideal, the New Urbanists have primarily focused on the small town and the village, which made a more or less self-sufficient and socially fine-meshed community.

The ideal "good city" is good because it is both an organic, continuous and centred community and defined as an entity closed towards the outside, no longer defined by nature but by the rest of the city, which is not the good city, but the formless, scary and unharmonic urban jungle. (Diken & Laustsen 2002)

Jacobs wrote in The Death and Life of the Great American City:

> Human beings are, of course, a part of nature, as much so as grizzly bears or bees or whales or sorghum cane. The cities of human beings are as natural, being a product of one form of nature, as are the colonies of prairie dogs or the beds of oysters.
>
> (Jacobs 1961: 443)

For Jacobs, a natural balance between city and nature is the ideal, just as it was for Plato and his ideas of the good city in The Republic.

For Plato the good is beautiful, and the beautiful to him is the balanced and harmonic. In relation to this, ethics in pre-modern philosophy was concerned about what could be called "the art of life", or how to act to become good.

For Plato the beautiful or the aesthetic (as ideas of the beautiful in modern thinking has been described as aesthetic), can help and give access to the good. The good that is reason the eternal and true logos, which is the foundation that the Gods build the world on.

Such lofty ideas is not the basis of the urban development models discussed here, but the assumption that specific form can give access to and accommodate "the good life" is significant.

As is the idea that everything from social dissolution, potential ecological disasters and rising crime rates can be partially solved by the application of these formal ideas of beauty and harmony.

Through the proper blend of programmes and the specific formal detailing of the containers of these programmes as, for instance, the profile on the specific street or the facades of the buildings lining it, "good city" strategies try to design good cities. In this way the ethical arguments are based on aesthetic ideas, on ideas of the beautiful. This again makes the "good city" a highly sell-able product of, for instance, clear and clean neighbourhood-identity, to the consumers of cities.

Opportunism: The pragmatic turn

During the 1990s parts of the discussions about urban development turned away form the "reform-oriented" strategies and the belief in a strong planning-authority that had dominated both the modern tradition of urban planning and the "godd city" built on a critique of this.

Within this new trend or tradition, models for urban development have shifted their focus, from the specific formal approach and the idea that planning (or architecture) can solve in any way basic societal problems.

This shift has been motivated by what is seen as the increasing impotence of planning authorities and the uselessness of their tools in the attempted response to the challenges posed by continued growth of the urban regions, the increasing demand for mobility and other factors related to what is called globalisation.

The ideas originate in the recognition of the limitations of planning. After many years of planning, and after an immense amount of resources has been spent on the project of planning the cities, it is increasingly acknowledged that complete control and "good design" do not create "good" cities. Instead the city is seen as an infinite and complex network of processes neither good nor controllable, a network inside which the planner can act, but only as one of many actors. This has resulted in the interest of dealing with subjects and phenomena outside what has earlier been considered the field of the planner, and to cooperate more directly with different actors, private as well as public, representing a large spectrum of interests and skills.

As a result, a series of projects with programmes and problems not confined to the question of form or aesthetics has been presented. Dutch planners and architects, like Rem Koolhaas, MVRDV and CHORA have been the most prominent examples, but the ideas can be found at numerous different, mainly small, planning offices everywhere, as well as in the proposals and discussions of larger firms and authorities. This has been described as an interest in the ethical implications and questions concerning architecture and planning.

Despite this, Rem Koolhaas the most influential architect and critic that can be put under the label of the "pragmatic turn", claims that he is uninterested in "the good." Actually, to some critics (for instance Juhanni Pallasma) he exemplifies a species of "euro-capitalism" opportunists that has made the market and the so-called market-made freedom its guiding star and symbol of truth.

The pragmatic, strategic approach seems to try to avoid departing from aesthetic or ethical preferences. The idea is to remain open-minded, or with no prejudice to the circumstances or limitations preconditioned outside the domain of the planner. Negotiation, investigation and accumulation of knowledge throughout the process are the way urban problems are being dealt with.

"The good" is replaced as a predefined ideal, by "the possible" or "the achievable", and the objective is instruments to be used by the people who are going to build the city and by the people going to use the city, rather than solutions. As opposed to "the good city" strategies, the good is not believed to be something that can be planned or constructed.

That does not mean that there is no design or any aesthetic preferences or values. It just means that opportunism as opposed to rejection creates different potentials and flexibilities.

The possibility of urban planning in the welfare society

To conclude, two central "planning-trends" can be seen at present. What here is generally labelled "the good city"-strategies that with very different architectonical results seeks to design "good" cities. These are coherent, harmonic, legible, in balance (also with nature), and based on formal typologies in "a human scale", that have been quality-tested in other settings and times.

In short they are strategies that try to resist and avoid the phenomena that result in sprawling, formless cities.

Secondly there is the "pragmatic" tendency seeking the possible in the given, by trying positively and concretely to create working and interesting cities within the premises set by the current relationship between state, market and individual. That is done through the "re-negotiation" of the planners traditional professional fields of competence.

The differences between the approaches seem to be justified from arguments valuing respectively homogeneity and naturalness, and heterogeneity and mediation.

The "Ethics, Aesthetics and Urban Welfare" research project seeks to investigate how these different strategies relate to the formlessness and uncertainty that the world and all ideas about the future in it seem to share. The question is not which approach is more "ethical" or which is more "aesthetic". Rather the ambition is to analyze and problematize relations between the ethical and aesthetical in the normative foundations and arguments of the different projects and strategies, in relation to the contemporary problems of planning. The results of the project is published during 2004, in publications focusing on the discussion of the possibilities of urban planning in the context of the contemporary welfare society. (See Nielsen 2004a, 2004b, 2004c.)

References

Bocock, R. (1995) (1993) *Consumption*, London: Routledge

Driessen, O. (1998) "Space Plus – Houston and Randstad Holland", in *archis*, nr. 4

Diken, B. & Lausten, C. (2002) "Zones of Indistinction – security, terror, and bare life" in *Space & Culture*

Jacobs, J. (1961) *The Death and Life of Great American Cities*, New York: Random House

Koolhaas, R./Mau, B. (1995) *S, M, L, XL*, Rotterdam: 010 Publishers

Koolhaas, R./Obrist, H. U. (1998) "Chinese City" in *Berlin/Berlin*, Cantz Verlag, pp. 18-19

Nielsen, T. (2001) *Formløs – den moderne bys overskudslandskaber,* Aarhus: Arkitektskolens Forlag

Nielsen, T. (2004a) "Ethics, Aesthetics and Contemporary Urbanism" in *Nordisk arkitekturforskning*, No. 2 (Welfare City Theory)

Nielsen, T. (2004b) "Byudvikling og velfærd" (Urban Development and Welfare), in *Velfærdsbegrebets betydninger – Om forholdet mellem velfærd, velfærdsstat og velfærdssamfund,* ed. Jensen, P. H., Copenhagen: Hans Reitzels Forlag, (forthcoming)

Nielsen, T. (2005) *Gode intentioner og uregerlige byer* (Good intentions, Unruly Cities), Aarhus: Arkitektskolens Forlag, (forthcoming)

SEA-ING SPIRIT
Ecotheology and a coastal sense of place

NANCY M. VICTORIN-VANGERUD

Islands and oceans
Oceans and islands always
Did they fall into the child's eye?

                        Arnold Eidslott[1]

His days are lived according to the tide. From the spit he casts for queenfish and trevally and now and then he takes a spanish mackerel ... He labours all one morning to make the mesa's summit and traverse its windblown gutters to look out oceanward and see the archipelago backed up like a jack-knifed train in the gulf below ... Fox begins to grow expansive.

                        Tim Winton[2]

Introduction: Learning to see

We live in a "world of waters", as Rachel Carson knew so well.[3] The vast ocean, covering over 71% of our earth's surface, ebbs and flows to cosmic currents within and beyond. It is home to myriads of creatures living in shallow warm tidepools all the way down to cold abysmal depths. Humans though, have lived along the edge of the land, venturing out across the ocean only by learning the language of wind, stars, islands and waves. Seascape captured the imagination of our foremothers and forefathers as evidenced by the stone labrynths of the fjord near Alta, Norway or the grooved rock carvings of the South Bondi headland in Sydney, Australia. This liminal place where sea and land meet has given rise to deep dreaming throughout time and the breadth of human cultures.

Today, we continue to dream in coastal places. Contemplating the colours of the shimmering sea and far-reaching sky, we may have wondered as children, "Is the sea the sky, or the sky the sea?"[4] Such was the seascape of my childhood and it reached deeply into my eyes. Yet, inhabited by breeze or storm, sand or rocky reef, seascapes are many and express diverse, profound connections between people and place. What is it about the expansive coast that gives rise to such enchantment and engagement with the elemental? What is it about this "sacred edge" that draws us to discover the psalmist's spiritual longing, "Deep calls to deep..." (42:7)?[5] At this edge might we find ourselves encountered by the very Spirit of God?

I bring to this collection the reflections of a Christian theologian who grew up near the coast of New Jersey in the United States, but for the last six years has been living in Perth, along the southwest coast of Western Australia. This littoral love brought me to Norway as I am interested in how people practice and understand a coastal sense of place. For this research, I am drawing on George Seddon's understanding that sense of place has to do with "learning to see" our relationship with our environment through the particular geology, landforms, soil, water, species, and cultural narratives of our dwelling places, which he claims may be interpreted today as the "genius loci" of a place.[6] I am learning to see what Brian Elliott calls the "subtler enquiries" about landscape:

> What spiritual and emotional qualities do such a people develop in such an environment? In what way do the forces of nature impinge upon the imagination? How do aesthetic evaluations grow?[7]

But where Seddon and Elliot focus primarily on the relation of seeing and landscape, I am concerned about seeing seascape, about seeing the sea! I am curious about the subtler enquiries of a coastal sense of place, and how seeing the sea resonates with the theologies and spiritualities of coastal people. Is it possible that people see/sea God's Spirit in ways significant to the artistry of thinking theologically?

In recent years, theology has made a contextual turn to address the challenges of our environment, gaining inspiration from Hildegard of Bingen's vision of God's Spirit bringing forth the "greening of life".[8] Ecotheology, thus explores the significance of God's healing, liberating, and whole-making relation to the whole of creation. But what if we extend Hildegard's inspiration to include the ocean in our spiritual vision and imagination; what if we immerse ourselves in the "blue-ing" of life and affirm the ecological connectedness of land and sea, fresh water and salt water, and terrestrial and aquatic life, particularly from our own specific senses of coastal place? What if we learn to see our seascapes as places where God's Spirit continues to sweep "across the face of the waters" (Genesis 1:1)? What might a coastal sense of place illumine for ecotheology's contributions to the flowing currents of aesth/ethics, architecture and spirituality?

I claim that attentiveness to a coastal sense of place opens up ecotheology's horizons of hope by challenging the arrogant and triumphalistic narrative of human being in relation to the elemental, which is often presented in Christian myth as the evil and chaotic sea. As "feminists have to find new configurations of old myths continually", I invite us to consider that a coastal sense of place enables us to renew a myth of human humility and finitude, but in ways that are edged with openness and possibility, rather than closed and triumphal endings.[9] Imagining the coast as a sacred edge of the Spirit enables us to map a new "geography of faith", one that does not place the elemental outside or beyond God.[10] As Jay McDaniel suggests, "We need new maps of God, ways of thinking about God ... They help orient us, however fallible and finite, to the Mystery".[11] When we learn to see/sea our place, we are drawn not up and out to another world, but deeper and deeper into an encounter with God's Spirit, the "giver of life" and creator of "the life of the world to come".[12]

The wisdom of place

Stories of people and place are beginning to make a difference to the ways we contextualize our talk of God and God's relation to the world. Theologians are learning to see that our habits of our hearts and our habitats are deeply related.[13] As feminist theologian Catherine Keller claims, "Place is inseparable from self, at least from a self which knows itself as bodily and communal."[14] The model of contextual theology that I am employing for this coastal exploration has been termed the "anthropological model" by Stephen Bevans, who claims that theology begins "where the faith actually lives, in the midst of people's lives. It is in the world as it is, a world bounded by history and culture and a particular language, that God speaks."[15] According to this model, human culture is not the object or destination for a pre-determined message. Here, the "goodness of all creation and … the lovability of the world" are taken with utmost seriousness, resulting in our "encounter with God's loving and healing power in the midst of the ordinariness of life."[16] Valuing the diversity of human cultures can be extended to also valuing the diversity of places in which people live and have their being. In fact, we need to explore how culture and place are interconnected. As Peter Hodgson observes, the challenge before us is to think theologically "in relation to our own time and place, not just to repeat what has gone before."[17] It is time now to take culture and its relation to place seriously in our theological construction.

The problem, though, according to philosopher Edward Casey, is that place has lain "so deeply dormant in modern Western thinking".[18] In the past, Enlightenment rationalism celebrated an anthropocentric and dualistic worldview that drew an impermeable, self-contained boundary between the human and "his" surrounding environment, separating subject and object, spirit and nature, civilized people and primitives, mind and matter, and male and female. Armed with this map, the empires of Western science and colonialism came to view "the environment as an outside force or field to be attacked, conquered and domesticated", according to cultural ecologists Elisabeth Croll and David Parkin.[19] In contrast to modernity's "development gaze", they claim we can learn to see our places according to holistic, complementary perspectives, based on the wisdom of indigenous cosmologies, "which treat tree, plant, animal and human interaction as a single spiritual, moral and regenerative system."[20] By renewing a sense of place to heal our dualistic sight, Tim Ingold proposes a "synergistic" and "mutual envelopment" between persons and environment, so that "enfolded within persons are the histories of their environmental relations, (and) enfolded within the environment are the histories of the activities of persons."[21] Thus, attending to a sense of place means that individuals and communities recognize their inheritance of a past – historical and environmental – and responsibility for the future. Who we are as spiritual beings draws sustenance, meaning and purpose when we learn to see ourselves as "belonging" to a place, including

Contemporary Beach Home, Dunsborough, Western Australia, photo by the author

the ambiguous legacy of others' (and our own) hopes and losses, dreams and destruction.[22] As Casey has come to see:

> Place is as requisite as the air we breathe, the ground on which we stand, the bodies we have. We are surrounded by places, we walk over them and through them. We live in places, relate to others in them, die in them. Nothing we do is unplaced, how could it be otherwise? How could we fail to recognize this primal fact?[23]

When we learn that we are "in" place, and place is "in" us, we discover that our belonging opens us to wisdom that we may not have been able to discern before. Like anthropologist Keith Basso, who learned from his Western Apache mentor Dudley Patterson that "wisdom sits in places":

> It's like water that never dries up. You need to drink water to stay alive, don't you? Well, you also need to drink from places. You must remember everything about them. You must learn their names. You must remember what happened at them long ago. You must think about it and keep on thinking about it.[24]

Drinking from places we have learned to see leads to living with attentiveness and sensitivity to a particular place. Practical wisdom becomes the horizon of sensing one's place. Reflecting on his thirty-five years of drinking from places with the Western Apache people of Cibecue, New Mexico, Basso has learned the following about place-making:

> Places possess a marked capacity for triggering acts of self-reflection, inspiring thoughts about who one presently is, or memories of who one used to be, or musings on who one might become. And that is not all. Place-based thoughts about the self lead commonly to thoughts of other things – other places, other people, other times, whole networks of associations … The experience of sensing places, then, is thus both thoroughly reciprocal and incorrigibly dynamic … When places are actively sensed, the physical landscape becomes wedded to the landscape of the mind, to the roving imagination.[25]

In contrast to modernity's core value of autonomy, Patterson's and Basso's way of seeing focuses on relationships, or the "interbeing" of self and other through vast networks of ecological associations.[26] For example, we can learn from the plea of Leslie Boseto, who expresses a Melanesian sense of place: "Our land and sea are us and we are them. Do not separate us, if you do so, you are murdering us!"[27] As a contextual theologian, Boseto shares the perspective of the Inaugural Pacific Consultation of the Ecumenical Association of Third World Theologians:

> Developers from the outside come into the region, they look at the forests and think the forests are empty, they look at the beaches, reefs, lagoons and think they are empty. They are not empty. They maintain the history of the Island people. They keep our identity, they speak to us everyday of the past; and it is our library, our diary that speaks to us everyday of our own identity and who we are within our island nations.[28]

The interbeing of people and place, community and cosmos, challenges those with the developer's gaze to see anew and drink more deeply. Communities are implicated in environments and environments are implicated in communities as part of a dynamic process. Modernity's obeisance to autonomous reason can give way to a postmodern receptivity to the wisdom of places, an embodied knowledge for practical living. As Keller, Boseto and contextual theologians of Oceania claim, theology needs to recognize its

Cottesloe Beach Horizon, Western Australia, photo by the author

neglect and impoverishment of place. But curiously, Edward Farley recollects that Christian theology was originally understood as a "habit (habitus) of the human soul ... having the primary character of wisdom."[29] Perhaps in revaluing the deep interbeing of people and place, culture and environment, theology has a chance to save its soul. It can learn to see the vast network of relations constituting who we are in our times and places, inviting us drink more deeply of God's wisdom for the whole of creation.

Maritime myth and memory

We can gain insight regarding coastal wisdom from artists working at the interface of water, stone and air. Scattered along the long coast of Northern Norway, thirty three sculptures comprise the collection *Artscape Nordland*, providing opportunities for people to reflect on the "dialogue with landscape" and our "projected future world".[30] Set atop a rocky outcrop along the fjord near the community of Bø, stands a sculpture by Kjell Erik Killi Olsen, entitled "The Man from the Sea".[31] The dark, tall, cast-iron figure faces the water holding forth in his hands an obelisk-shaped crystal. Maaretta Jaukkuri provides the following commentary:

> It has been said that myths are like invisible threads that weave societies together. At the same time they are also stories that gently help us to understand the reality of the situation we are living in. Killi Olsen's sculpture…reflects both of these definitions of myth, while also creating a new myth. We find ourselves spinning a story of a man who has left the sea and trodden on firm ground, holding…an offering – the artist has suggested – to his former abode.[32]

Yet, the sculpture does more than mark human tribute to the sea. From the site of the sculpture, the local community can be seen in the background, including the museum that gathers together the memories of the people. Jaukkuri reflects that the sculpture evokes myth and memory, which constitute our lives as human beings in community and through which we come to understand our deep connections with our environment. Through Killi Olsen's sculpture, people honour the sea from which life has evolved, and with which communities continue to live in deep connection. The communal wisdom tells us that human beings cannot cut our ties to the sea.

Traveling to the southern hemisphere, half a world away, we find another sculpture exhibition at Bondi Beach, along the coast of Sydney. The annual *Sculpture by the Sea*, running in November, includes over one hundred sculptors who illumine the interplay between cultural and environmental sustainability, particularly in relation to the sun, sea, wind and rain.[33] Like *Artscape Nordland*, the Bondi exhibition includes artists from many nations. In 2001, Steinunn Thorarinsdottir of Iceland contributed an exhibit entitled "Thought", an aluminium figure of a person, seated, with arms wrapped around the knees in contemplation.[34] Thorarinsdottir invites people to their own contemplation beside the sea, like the sculpted figure along the coastal pathway. She suggests, "Let the mind flow with the waves."[35] Because she believes that "everything a person does, sees and experiences is informed by previous experiences and knowledge", Thorarinsdottir offers a "narrative of humanity" through her exhibit.[36] Again we hear the importance of memory and myth in her artistic vision, as people contemplate their origin and future.

Writing especially for the Bondi 2002 *Sculpture by the Sea*, Paul Taçon of the Australian Museum explains that because the coast is a place of dynamism and change, "inspiration and revelation about who we really are and where we might be going" may be encountered there.[37] Taçon notes that the coast is a place where water, stone and air intersect, forming sand, clay and earth, the soils that support terrestrial and marine life; thus, "ultimately life is nourished or born" and remembered in these places.[38] Throughout history, humans have marked special coastal places, reflecting a "bonding process" in which people come to terms with their natural environment.[39] As Taçon explains, "We change the land; the land changes us. Artists, the world over are good at this, but all of us engage in this activity …(to) reaffirm relationship with both land and sea."[40] Coastal places are marked with art and architecture, manifesting an aspect of sacredness: "Natural place thus has deep roots in our psychology … our paintings, engravings, sculptures and architecture are extensions of a place's natural significance."[41] Thus, as we have seen in the coastal sculptures of Killi Olsen and Thoranisdottir, human wisdom and aesthetics are intimately bound together in the connection of people and place. The coast offers a place where myth and memory flow together.

Place and Spirit

So what about theology? What if ecotheology took seriously the possibilities of learning to see/sea, then drink deeply from places of coastal wisdom, places of coastal myth and memory? Curiously, the opening verse of Jewish and Christian canonical memory (Genesis 1:1) invites us into a flowing and dynamic myth of cosmological origins:

> In the beginning when God created the sky and the land, the earth was a formless void and darkness covered the face of the deep, while the wind (*ruach*) of God swept over the face of the waters.[42]

In this text, the *ruach* of God – the wind or living spirit, the very breath of God – hovers like a mother bird with warm anticipation for the emergence of creation from the mysterious abyss.[43] The myth challenges the notion of

Cottesloe Beach and the Indiana Tea Room, Cottesloe, Western Australia, photo by the author

theistic separation with the flowing relatedness of God and the deep, the land and the sky, life and all the elements. Calling our attention to these cosmic and female symbols of the Creator Spirit, Elizabeth Johnson writes:

> The One who blows the wild wind of life…, who gives birth to the world, or who midwifes it into existence does not stand over against it or rule it hierarchically from afar but dwells in intimate, quickening relationship with humanity and the life of the earth.[44]

The mythical linking of water and spirit in Genesis 1:1, which Christianity continues to invoke through the ritual of baptism, narrates an open, hopeful relation between God's Spirit and creation. Throughout the seven days of creation, we hear the dreamtime blessing on the emergence of life: "And God saw that it was good." (Gen. 1: 4, 10, 12, 18, 21, 25, 31) In the beginning, the spiritual inter/face along the waves of the deep or *tehom*, symbolizes a hopeful "edge" of cosmic possibility and cosmic actuality for all beings in creation.[45] According to Catherine Keller, this is a far cry from the evil, monstrous and chaotic image of the deep functioning in the *Enuma Elish* and Ugaritic texts.[46] This is also a far cry from the doctrine of *creatio ex nihilo* in the classical tradition of Christian theism, where the *tehom* functions as a negative emptiness or absence. For Keller, the wind or breath of God hovers hopefully along the edge, "preparing to unfold the deep into the upper darkness of outer space and the lower darkness of the terrestrial sea – a relation of interdependence by which the no-thingness of the indeterminate yields potentiality for difference, and actualization."[47]

Keller's edgy image of spiritual life resonates with Johnson's proposal that the language of Spirit becomes meaningful through our experience of living along the horizon of life:

> Wherever we encounter the world and ourselves as held by, open to, gifted by, mourning the absence of, or yearning for something ineffably more than immediately appears, whether that "more" be mediated by beauty and joy or in contrast to powers that crush, there the experience of the Spirit transpires. Within this wide horizon of historical experience language about the Spirit of God finds it origin and home.[48]

In light of our explorations of people and place, I would like to localise Keller's and Johnson's cosmic metaphors of edge and horizon to reflect a coastal sense of spiritual place. Rather than map "life in the Spirit" as a vertical ascent for individual human souls from one earthly world to another heavenly world, what if we see/sea the relation of Spirit and life as a littoral journey in which we dive deeper and deeper into the heart of God's oceanic mystery?[49] What might seeing/sea-ing Spirit mean for a theology of the Spirit, or pneumatology?

Two theologians help us make a topophilic turn in ecotheology that open up the possibilities for the relation of Spirit and a coastal sense of place. Taking seriously his own sense of place in Northern Norway, Roald Kristiansen advocates an "ecology of Spirit" in which sacred places enable people to meet the challenges of transcendence, where "life is given and taken away without oneself being able to be the Master of life".[50] He describes the presuppositions of his method as the following:

> To speak about an "ecology of Spirit," one has to think in terms of how humans and nature are woven together in an intricate web of existence, thus creating an intimate bond between the natural, the cultural, and the mental landscape … The fusion of natural and cultural landscapes creates an inner world, a mental space, in which the natural and the cultural landscapes are interpreted and attributed a religious significance and meaning, thus creating a religious landscape.[51]

Kristiansen's Northern Norwegian sense of "holy nature" draws meaning from not only pre-Christian Sámi religion, but from a creation-centred Christian theology that affirms "the conviction that God is present in all realms of life".[52] Even at what may seem like to others the "edge of the world", an "Arctic ecotheology" affirms the presence of God's Spirit in nature as our home. But for Kristiansen, a religious landscape doesn't exclude the sea:

> Life in the North is very much marked by the close relationship to nature, especially to the sea; which sometimes gives food in abundance, while other times claims its right to take human life away from those who depend on its gifts.[53]

Because of the close relationship between people and the sea, life and death, culture and the elements, "stories about the sea are extremely important for maintaining a sense of personal identity and belonging".[54] Attending to the stories of abundance and loss enable people to live wisely in their home and contribute care-fully to the "ecology of the Spirit".

Theologian Sigurd Bergmann also sees connections between cultural belonging, landscape and Spirit, which inspires him to recognize a "deep identification" between the Christian gospel and the context of Northern Norway.[55] Where modernity has decontextualised the holiness and wholeness of landscape, fragmenting the land into discrete functional uses, the arts of the Sámi express a sense of place characterised by "great openness".[56] Bergmann wonders, "One could ask whether the experience of the (sub)artic landscape is related to the openness of the cultural and historical landscape."[57] Where the view of modernity would see living in the windy tundra and being exposed to the elemental expanse as alienating, Sámi painting and poetry express feelings of being at home in what Nils-Aslak Valkeapää imagines as the "warm soft arms" of the tundra.[58]

Sámi arts have inspired Bergmann to construct an "ecological, liberating pneumatology", in which human destructiveness of nature as the sacrificial other of modernity is challenged toward a "life-enhancing, transmodern future".[59] From the Christian tradition, Bergmann retrieves the Constantinopolitan affirmation (381 ACE) of the Spirit as "the Life-giver" and Creator of "the life of the world to come". He further draws on Gregory of Nazianzen's theological interpretation of the four elements (*ta stoicheia*) to affirm the soteriological relation between God and creation.[60] Against the hypostazing, metaphysical and pantheistic understandings of the elements, Gregory made a distinction between the Creator and creation, but he "proposed the theory that God's work could be recognized in the elemental nature of the world".⁶¹ Thus, for Gregory, the whole of nature participates in God's creative, liberating and transforming economy (*oikonomia* – linked with *oikos*, or household). In contrast to modernity's attitude of "mammonism" and Christian mission's colonization of historical and natural others, Bergmann re-imagines the economy of "Sister Spirit":

> I would rather advocate a trinitarian approach which – with historical roots in Cappadocian apophatic theology – considers the world a mirror, work and love of the whole Trinity, and the Spirit as a life-giving God and an "earth-keeping Spirit".⁶²

Both Kristiansen and Bergmann construct pan-en-theistic pneumatologies (God in the world, the world in God) that hold in intimate tension the connections of people, place, Spirit and transformation, including the world of waters. Drawing on Kristiansen, we can honour people's elemental and ecological senses of belonging and identity in relation to the sea and the coast. Drawing on Bergmann, we can learn from Gregory's elemental and ecological perspective on water, which includes a "fourfold harmony of springs, seas, rivers and the waters of the air", thus we can expand the earthkeeping Spirit to be a water-keeping Spirit as well.⁶³

Horizons of hope

This sense of the *seascape of the Spirit* challenges the "tehomophobic" theology of Revelation 21:1, one of the privileged texts of hope in the Christian tradition.⁶⁴ Here, John of Patmos envisions a "new heaven and new earth", but the "sea is no more". Keller argues that this vision of oceanic evacuation leaves us with "an ecologically degraded Christian eschatology".⁶⁵ Is there no hope for the sea and all the beings of its watery depths? Geiko Müller-Fahrenholz observes that rather than continue hope for their world as the *oikos* or dwelling place of God, the early churches adopted instead another oikos-related word, *paroikia*, meaning "living away from home" to reflect their apocalyptic longing.⁶⁶ As this tradition gained in hermeneutical privilege and power, it fostered "parochial" theologies and spiritualities of living as "aliens and exiles in a hostile world".⁶⁷ For these theologies, the sea continued to function as the churning, evil and chaotic element, in need of closure and evacuation, providing the basis for emerging theologies of human mastery. But echoing images from the biblical book of Job, Keller claims:

> When we set ourselves apart from and above nature, hoping to transcend finitude, we only set ourselves at odds with a creator not made in our image: one who in the image of a whirlwind and a whale parodies human political economy based on the conquest and exploitation of the nonhuman.[68]

As we have seen, Kristiansen and Bergmann invite us to re-imagine the relation of God's Spirit and the earth in ways that honour our human connection with the elemental. In fact, it may be those watery elements most marginalized as the abysmal others of human mastery that challenge us today to new practices of *oikodomé* or "ecodomy" – building the house of the earth in sustainable ways of earthkeeping, rather than earth-domination.[69] Can we re-imagine a more humble and vulnerable place for ourselves in creation, rather than re-entrench our attitudes of invulnerability and transcendence? Can we re-new our relation to the elemental as part of our dwelling, identity and belonging, and thus re-image our "life in the Spirit" as open to and inclusive of the vast land, sea, fire and air? Bergmann's and Kristiansen's contextual pneumatologies bring forth possibilities for dwelling in relation to the vast sea and flowing waters of life by valuing these waters as part of God's divine economy. Thus, for God's *oikos,* we need more than the "greening power of the Spirit" to inspire new architectural and aesth/ethic visions – in relation to the world of waters, we need a blue-green renovation as well![70]

Bach to coastal aesth/ethics

It's funny what you learn by reading airline magazines. Recently, while flying over the Pacific Ocean, I came across an article about the traditional New Zealand holiday home, the bach. As the writer explains, "It's a local custom. Where other cultures have tea ceremonies, war dances and peace pipes, New Zealanders have their beach houses."[71] This resonates with my experience of Australian culture, because in Australia, the beach shack also has its special place. In fact as Australian architect Philip Drew claims, the shack is a "branch of religious architecture", a form of "white dreaming" that "paints a picture of the Australian soul."[72] But according to the article, over the last few years the traditional clapboard bach with its fading, second-hand furniture has been given an architectural make-over into designer homes with fabulous views worth thousands, even millions, of dollars. Yet, the new bachs (like the new shacks) still reflect the old values – simplicity, ease, casualness, and open air living. As architect Lance Herbst explains,

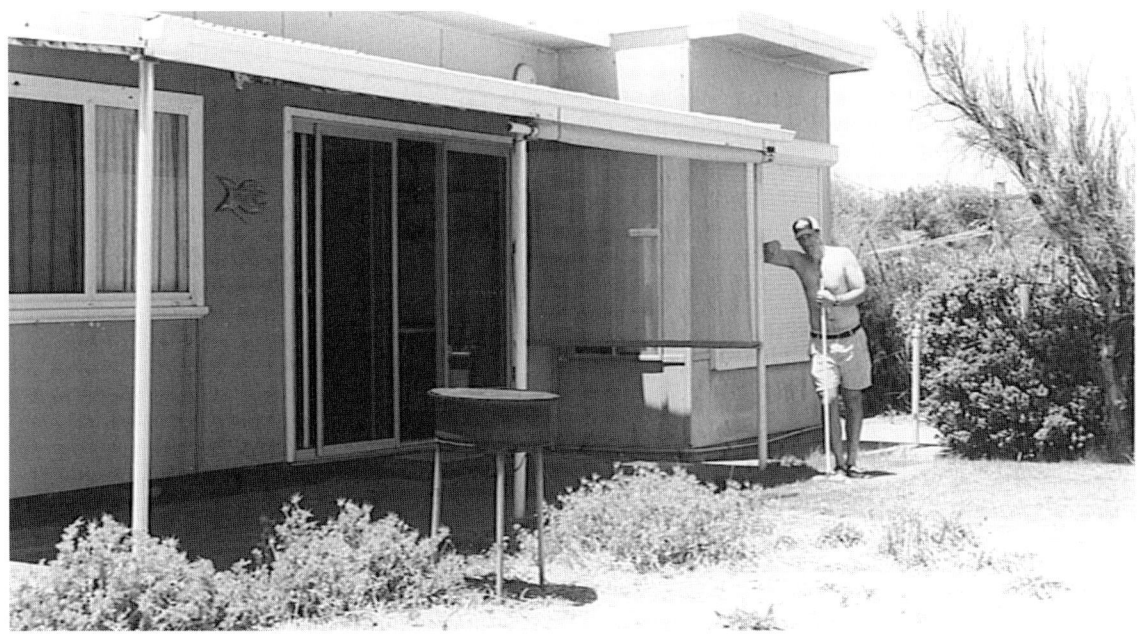

*Old Fibro Beach Shack,
Peppermint Grove Beach,
Western Australia,
photo by the author*

"When you get there, you can hear the ocean and you realise it's a beautiful starry night. It's all about retaining the magic of the bach experience."[73]

While the new bach and the new shack may be simple, yet sophisticated (and beyond the financial means of most people), they continue to point to what is of value to many coastal dwellers, that there is something about the sea that evokes beauty, awe, mystery and contemplation. As Meaghan Morris observes, the beach is "one of the deepest-laid 'realities' of life" in Australia.[74] For example, novelist Robert Drewe claims, he feels "most Australian" when he sees "a patch of ocean framed in the branches of a gum-tree … or catch my first glimpse of Little Parakeet Bay on Rottnest Island, off the Western Australian coast, on an early morning bike ride."[75] In the last two centuries of Western colonization, the desert and the bush have served as the primary icons of spiritual identity, with the coast functioning as the secular "edge of the sacred" for non-Indigenous Australians.[76] This leads Australian spirituality and aesth/ethics to be mapped through the concepts of core and periphery, with the desert as the sacred symbolic space.[77] But what is it about the lure of the sea? Is it possible that Philip Drew's observation about the spiritual character of the beach home is indicative of a newly emerging sea aesth/ethics in Australian consciousness?

But the Australian sense of coastal place needs to be seen in historical perspective. Immigrant Australians brought with them attitudes and values influenced by what Alain Corbin names the "discovery of the seaside" in the Western World during the period 1750-1840.[78] During this time, a shift in perspective was made from the catastrophist view of the 1600's and early 1700's to the Romantic view of the sea. According to Corbin, the former provided an aesthetics of fear and repulsion, because the coast was viewed as a place of ruin following the biblical flood, when the abyss surged up over the smooth paradise to erode the land and clean away the sin of human beings. Angry storms, sea-monsters, and the flotsam and jetsam of the beach reminded people of God's judgment against sin. The sands signified this fragile boundary between the demonic and civilization, death and life, madness and sanity, damnation and salvation.

But around the turn of the 18th century, a constellation of new developments brought about a sea-change in perspective. Nature began to be viewed as a spectacle that human beings could admire, understand and encounter, because according to natural or physico-theology, God had providentially ordered and purposed the sea for human use. The sands were now perceived as a solid border set by the Creator for the flourishing of human life. New medical knowledge suggested the therapy of ocean swimming for melancholia, invalidism, pallidness and other afflictions of the urban, leisured elite. For relief from the polluted and degenerate cities, the coast provided purification and restoration. Thus for men, the remedy involved heroically swimming alone against the waves until exhaustion ensued. Women, though, were submerged under the waves by bathing assistants, who then lifted them out to the awaiting carriages. Corbin explains that this Romantic shift to an aesthetics of the sublime involved …

> facing the violent water, but without risk, enjoying the pretence that one could be swept under, and being struck by the full force of the waves, but without losing one's footing. This explains the preoccupation with safety. Everything – the detailed medical prescription, the services of expert bathers, the attendants, and a hard sandy soil whose slope had been carefully assessed – contributed to removing any peril, leaving only the emotion.[79]

Whether submerging under the coastal waves, walking along the cliffs to watch a storm at sea, galloping on horseback along the beach, venturing into dark caverns or contemplating the immensity of an ocean whose limits one is incapable of grasping, Romantics could safely be lured to the edge, sense the experience of entering the abyss, yet overcome it through human and divine resources. Corbin explains the Romantic fascination with the dizzying sense of boundlessness and emptiness:

> Unlike the cool valley, which had once been the image of the golden age, the sea-shore allows an accumulation of simultaneous emotions. The infinite view, the emptiness of the horizon, and the proximity of the abyss all emphasize the horror of the void, and lay the foundations for fantasies of being swallowed up ... The sea as grave fuels dreams of regression ... Yet the romantic walker likes to stand atop a rock as if rooted there, in a defiant attitude in the face of the elements assailing the headland. This is a heroic posture, which at the same time fosters meditation and seems to foreshadow a plan for domination.[80]

As Corbin traces the emerging constellation of aesthetics, therapeutics and ethics in the Romantic lure of the sea, we can hear an opposition between the sea as void or abyss and the autonomous, modern subject. The Romantic is lured by the horrible, yet pleasurable loss of the ego in contemplative confrontation with the elemental. Yet he emerges from his sublime journey with a sense of self-mastery and self-knowledge. He has experienced the ecstasy of standing out of the elemental, by withstanding the lure of the sea, the dark, the abyss, the other, the mother, the void that reduces all things to itself.

Sublime subversions

Yet, is the Romantic code of losing and mastering ourselves, the only way to way to construct the lure of the sea? Are there other ways to theorize an aesth/ethics of the sublime? Are there other ways to configure the deep identification between humans and the elemental? Keller suggests that Western history has been haunted by its own oppositional thinking between the masculine "separative self" and the feminine "soluable self".[81] For men, maturity follows the narrative of the hero, who must differentiate himself over against others, so that his perfection is found in his aseity. The separative self is externally related to others, like the Father God, in whose image he is created. Woman's subjectivity is internalized as the emotional and devotional tendency to dissolve into the other, so that she passively participates in and through the activity of others. With the soluable self, she is always giving herself away, while he, the separative self, is ontologically belligerent. Yet both of these roles presuppose the other in a co-dependent, deceptive way.

In seeking to move beyond this epic polarization, Keller conceptualizes a third subjectivity, the "oceanic self", which is her own positive re-imaging of Freud's dreaded oceanic feeling.[82] For Keller, selves are internally related, yet not reduced to their relations. Thus, subjectivity is dynamic, fluid, and porous, not simple, static or unitary. For better and for worse, we flow into others and others flow into us. We are complex beings, immersed in ecologies of relations. Thus maturity and growth involve freedom and possibility within relations, not in abstracting ourselves from relations and emotional life, then turning the "chaotic" matrix into an abject to rise above, debase or slay. For Keller, the oceanic self follows tidal patterns of connection based on empathy. Rather than slaying Tiamat (the primal mother of Babylonian myth), Keller's oceanic self seeks to swim with Tiamat, the face of the deep, neither assimiliating her nor becoming dissolved in her.[83]

Keller's oceanic subjectivity helps subvert the Romantic selfhood of sublime submersions. What if the heroic man allowed himself to be carried along with others by the swells and currents of the ocean? What if the pallid woman learned to swim herself within and under the waves breaking on the shore? Perhaps both needed a lesson in body surfing! Barbara Claire Freeman also questions the Romantic logic of identity that conceives the self in exclusive terms of either presence or absence.[84] For a sublime subversion, Freeman envisions the possibility of an identity that "neither possesses nor merges with the other but attests to a relation with it."[85] Thus, a feminist theory of sublimity resists the masculinist narrative of infantilism and mastery in regard to the oceanic elemental, imaged as an evil, consuming mother. Why not a relation to the elemental as a lover, friend, or source, rather than enemy? Bergmann and Kristiansen attest to the deep identification of people and the elements of Northern Norway. At times the sea is a powerful force of death and destruction, but it is also the giver and sustainer of life. Thus, people dwell along the coast with the sea, neither as masters or slaves, but as kin. This coastal sense of place resonates with the elemental subliminity of the sea as seen by Luce Irigaray, as she reminds sun-aspiring Friedrich Nietzsche of his maritime lover:

> Yet is there any greater rapture than the sea? For he who climbs high to set his senses areel as if from good wine must still climb down again at last. And his rapture lasts only so long. And all kinds of depressions lie in wait, and the spell is often broken.

> But endless rapture awaits whoever trusts the sea. For as she rises and falls, so one's rapture swells and sinks. Whether the sea is rising or falling, nothing changes in the enchantment of living – moving about endlessly. And does it matter if the sea is pouring over the beaches or sinking back into its bed? Doesn't the one will the other, and the other the one? And isn't it the passage from one to the other that makes for eternal good fortune?[86]

Conclusion: Water Wisdom

This chapter has journeyed to many people and places, but when we "think like an archipelago" rather than an island, we find that the sea connects us.[87] I have shown that in taking seriously the connection between people and a coastal sense of place, we come to a new "water-wisdom" about living with the elemental.[88] A sea aesth/ethics in our time illumines new models of ecotheology and earthkeeping that do not pit humans against the elemental. Dwelling along the edge, we are invited to participate in the ebbing and flowing of the Spirit. Rather than fear the deep and fortify ourselves with practices and attitudes of mastery, we can dwell in much more humble and hopeful ways.

I would like to close with the words of Tim Winton, who has given voice to the coastal belonging of many Australians. He has learned to see/sea the Spirit and drink deeply from coastal places in ways that place himself within a cosmic community of kinship. Winton draws from the Romantic tradition, yet he subverts the heroics of mastery with his own water-wisdom:

> I trekked and camped along the coast, fished for groper from dolerite bluffs, climber the Stirling and Porongorup Ranges, wriggled into caves and canoed creeks and inlets to feel the places eating into me, making marks I could feel more than understand. Even though I left at sixteen, I return often to this region to drink places in. Not simply to revisit my lost youth, but to reacquaint myself with the particularities of the region, the odd smell of the heath scrub, the bloody flowers of the red flowering gum, the turquoise bays unlike any other in the world …
>
> It was these places that taught me how small I was. Not small the way a child often feels, wanting desperately to be big and thereby earn the privileges of citizenship and adulthood. Small in a way that was illuminating and entirely satisfactory. Scrambling up a rockface, tumbling blind along

the seabed and pressed down by waves beyond the limits of breath and strength, or fumbling, numb-knuckled with matches and twigs to make a fire in the rain, you learn a kind of humility which schooling, politics and television couldn't provide. All the talk around me insisted that I was a master of the universe, a human, and a white one at that. I was the whole point of things. That strange dark landscape around Albany told me otherwise and it was a relief to know.[89]

Notes

[1] The lines are from Arnold Eidslott's poem "The Coast of Childhood", cited by Holger Koefoed in *Ørnulf Opdahl* (Oslo: Labyrinth Press 1994), 46. In Norwegian, the lines are "Øyer og hav/hav og oyer bestandig/falt de inn i barneøyet". I am grateful to Tove Bull, who translated these words with me while on her study leave in Perth, January 2003. I am also grateful to Helge Nordahl, who shared with me his admiration and understanding of Eidslott's poetry while I was on study leave in Oslo, April 2001. Along with Asbjørn Aarnes, Nordahl edited the book *Hellig Hav: Øm Arnold Eidslotts Diktning* (Oslo: Verbum 2000). And most of all, I am grateful to Arnold Eidslott for talking with me about his "praise to the ocean" in his home in Ålesund, May 2001. For one of his many collections of poetry, see *Nettene under Kapp Hoorn* (Oslo: Gyldendal 2000).

[2] In his recent book *Dirt Music* (Sydney: Picador 2001), Western Australian novelist Tim Winton tells the story of a heart-broken and grieving musician named Luther Fox, who finds the possibility of healing and new life – re-creation – along the Australian coast, a seascape of holy transformation (352-4).

[3] Carson is best known for her prophetic work of environmentalism in *Silent Spring*. But as her editor Linda Lear writes in *Lost Woods: The Discovered Writing of Rachel Carson* (Boston: Beacon 1998), Carson's "environmental ontology" from which "everything else followed" can be found in the introduction Carson wrote in 1935 for a U.S. Bureau of Fisheries brochure entitled "The World of Waters" (xiii). Deemed by her supervisor as too lyrical for a government report, Carson was encouraged to submit it to the *Atlantic Monthly*, where it was published in 1937 as "Undersea", and included in the collection *Lost Woods*, 3-11.

[4] Thus, I am affirming an "ocularcentric" relation to the coast that privileges human vision, but does not exclude the other senses – who could imagine the coast without the feel of the breeze upon one's skin, the smell of the scrub, the taste of the salty foam, or the touch of rough rock faces? As Martin Jay concludes: "Vision and visuality in all their rich and contradictory variety can still provide us mere mortals with insights and perspectives, speculations and observations, enlightenments and illuminations, that even a god might envy." (594).

5   The image of the sacred edge comes from my attempt to map Australian spirituality in a way that resonates with how I hear many people talk about their sense of belonging and connection to seascape, in addition to landscape. In the past, the desert and bush have been the central icons of the spiritual journey for many Australian theologians, poets and novelists. But in recent years, writers like Robert Drewe, Dorothy Hewitt, Kim Scott and Tim Winton have offered alternative visions of belonging and enchantment. See any of my articles, (2001ab) (2001/02) (2002).

6   Seddon (1997a), 111, and (1997b), 113-118.

7   Elliot, quoted in Seddon (1997a), xiv.

8   On Hildegard's image of the *viriditas* of the Holy Spirit, see Moltmann, 148.

9   Anderson, 139.

10 Cochrane, 166. I use Cochrane's concept of "geography of faith", but in relation to place, instead of space. The latter he claims is "continually shifting sites and boundaries" (166). In attempting to contextualize ecotheology within a coastal sense of place, one learns that the sands, sea and shoreline are always shifting, never stationary.

11 McDaniel, 38.

12 This is the language of the Constantinopolitan Creed, 381 ACE, in *Creeds of the Church*, in Leith, 33, which inspires Sigurd Bergmann's ecological and liberating pneumatology in Bergmann (1997a), 161-3.

13 Beldon C. Lane explores the spiritual connection of "*habitus* and habitat" in Lane, 9.

14 Keller (1996), 174.

15 Bevans, 54.

16 Ibid., 52. Certainly there is a danger in this model with viewing culture as static and homogeneous. As Delwin Brown points out, cultures are complex, dynamic entities engaged in processes of negotiation, continuity and change. Still, with this critical recognition, we can draw on Bevans' anthropological model as a way of constructing "local" or emplaced theologies. See Schreiter or Barr.

17 Hodgson, 42. Emphasis added.

18 Casey, xi.

19 Croll and Parkin, 17.

20 Ibid., 17, 19, 32.

21 Ingold, 44, 51.

22 Read.

23 Casey, ix.

24 Basso, 27.

25 Basso, 107.

26 The word "interbeing" is used by John A. Grim, who credits the term to Thich Nhât Hahn.

[27] Boseto, 69-70.

[28] Cited in *The Pacific Journal of Theology* Series II, No. 13 (1995), 14.

[29] Farley distinguishes between theology as a theoretical and scholarly discipline and theology as the Christian community's knowledge of divine being whose end is salvation. See Farley, 29-44.

[30] Jaukkuri, 5-6. Garner translates Jaukkuri's title as "Art takes place".

[31] Jaukkuri, 36-9.

[32] Ibid., 38.

[33] See the website *www.sculpturebythesea.com* for a history by the exhibition's director, David Handley, and on-line presentation of the recent and past years' entries.

[34] See her entry in the "Bondi 2001Exhibition" at *www.sculpturebythesea.com* .

[35] Cited in *Bondi 2001: Sculpture by the Sea Catalogue and Site Map*, 14.

[36] Ibid.

[37] Taçon, 56-7.

[38] Ibid., 57.

[39] Ibid., 56.

[40] Ibid., 56.

[41] Ibid., 57.

[42] The phrase traditionally rendered as "heaven and earth" and interpreted in hierarchical, dualistic ways, has been translated here as "sky and land" according to Habel, 43.

[43] See Jürgen Moltmann's study of the Hebrew word *ruach* in Moltmann, 40-3. The cosmic breadth of God's ruach-spirit leads Moltmann to challenge the anthropocentric and dualistic legacy in much of Christian theology's doctrinal understandings of the Spirit (pneumatology). By recovering the flowing associations of ruach, Moltmann offers an ecological and immanent model of life in the Spirit that is universal in scope and invigorating towards new human practices of sustainability. Within creation, the Spirit of God is "the confronting event of God's efficacious presence" and "the power from which everything that has life lives" (42). God's presence and power as wind and breath also links ruach with breadth to imagine "the space of freedom in which the living being can unfold" (43). For living beings, life in the Spirit is experienced as emergence into an open and broad space that is life-sustaining and liberating. Moltmann's pneumatological interpretation of space can lead us to look more seriously at the relation of Spirit and place.

[44] Johnson, 57.

[45] Catherine Keller claims that the Greek meaning of *eschaton* is "edge", as either "spatial or temporal rim" in Keller (2000), 195. See also her new book, Keller (2002).

[46] Keller (2000), 187. In the Babylonian creation text *Enuma Elish,* which dates from the time of Babylon's rise to political supremacy (2057-1758 BCE), Tiamat

is the great mother sea-goddess slain by her grandson, the warrior Marduk. Her dismembered body becomes the cosmos.

[47] Ibid.

[48] Johnson, 124-5. Emphasis added.

[49] Paul Santmire examines the conflict between the "spiritual" metaphor of ascent and the "ecological" metaphors of fecundity and good land in the work of classic theologians of the Christian tradition and concludes, "The root metaphor of ascent, by itself, is not suitable for a viable theology of nature." See Santmire, 73. In contrast, I am proposing metaphors of ecological descent!

[50] Kristiansen (1998), 17. I am grateful for Roald Kristiansen's hospitality and insight while I was researching at the University of Tromsø (May, 2001).

[51] Kristiansen (1998), 17. See also Kristiansen (2000), 8-26.

[52] Kristiansen (1998), 55-6. See also Kristiansen (1997), 7-31.

[53] Kristiansen (2000), 9. See also Kristiansen (1993).

[54] Kristiansen (2000), 21.

[55] Bergmann (1998), 107. I am also grateful for the hospitality and insight of Sigurd Bergmann while I was researching in Trondheim at the Norwegian University of Science and Technology (April 2001).

[56] Bergmann (1998), 109.

[57] Ibid.

[58] Ibid. Bergmann cites Valkeapää's words from *Sámi Eatnan Duoddarat, Samelands vidder,* Music text on the CD *Goaskimiellja, Ørnebror* produced by Mari Boine et al., 1993.

[59] Bergmann (1997a), 161, 163.

[60] See Bergmann (1997b). See Bergmann's forthcoming book, *Creation Set Free: The Spirit as Liberator of Nature* (Grand Rapids, Mich.: William B. Eerdmans (2005), in which he has revised his earlier work (1995).

[61] Bergmann (1997b), 86.

[62] Bergmann (1997a), 162. In this passage, he draws on the "earth keeping" work of M. L. Daneel (1991) (1993).

[63] Bergmann (1997b), 87.

[64] Keller (2000), 196.

[65] Ibid., 183.

[66] Müller-Fahrenholz, 109.

[67] Ibid.

[68] Keller (2000), 190.

[69] Müller-Fahrenholz, 108-112.

[70] Catherine Keller calls for a "green ecumenacy" based on the "greening power of the Spirit" inspired by Hildegaard von Bingen's mystical image of *viriditas*. See Keller (1994), 345.

71 Schaer, 62-6.
72 Drew, 5.
73 Quoted in Schaer, 64.
74 Morris, 105.
75 Drewe, 4-5.
76 See Tacey.
77 See Yi-Fu Tuan's discussion of Australian sacred space in Tuan, 177-79.
78 Corbin.
79 Ibid., 73.
80 Ibid., 167, 177, 128.
81 Keller (1986), 7-46.
82 Ibid., 93.
83 Ibid., 148.
84 Freeman, 331-34.
85 Ibid, 333.
86 Irigaray, 13.
87 See my article, (2003) I am playing with Aldo Leopold's vision of community in "Thinking like a Mountain" from Leopold, 132.
88 Elizabeth Johnson (1993) suggests, "As a symbol of the Spirit, water points to the bottomless wellspring of the source of life and to the refreshment and gladness that result from deep immersion in this mystery." (48-9).
89 Winton (2000), xxi-xxii. Winton is most known for his novel *Cloudstreet* from 1991, which has now become an internationally acclaimed play.

References

Anderson, Pamela Sue (1998) *A Feminist Philosophy of Religion: The Rationality and Myths of Religious Belief,* Oxford: Blackwell

Barr, William R. (ed.) (1997) *Constructive Christian Theology in the Worldwide Church,* Grand Rapids, Mich.: Eerdmans

Basso (1996) *Wisdom Sits in Places: Landscape and Language Among the Western Apache,* Albuquerque: University of New Mexico Press

Sigurd Bergmann (1995) *Geist, der Natur befreit: Die trinitarische Kosmologie Gregors von Nazianz im Horizont einer ökologischen Theologie der Befreiung,* Mainz: Matthias-Grünewald-Verlag

---, (1997a) "History of Mission – History of Liberation?", in *Geist, der lebendig macht: Lavierungen zur ökologischen Befreiungstheologie,* Frankfurt: IKO

---, (1997b) "Gregory of Nazianzen's Theological Interpretation of the Philosophy of Nature in the Doctrine of the Four Elements," in *Geist, der lebendig macht: Lavierungen zur ökologischen Befreiungstheologie,* Frankfurt: IKO

---, (1998) "Cold Cradle of Stone, Warm Soft Arms – Cultural Landscape in Sápmi", in Kristiansen/Terebikhin

---, (2005) *Creation Set Free: The Spirit as Liberator of Nature,* Grand Rapids, Mich.: Eerdmans, (forthcoming)

Bevans, Stephen B. (2000) *Models of Contextual Theology,* Maryknoll, New York: Orbis

Bondi 2001: Sculpture by the Sea Catalogue and Site Map

Boseto, Leslie (1995) "Do not Separate Us from Our Land and Sea" in *The Pacific Journal of Theology,* Series II, No. 13, pp. 69-70

Brown, Delwin (1994) *Boundaries of Our Habitation: Tradition and Theological Construction* Albany, New York: SUNY

Carson, Rachel (1937) "Undersea", in *Atlantic Monthly, Lost Woods,* pp. 3-11

---, (1982) *Silent Spring,* London: Penguin Books (1965)

Casey, Edward S. *The Fate of Place: A Philosophical History,* Berkeley: University of California Press

Croll, Elisabeth and Parkin, David (1992) "Cultural Understandings of the Environment", in Croll, Parkin (eds.), *Bush Base: Forest Farm – Culture, Environment and Development,* London: Routledge

Cochrane, James R. (1999) *Circles of Dignity: Community Wisdom and Theological Reflection,* Minneapolis, Minn.: Fortress Press

Corbin, Alain (1994) *The Lure of the Sea: The Discovery of the Seaside in the Western World 1750-1840,* translated by Jocelyn Phelps Berkley, University of California Press

Daneel, M. L. (1991) "African Christian Theology and the Challenge of Earthkeeping", in *Neue Zeitschrift für Missionswissenschaft,* 47, pp. 2-3, 129-142, 225-246

---, (1993) "African Independent Church Pneumatology and the Salvation of All Creation", in *International Review of Mission,* Vol. LXXXII, No. 326, pp. 143-166

Drew, Philip (1999) "Foreword", in Reed Burns, Jenna (compiled by) *Australian Beach Houses: Living by the Sea,* Sydney: New Holland Publishers

Drewe, Robert (1998) "Forward: The lure of the beach," in Matthew, Anne (compiled by) *Australian Beaches,* Sydney: Landsdown Publishing, pp. 4-5

Eidslott, Arnold (1994) "The Coast of Childhood", in Koefoed, Holger Ørnulf *Opdahl,* Oslo: Labyrinth Press, p. 46

---, (2000) *Nettene under Kapp Hoorn,* Oslo: Gyldendal

Elliot, Brian (1967) *The Landscape of Poetry* Melbourne: F. W. Cheshire

Farley, Edward (1983) *Theologia: The Fragmentation and Unity of Theological Education,* Philadelphia: Fortress

Freeman, Barbara Clair (1998) "Feminine Sublime", in *The Encyclopedia of Aesthetics*, Kelly, Michael (ed.) Vol. 4, New York: Oxford University Press, pp. 331-334

Grim, John A. (2001) *Indigenous Traditions and Ecology: The Interbeing of Cosmology and Community,* Cambridge, Mass.: Harvard University Press

Habel, Norman (2000) "Guiding Ecojustice Principles," in Habel, Norman (ed.) *The Earth Bible: Readings from the Perspective of Earth*, Vol. 1, Sheffield: Sheffield Academic Press, p. 43

Hodgson, Peter C. (2001) *Christian Faith: A Brief Introduction*, Louisville: Westminster John Knox Press

Ingold, Tim "Culture and the Perception of the Environment", in Croll/Parkin (eds.)

Irigaray, Luce (1991) *Marine Lover of Friedrich Nietzsche,* New York: Columbia University Press

Jaukkuri, Maaretta (1999) "Kunst finner sted", in *Skulpturlandskap Nordland*, Kiese: Forlaget Geelmuyden

Jay, Martin (1993) *Downcast Eyes: The Denigration of Vision in Twentieth-Century French Thought,* Berkeley: University of California Press

Johnson, Elizabeth A. (1992) *She Who Is: The Mystery of God in Feminist Theological Discourse,* New York: Crossroad

---, (1993) *Women, Earth and Creator Spirit,* New York: Paulist Press

Keller, Catherine (1986) *From a Broken Web: Separation, Sexism and Self,* Boston: Beacon

---, (1994) "Eschatology, Ecology and a Green Ecumenacy", in Chopp, Rebecca S. and Taylor, Mark Lewis (eds.), *Reconstructing Christian Theology*, Minneapolis, Minn.: Fortress Press

---, (1996) *Apocalypse Now and Then,* Boston: Beacon Press

---, (2000) "No More Sea: The Lost Chaos of the Eschaton" in Hessel, Dieter T. and Radford Ruether, Rosemary (eds.), *Christianity and Ecology: Seeking the Well-Being of Earth and Humans,* Cambridge, Mass.: Harvard University Press

---, (2002) *The Face of the Deep,* London: Routledge

Kristiansen, Roald E. (1993) *Økoteologi,* Frederiksberg: Anis

---, (1997) "Sacred Space: Towards a Theology of Place and Sacred Space," in Kristiansen, Roald E. and Terebikhin, Nickolai M. (eds.) *Religion, Church, and Education in the Barents Region*, Arkhangelsk: Pomor State University

---, (1998) "An Agenda for the Ecology of Spirit", in Kristiansen/Terebikhin (eds.)

---, (1998) "Religion in the North: Towards a Contextual Theology of the Arctic," in Kristiansen/Terebikhin (eds.)

---, (2000) "Artic Ecotheology," in *Ecotheology*, Vol. 9 July, pp. 8-26

Kristiansen, R. E., Terebikhin, N. M. (eds.) (1998) *Ecology of Spirit: Cultural Plurality and Religous Identity in the Barents Region,* Umeå

Lane, Beldon C. (1998) *The Solace of Fierce Landscapes: Exploring Desert and Mountain Spirituality,* New York: Oxford University Press

Lear, Linda (1998) *Lost Woods*: *The Discovered Writing of Rachel Carson,* Boston: Beacon

Leith, John H. (ed.) (1982) *Creeds of the Church*, Atlanta: John Knox Press

Leopold, Aldo (1968) *A Sand Country Almanac and Sketches Here and There,* London: Oxford University Press (1949)

McDaniel, Jay B. (1990) *Earth, Sky, Gods & Mortals: Developing an Ecological Spirituality* Mystic, Conn.: Twenty-Third Publications

Morris, Meaghan (1998) *Too Soon, Too Late: History in Popular Culture,* Bloomington, Indiana: Indiana University Press

Moltmann, Jürgen (1992) *The Spirit of Life: A Universal Affirmation,* Minneapolis, Minn.: Fortress Press

Müller-Fahrenholz, Geiko (1995) *God's Spirit: Transforming a World in Crisis,* New York: Continuum

Nordahl, Helge and Aarnes, Asbjørn (eds.) (2000) *Hellig Hav: Øm Arnold Eidslotts Diktning,* Oslo: Verbum

Read, Peter (2000) *Belonging: Australians, Place and Aboriginal Ownership,* Cambridge: Cambridge University Press

Santmire, Paul (1985) *The Travail of Nature: The Ambiguous Ecological Promise of Christian Theology,* Minneapolis: Fortress Press

Schaer, Cathrine (2002) "Bach Dated", in *Air New Zealand Panorama*

Schreiter, Robert J. (1986) *Constructing Local Theologies,* Maryknoll, New York: Orbis

Seddon, George (1972) "Forward", in *Sense of Place: A Response to an Environment* Nedlands, Western Australia: University of Western Australia Press

---, (1997a) "Sense of Place", in *Landprints: Reflections on Place and Landscape* Cambridge: Cambridge University Press

---, (1997b) "The *genius loci* and the Australian Landscape", in *Landprints, Reflections on Place and Landscape,* Cambridge: Cambridge University Press

Tacey, David (1995) *Edge of the Sacred*, Melbourne: HarperCollins

Taçon, Paul S. C. (2002) "By the Sea: A History of Human Engagement", in *Bondi 2002: Sculpture by the Sea Catalogue,* pp. 56-57

Tuan, Yi-Fu (1995) *Passing Strange and Wonderful: Aesthetics, Nature and Culture,* New York: Kodansha International

Victorin-Vangerud, Nancy M. (2001a) "The Sacred Edge: Women, Sea and Spirit", in *Seachanges: Journal of Women Scholars of Religion and Theology*, Vol. 1, www.wsrt.com.au, pp. 1-28

---, (2001b) " 'The Sea is Our Life!' Cross-Cultural Reflections on a Coastal Sense of Place", in *In God's Image: Journal of Asian Women's Resource Centre for Culture and Theology* 20/4, pp. 34-8

---, (2001/02) "The Sacred Edge: Seascape as Spiritual Resource toward an Australian Eco-eschatology", in *Ecotheology*, Vol. 6, pp. 167-185

---, (2002) "Sea-ing Faith, Fathoming Faith: Reflections on a Coastal Sense of Place", in *Eremos: Exploring Spirituality in Australia*, No. 79, pp. 17-21

---, (2003) "Thinking like an Archipelago: Beyond Tehomophobic Theology", in *Pacifica: Australian Theological Studies* 16/2, pp. 153-192

Winton, Tim (2000) "Strange Passion: A Landscape Memoir", in Woldendorp, Richard, *Down to Earth: Australian Landscapes*, North Fremantle, Western Australia: Fremantle Arts Centre Press (1999)

---, (1998) *Cloudstreet*, Ringwood, Victoria: Penguin (1991)

---, (2001) Dirt Music, Sydney: Picador

Used webpage

www.sculpturebythesea.com

SPIRITUAL EXPERIENCE

CHRISTIANE JOHANNSEN

The relation and meeting of the different religions, together with their acceptance and tolerance of each other, is a topic that becomes more and more important in our society. Places for all religions such as Tadao Ando's Meditation Space within the UNESCO Headquarters in Paris, which is dedicated to global peace, already exist and there will be more need for places like that in future. As an architect, I am interested in the question if and how architecture can take part in the meeting of different religions. Can we actually achieve spiritual experience through architecture and how is such an aesthetic experience possible?

The Japanese internationally recognized architect Tadao Ando, is known for the non-confessional spiritual or religious belief related to his work. He is interested in the meeting of different cultures and wants people to experience his buildings in a special way.

> What I have sought to achieve is a spatiality that stimulates the human spirit, awakens the sensitivity and communicates with the deeper soul.
>
> (Ando, 1995)

CHRISTIANE JOHANNSEN

1   Tadao Ando, Koshino House.

In this connection spirituality is not necessarily part only of religion or sacred buildings. In my research project, called "Spirituality in Architecture", it is the aesthetic or spiritual experience of beauty in all kinds of architecture that interests me. I want to find out both how Tadao Ando tries to create spirituality in his buildings and if and how this spirituality is experienced.

In this article I want to introduce Tadao Ando's architecture, the way he thinks and works, besides discussing how spiritual experience in architecture could be possible. First I will explain experience as a phenomenological problem in the different disciplines of philosophy (Husserl), social science (Schutz and Luckmann) and architecture (Norberg-Schulz and Holl). Then I will focus on aesthetic experience in art and architecture (Soetsu and Cold) and relate to it to ideas of both philosophy and social science.

Ando's work

Tadao Ando's architecture is famous for its style of minimalism – "a world of nothingness" as Peter Eisenman called it. The wall is the main element in Ando's architecture, which is characterized by geometry and follows Mies van der Rohe's principle "less is more" in a new way. The three elements of diversity, complexity and contradiction coexist in their most reduced form. In "A Study in Walls" Masao Furuyama wrote: "In Ando's architecture, walls assert themselves by themselves." The wall's structural attributes become less important – the wall itself is architecture. It functions as a screen, leading and breaking the entering light and creating its shadows. It is the relationship between man and nature through architecture that is most important for Ando. In an abstract form he works with man's/woman's communication with nature – the elements of rain, wind, topography, light and water are integrated in the projects. "My goal has not been to commune with nature as it is, but rather to try to change the meaning of nature through architecture." (Ando, 1989, 19)

2

Tadao Ando, Church of the Light.

In his acceptance speech for the Pritzker Prize in 1995, Ando spoke about two dimensions he wants to integrate in his work – ideals and reality, the fictive and the substantive. The fictive aspect of architecture, Ando (1995) defined as "the quality of a spatial experience composed of architectonic elements aimed at aesthetic perfection." Therefore architecture has to contain both human life and human expression – it is both science and art. He compared these dimensions with the three principles of architecture – utilitas, venustas, firmitas – that had been developed by Vitrivius, the architectural theoretician of ancient Rome.

> ...utilitas is function (commodity) and firmitas is strength (firmness), both are measures of architectonic potential, while venustas (delight or beauty) resides in the dimension of imagination.
>
> (Ando, 1995)

Ando called the synthesis of these two dimensions – the one of fiction and of reality – as the element "which deeply affects human spirituality". Fiction and reality together make it possible to create a space of a higher dimension.

Ando uses the spatial manipulation techniques of traditional Japanese architecture in a contemporary context. A well-known example is the passageway within the Shisen-do complex where different feelings are created in order to try to lead the visitors in their behaviour of how they explore space (actively). Within the Shisen-do an esoteric technique is used to create a space for meditating.

> First objects slowly disappear, and with the objects the (perceiving) subjects also disappear. We are made aware of awareness, which is empty, the ultimate extension of space ... As a mystic, Ishikawa Jozan knew that what is to be empty must first be filled. All meditating techniques are based on this principle. Only a place inducing such an experience (or better, non-experience) is sacred. It gives us a taste of who we are.
>
> (Nitschke, 41)

Yanagi Soetsu described the Japanese contribution to world culture as the ability to see beauty in things that seem to be trivial.

Experience – a phenomenological aspect

Experience is an important aspect in phenomenology, which in general can be said to be about the study of appearances. Phenomenology recognizes the reality and truth of phenomena – of things that appear and manifest themselves as what they are – as objects of experience. Physical things are real but they are not what they seem – they are appearances, actual or possible. Phenomenology has the goal of rational and systematic understanding of human action and experience. Its doctrine can be described as:

> The teaching that every act of consciousness we perform, every experience that we have, is intentional: it is essentially "consciousness of" or an "experience of" something or other ... Every act of consciousness, every experience, is correlated with an object. Every intending has its intended object.
>
> (Sokolowski, 8)

In order to describe man's perception of things, Edmund Husserl, the founder and leading figure of the philosophical direction, developed the three aspects of *life-world, phenomenological reduction* and *intentionality*. The pre-scientific *life-world*, which is the basis of meaning in every science, is understood as a concept in the mental sphere, which has the naïve human being, the *ego*, in its centre. Through the change to the *phenomenological attitude*, which is the changing from natural targets of our concern to simple ones (the *intentionalities* themselves), the mental process of experiencing becomes possible. It is a return to the original experience of the *life-world*, in which facts can be grasped directly with focus on the single human being's consciousness of the world. In Husserl's opinion only thought, human thinking that arises from experience, is absolute, everything else is relative. Experiencing is characterized by intentionality, which is the main phenomenological theme. It helps us to describe a number of different experiences as the unity of one consciousness. The process of experiencing an object is an intentional act. It is the starting point and the most characteristic of consciousness – a pure and simple awareness of the human.

In social science the ideas of Husserl's phenomenology were taken up and further developed by Schutz, who described it as the science of mind and the only method that explains the world through mind – world and mind are correlated with each other. According to this, Luckmann, assistant to Schutz, described the experience of the individual human being, which is the centre of the system, as the first condition for the world. In studying social phenomena it is most important to describe situations as they "really" are and so both Schutz and Luckmann demanded that the researcher must not add information, interpret situations or jump to conclusions at all.

The connection of phenomenology to art seems logical as the following quote of Natanson shows: *"…as the discipline of subjectivity it could hardly avoid one of the richest expressions of consciousness – the domain of art."* (Natanson in Luckmann, 198).

Christian Norberg-Schulz used the term phenomenology in architecture in order to describe a theory for understanding architecture in concrete, existential terms. He understands architecture as a concrete phenomenon and sees the purpose of man-made places in visualizing and symbolizing man's understanding of his environment. Through orientation, how man is located in space, and identification, how man is exposed to the place's character, man is able to live. It is the task of architecture to create meaningful places in order to make dwelling possible and give man existential foothold. Every place has its particular identity, its spatial character – the spirit of place or *genius loci*. Norberg-Schulz described the basic act of architecture as the

3

Tadao Ando, Church on the Water

vocation of a place, a phenomenon that has to be seen in its qualitative totality. The essence of place (atmosphere) consists of different aspects such as material substance, shape, texture or colour. It is impossible to describe a place only with methods of natural science – the environmental character, which is most important for man's identification, would be lost.

Experience of art in general and particularly architecture as part of it can be understood as a private dialogue and interaction between the work and the viewer. Alvar Aalto explained this identification of the human being with space, place or architecture, through the fact of the *"verb essence of architectural experience."* (Aalto quoted in Holl, Pallasmaa, Pérez-Gomez, 35). Also Juhani Pallasmaa described the experience of place or architecture as multi-sensory – containing the five senses of vision (fire, light), hearing (air), smell (vapour), taste (water) and touch (earth).

> A walk through a forest or a Japanese garden is invigorating and healing because of the essential interaction of all sense modalities reinforcing each other; our sense of reality is thus strengthened and articulated.
>
> (Pallasmaa in Holl, Pallasmaa, Pérez-Gomez, 30)

Steven Holl brought up these questions of perception in connection to questions of intention in his writings about phenomenology of architecture. The experience of architecture awakes all senses and includes different aspects such as time, shadow and transparency, colour, texture, material or detail. He took up the empirical distinguishing of inner and outer perception, which has already been discussed by Brentano, an important figure in the beginning of phenomenology in philosophy. Holl demanded that both the outer perception of physical phenomena and the inner perception of mental phenomena should be simulated by architecture.

Also Norberg-Schulz described the physical aspect and practical side of architecture in relation to two different sorts of phenomena – concrete objects, which are part of our life-world (people, animals, flowers) and feelings, the content of our experience. The interplay of the real and the intentional existence can be understood by intention through dividing the whole and analyzing the partial perceptions.

"As in direct perceptual experience, architecture is initially understood as a series of partial experiences, rather than a totality." (Holl, Pallasmaa, Pérez-Gomez. 42)

4

Tadao Ando: Meditation Space

Aesthetic experience

Beauty is understood as an attribute of objects, surrounding or art, which we are able to experience. The aesthetic quality of the surrounding, either experienced as positive or negative, is a unity that consists of different aspects such as space, form, nature, furniture, materials, colours, light, decoration and detail. Aesthetic experience is created by impressions we get through our senses such as sight, smell, hearing, the way we move through the room or how we come into contact with surfaces.

Many opinions have been developed as to how aesthetic experience is possible. Kant was of the opinion that in aesthetic experience an object has to be seen in a direct way without any thought about its purpose, worth or symbolic meaning. Nørretranders and Gombrich, on the other hand, reasoned that it is difficult for us to separate the aesthetic part from our conscious knowledge and unconscious feelings. Nørretranders focused on our unconscious knowledge and Gombrich argued with the difficulty of separating what we see from what we know. This discussion is also known from social science where, for instance, Luckmann demanded the bracketing of all background information – nothing must be added. He was criticized because this seemed to be impossible to realize. Yanagi Soetsu, a Japanese artist and founder of the modern folk-art movement in Japan, saw the only possibility to see beauty through intuition rather than through intellect.

> He who lets knowledge precede seeing can not achieve a sense of beauty. The ability to see penetrates to the inner man, while knowledge circles around what is real. In order to understand beauty one must let the intuition work before one begins to judge. Finding the essential depends on intuition not the intellect. In other words, one achieves real understanding by seeing rather than through knowledge. Often the achievement of reaching the truth is unexplainable … beauty is in some way mystical. It can not, therefore, be explained adequately by the intellect. A pure intellectual understanding lacks depth.
>
> (Soetsu, 1940, in Thomsen)

As an attribute of an object, beauty is always here waiting for us to be perceived and experienced. In that sense, can it be compared with the identity of an object, as it is described within Husserl's phenomenology? In the earlier quote Soetsu said that the only way of experiencing beauty is to use intuition rather than intellect. This seems to be an obvious parallel to phenomenology, where Husserl described intentionality as the most important attitude of our consciousness in the process of intending an object's identity. Although the object's presentation and appearances can change, the object's identity never changes – it is always there and can be perceived through the act of *"cognito"*. This moment when the human being turns to an object in order to perceive it was described by Husserl in a very poetic way: "In every wakeful cogito a 'glancing' ray from the pure Ego is directed upon the 'object' …" (Husserl 243). It is important that the human being has this direct concentrated connection to the one object and separates it from its objective background, where it exists next to other things. Also Soetsu underlined this special relationship between the observer and the object as the following quote shows:

SPIRITUAL EXPERIENCE

5   Tadao Ando, Nariwa Museum   6   Tadao Ando, Koshino House

> Among the few were the former tea masters. They saw genuinely ... they saw directly. "Directly" is different than other ways of seeing... "Directly" is an unbroken line between the eye and the object. If one does not see into the core of the object, it is difficult to understand the object itself... Seeing directly means seeing before thinking. To see the object through one's thoughts means that seeing is only partial. He who depends on intellect before seeing will achieve only a vague understanding... A well know religious scripture says: "He who wishes to know before he believes will never achieve a full understanding of God." The same is true of beauty. He who depends on intellect before seeing can not achieve a full understanding of beauty.
>
> (Soetsu, 1936, in Thomsen)

In phenomenology in architecture both Norberg-Schulz and Holl focused on the experience of the special character of place, which Norberg-Schulz called *genius loci*. There are two main points which are important for the perception of architecture. One is that a place contains several aspects, which all have to be experienced in order to understand the identity of a place – the qualitative totality of the environmental character. The other one is that this experience can only be achieved through five senses rather than through knowledge or intellect. This makes it possible for the observer to be in direct contact with the objects of perception, or as Soetsu described it – to see things directly.

In Birgit Cold's opinion, both cultural ideas and individual taste are basis for the creation and experience – through both senses and feelings – of beauty. Our knowledge about a topic or an example of architecture is background and basis for our aesthetic judgements. Our experiences are dependent on who we are, which culture we come from, our education and previous knowledge. This variety of how different people experience things differently was also mentioned by Soetsu:

> Everyone sees things but the way one sees is not the same, and the object seen is therefore not the same. There are those who naturally see in dept, those who naturally see in depth, those who classify the object, seeing both good and bad. To misunderstand what one sees is the sme as not seeing… .
>
> (Soetsu, 1936, in Thomsen)

In philosophical phenomenology this variety was also taken up in the description of the *life-world* in the concept of the mental sphere. Husserl described the human being, the *ego*, which lives next to many other human beings, the *alter egos*, within a community of nature. Every *ego* builds the centre of its own mental *life-world* but has its own individual experience of things. That is why, according to Luckmann, it is important for the researcher not to be part of the *life-world* and to act as a disinterested observer. Through *phenomenological reduction* this change in attitude will help to put aside both his individual experience and his background knowledge.

Both social and aesthetic understanding is immediate, holistic and intuitive and stands always in social context. It transcends what is only sensory impression. The experience of an aesthetic object is dependent on the viewer's mood and frame of mind – it can differ every day. Speaking of experience as a phenomenological problem,[1] the principle of changing in attitude, the phenomenological reduction, seems to be basis for solving it in all the different directions I am writing about. Reduction, the change from the natural to the *phenomenological attitude*, is about bracketing all judgements about the ontological characteristics of the perceived objects. "Thus the experience is reduced to its 'essentials' of its form." (Schutz, 1970, p.321). Through bracketing of the original reality all knowledge and information, which serves normally as background, is put away. In social science that includes general information we have, for instance, about social structures or behaviour. In architecture it is basic knowledge we have about buildings – basic practical and technological information that is necessary for the function of architecture as a shelter. A special kind of perceiving – a spiritual experience of the spatial character – becomes possible.

Notes

[1] Based on Wittgenstein's statement "There is no such thing as phenomenology, but there are indeed phenomenological problems." (Wittgenstein in Holl, Pallasmaa, Pérez-Gomez, 41).

Illustrations

1. Ando, Tadao, *Koshino House,* Hiroshi Kobayashi (photographer), in Bertrand, P. (1990) *Tadao Ando: Das Haus Koshino*, Tübingen: Wasmuth
2. Ando, Tadao, *Church of the Light,* Mitsuo Matsuoka (photographer), in Bertrand, P. (1990) *Tadao Ando: Das Haus Koshino*, Tübingen: Wasmuth
3. Ando, Tadao, *Church on the Water,* Richard Pare (photographer), in Pare, R. & Ando, T. (1996) *The Colours of Light: Tadao Ando Architecture,* London: Phaidon
4. Ando, Tadao, *Meditation Space, UNESCO,* Richard Pare (photographer), in Pare, R. & Ando, T. (1996) *The Colours of Light: Tadao Ando Architecture,* London: Phaidon
5. Ando, Tadao, *Nariwa Museum,* Richard Pare (photographer), in Pare, R. & Ando, T. (1996) *The Colours of Light: Tadao Ando Architecture,* London: Phaidon
6. Ando, Tadao, *Koshino House,* Richard Pare (photographer), in Pare, R. & Ando, T. (1996) *The Colours of Light: Tadao Ando Architecture.* London: Phaidon

References

Ando, T. (1995) http://www.pritzkerprize.com/andore.htm

Cold, B. (1998) *Metode for opplevelse og bevisstgjøring av arkitektur og steder*, Trondheim: Institutt for byggekunst, Fakultet for arkitektur og billedkunst, NTNU

---, (2002) *Generelt om estetikk og omgivelsene,* Trondheim: Institutt for byggekunst, Fakultet for arkitektur og billedkunst, NTNU

Fields, D. W. (ed.) (1991) *Tadao Ando: Dormant Lines,* New York: Rizzoli

Frampton, K., Ando, T., Kunihiro, G. T., Eisenman, P. (1989) *Tadao Ando: The Yale Studio & Current Work*s, New York: Rizzoli

Gadamer, H.-G. (1999) *Truth and Method,* London: Sheed & Ward

Holl, St., Pallasmaa, J., Pérez-Gomez, A. (1994) *Questions of Perception – Phenomenology of Architecture,* Tokyo: A+u Publishing

Husserl, E. (1969) *Ideas: General Introduction to Pure Phenomenology,* London: Allen & Unwin

Luckmann, Th. (1978) *Phenomenology and Sociology,* Harmondsworth: Penguin Books

Mo, L. (2003) *Philosophy of Science for Architects,* Høvik: Kolofon

---, *Research Methods for Architects and Planners,* Trondheim: Department for Town and Regional Planning, Faculty for Architecture, Plan and Art, NTNU

Nitschke, G. (1993) *From Shinto to Ando: Studies in architectural anthropology in Japan,* London: Academy Editions, Ernst & Sohn

Norberg-Schulz, C. (1980) *Genius Loci – Towards a Phenomenology of Architecture,* London: Academy Editions

Pare, R., Ando, T. (2000) *The Colours of Light, Tadao Ando Architecture,* London: Phaidon

Schutz, A. (1970) *On Phenomenology and Social Relations,* Chicago: University of Chicago Press

Sokolowski, R. (2000) *Introduction to Phenomenology,* Cambridge: Cambridge University Press

Thomsen, S. (2002) *Japan-Kunsthåndverk – en guide til museets permamente Japanavdeling,* Trondheim: Nordenfjeldske Kunstindustrimuseum

Used webpages

http://www.archpedia.co/Architects/Ando.html

http://www.pritzkerprize.com/andore.htm

CLASSICISM, HISTORICISM AND MODERNISM

Architectural concepts as a gateway to Norwegian cultural debate 1920-30[1]

PER ANDERS AAS

The Norwegian twenties were a decade of *conflict*. The period 1920-30 has generally been viewed in terms of polarization between conservative and radical impulses: politically, ethically, theologically. But the twenties were also a decade of *classicism*. Neo-classicism appears in academic scholarship and text editions, in poetry and the visual arts, and most visibly in the architecture of the period, where the classic style gains practically supreme reign.[2] While radical intellectuals and conservative pietists fight on the front tradition/modernity, their external environment takes on a shape that is somewhat alien to this dichotomy.

The category of the classic may not be attributed unambiguously to either side of the axis tradition/modernity. It pretends an *a*-historicity that rather may lead us to question the value of chronological concepts in capturing the period's key concerns. Is the interwar debate simply a controversy between those looking back and those looking forward, or is something more crucial at stake?

Some European theorists, even in the twenties, have advocated the idea of architecture as the foremost manifestation of the *Zeitgeist*.[3] Any notion of a general spirit of the times is of course debatable, but this immodesty on behalf of architecture may encourage us to re-question what concepts prove most fruitful in capturing the essentials of an era. What is gained if we view the Norwegian twenties not in the flashing light of combat but in the light of classicism?

Three corner styles

For some time I have been working on a project about Norwegian moral and cultural debate in the interwar period, mainly the 1920s.[4] In my thesis *Cultivation in Crisis: Classical Humanism Approaching Modernity*, I examined different strategies of facing modernity at the idealist so-called "Second front" in the debate.[5] I have studied three neo-humanists: the art historian *Harry Fett*, the poet and essayist *Charles Kent* and the literary historian *A. H. Winsnes*, thinkers that may not be smoothly adapted to the radical/conservative axis that has been the prevalent perspective on the debate. Working with the sources, I have found myself in need of models that capture their ambiguities (and the ambiguities of their time) more fruitfully than a simple dichotomy.

What I suggest is to replace the dichotomy radial/conservative with three reference points: *historicism, classicism*, and *modernism*. The three entities are not taken out of thin air, but are very visibly manifested in the architecture of the period, representing explicit but not unambiguous positions. The question is whether the tension between the three elements, not by virtue of their chronological succession but by their position as conceptual cornerstones, provides a more dynamic frame of interpretation for the interwar debate, untying the simple binary opposition tradition/modernity that has guided the reading of this period.

Norwegian interwar architecture may roughly be divided into three styles: *historicism* as expressed, above all, in the national romanticism flourishing during the first world war and shortly after, the *neo-classicism* of the twenties and the *modernism* (functionalism) of the thirties.[6] The three alternatives all represent an ideologically conscious architecture, accompanied in contemporary debate by programme statements and polemical demarcations. In the early twenties Norwegian architectural debate was marked by an alternation of generations, a confrontation between an old national (historical) and a young international (classical) wing,[7] and, entering the thirties, modernism opposing both historicism and classicism appears as part of a radical reform programme.

The national romantic *historicism* reflects the national consciousness that emerged during the 19th century, culminating with the abolition of the union with Sweden 1905. This architecture carries on an interest in the particularity of tradition that characterizes 19th century romantic historicism. *Neo-classicism* aims at greater universality; idealizing not the particular, past and national but the eternal, international and rational. Hence it anticipates *modernism*, universal and rational, rejecting, at least theoretically, all utterances that do not follow from constructive demands.

It would be very easy to view neo-classicism simply as an exponent of tradition. Recent research, however, regards this as a narrowing of perspective.[8] As stated by an art historian: Classicism is not a kind of European traditionalism; it rather appears in the decisive moment when tradition is to be broken down.[9] Instead of viewing neo-classicism as late historicism, placing the decisive break tradition/modernity close to 1930, there is now a tendency to regard neo-classicism as pre-modernism and place the crucial break around 1920, when neo-classicism succeeds national romanticism. Through moving the watershed ten years ahead, this view maintains the focus on the binary opposition tradition/modernity.

But is it this *binarity* that is most crucially at stake in the interwar debate? Is it the transition from tradition to modernity, exposed in the succession of architectural styles, or is it something else, something that may be discussed *by means* of architectural concepts?

Three core values

The three styles are visually pronounced but theoretically ambiguous. *Classicism* lives by the historically particular – antiquity – but also has a universal ambition, hence a tension between tradition and universality. *Historicism* first occurs in the 19th century as a modern, individualizing romantic-expressive anti-classicism, taking the side of particularity against universality. Nevertheless, it shares with classicism the imitation codex committing it to a given tradition, hence a compound of tradition and subjectivity. *Modernism* appears with timeless, universal ambitions, like classicism, but also accents subjective expression, hence a tension between subjectivity and universality.

So what happens if we rotate the axis and focus on three concepts that are not linked unambiguosly to the styles, but may be discussed by means of them: *tradition, universality* and *subjectivity*?

Though the three corner styles may be regarded as ideologically ambiguous, they define themselves polemically against unambiguous entities: classicism against subjectivity, historicism against universality, and modernism against tradition. In my model they do not constitute themselves dichotomically against competing corner styles but against competing core values.

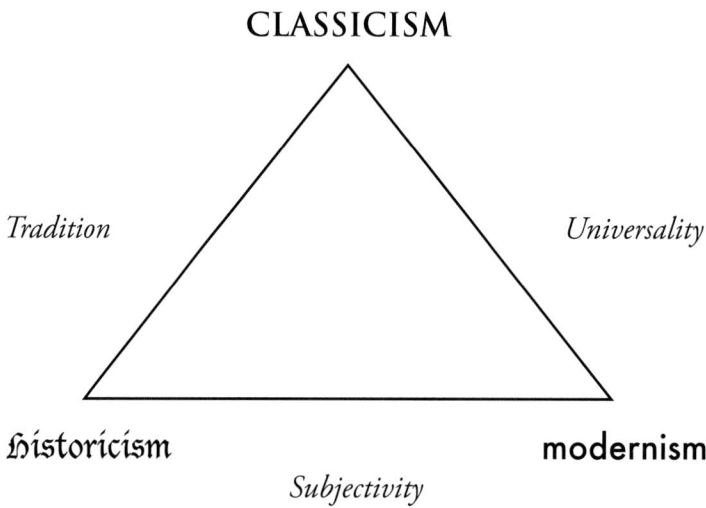

What do we learn, then, from this attempted alienation by rotation?

We are well familiar with a debate where *tradition* is at stake. Tradition is expressed in both historicism and classicism, which has led former research to focus on the breakthrough of modernism about 1930, supported by the modernists' self-understanding.

We may also be getting familiar with a debate where *universality* is at stake. Universality is expressed in both classicism and modernism, which has led recent research to focus the break around 1920, supported by the self-understanding of the old nationalist and the young internationalist architects shortly after 1920.

But we may not be that familiar with a position putting *subjectivism* at stake, treating both historicism and modernism alike. Why not?

Critical classicism

Perhaps because both historicism and modernism express modern Norwegian ways of thinking, i.e. thinking on the post-classic premises of the 19th century. This may be viewed as a hegemony of interpretation supported by strong ideological and social interests: the particularly national in political debate, the particularly psychological in moral debate (radical intellectuals versus conservative pietists).[10] But this subjectivity is exactly what classicism attacks.

Therefore, when neo-classicism appears as a strategy of cultural criticism At the "Second Front" in the 1920s, we may regard it as a fundamental attack on a hegemonic way of thinking constituted by 19th century subjectivism, i.e. a presupposition that embraces the dominant political-academic scholarly culture as well as both radical and pietist positions in the moral debate.[11]

My point is that a focus on chronology, pushed to the extreme in the binary opposition tradition/modernity, narrows our understanding of the interwar period. This applies to the discussion about when modernity starts (with neo-classicism around 1920 or with modernism around 1930), i.e. the discussion whether neo-classicism belongs to tradition or modernity. As long as our ultimate concern is this chronological binarity, the classic is reduced to an expression of transition, subsumed under something else and deprived of its alterity.

Replacing a binary model with a triangular, we may more easily recognize the classical as a self-contained entity, "wholly other" and alien to subjective ways of thinking. It combines *tradition* and universality in a time when tradition generally is occupied by particular interests (national, religious) and *universality* is emptied of moral and cultural content, both surrendered to subjectivism.

What I suggest is to apply this very conventionalized sketch, taking its starting point in architectural entities, to the interwar debate, particularly in order to understand the position of classical humanism, the "otherness" of the Second Front. This position may be viewed not as simply conservative but as combining tradition and univerality in a way that opposes both historicism and modernism but also interacts with them.

Notes

[1] This sketch is based on a paper entitled "Kritisk klassisisme: Klassisismen som kulturkritisk strategi på 'den annen front' i norsk mellomkrigstid, med særlig vekt på Harry Fett" delivered at a seminar on Norwegian Reception of Antiquity, Faculty of Theology, University of Oslo, 4 May, 1999. The historiographical discussion has been further developed in my paper, Aas (2003a).

[2] For a dicussion of classical impulses in various cultural fields of the period, cf. Skard, 128-151.

[3] On the primacy of architecture, cf. Källström, especially 136-137, 162-167 and 218-222.

[4] The work was carried out during my period as a research fellow financed by The Research Council of Norway at the Faculty of Theology, University of Oslo, 1996-2001, under the title "Hegemonies in Norwegian Moral Debate" (presented in NSD's database: http://www.nsd.uib.no/nfi/soek/get.cfm?SingleKey=7959) and has been published in my thesis, Aas (2003b). By studying the neo-humanists Harry Fett (1875-1962), Charles Kent (1880-1938) and A. H. Winsnes (1889-1972), I discuss how classical humanism, i.e. the neo-humanist ideal of cultivation (Bildung) is applied in a wide array of value orientations in order to cope with modernity. The fate of this worldview in Norwegian public debate (as opposed to the hegemonic academic culture and dominant radical and pietistic ways of thinking), and its potential confronted with upcoming anti-humanist threats, is also discussed. The employment of architectural concepts which I refer to in this presentation is not my overall approach, but it plays an important part in the sections of the thesis where I discuss the material in a historiographic perspective.

[5] For a short presentation of the "Second front" phenomenon, cf. Aas (1998). For a thorough examination, cf. Slagstad (1995), put into a larger historical context in Slagstad (1998), 392-400.

[6] For a detailed description of the three main style periods of the interwar era, cf. Norberg-Schulz.

[7] For the architectural debates, cf. Glambek.

[8] The breakthrough of a modern architecture is now by several art historians attached to the transition from national romanticism to classicism around 1920: neo-classicism is not regarded as prolonged historicism, but a predecessor of modernism. Cf. Hoel and Seip.

[9] Berczelly, 13.

[10] Gunnar Skirbekk has called attention to the hegemonic role of psychological ways of thinking in Norwegian cultural debate.

[11] This alliance is elegantly visualized in the architect Ove Bang's masterpiece, the headquarters of the Home mission (Staffeldts gt. 4, Oslo), characterized as the birth of modern Norwegian architecture.

References

Aas, Per Anders (1998) "Den annen front: idealister uten 'sak' ", in Johnsen, Egil Børre & Berg Eriksen, Trond (eds.) *Norsk litteraturhistorie: Sakprosa fra 1750 til 1995, vol. 2: 1920-1995*, Oslo: Universitetsforlaget, pp. 68-71, 702-703

---, (1999) "Kritisk klassisisme: Klassisismen som kulturkritisk strategi på 'den annen front' i norsk mellomkrigstid, med særlig vekt på Harry Fett", a seminar on Norwegian Reception of Antiquity, Faculty of Theology, University of Oslo, 4 May

---, (1996-2001) "Hegemonies in Norwegian Moral Debate" in NSD's database: http://www.nsd.uib.no/nfi/soek/get.cfm?SingleKey=7959

---, (2003a) "Modernity vs. tradition – or other axes?" in *Nordisk Arkitekturforskning/Nordic Journal of Architectural Research* 4/03, pp. 56-62, also published in Tostrup, Elisabeth and Hermansen, Christian (eds.) *(Theorising) History in Architecture*, Oslo: AHO, pp. 213-221

---, (2003b) *Dannelse i krise: Klassisk humanisme i møte med det moderne, Harry Fett, Charles Kent og A.H. Winsnes 1918-33*, Oslo: Unipub forlag

Berczelly, Lazlo (1998) "Klassisismens røtter i antikken", in Gundersen, Malmanger, pp. 11-26

Glambek, Ingeborg (1970) *Funksjonalismens gjennombrudd i Norge: Debatt og ideologisk bakgrunn*, (Mag. art.-thesis in Art history), University of Oslo

Gundersen, Karin, Malmanger, Magne (eds.) *I fortidens speil: Klassikk og klassisisme i Vestens kultur,* Oslo

Hoel, Kari (1998) "Etter 1900: En ny klassisisme – idé og debatt", in Gundersen, Malmanger, pp. 359-377

Källström, Staffan (2000) *Framtidens katedral: Medeltidsdröm och utopisk modernism,* Stockholm: Carlsson

Norberg-Schulz, Christian (1983) "Fra nasjonalromantikk til funksjonalisme: Norsk arkitektur 1914-1940", in *Mellomkrigstid: Norges kunsthistorie bd. 6*, Oslo: Gyldendal, pp. 7-111

Seip, Elisabeth (1998) "1920-tallsklassisismen: den foreløpig siste klassisismen", in Gundersen, Malmanger, pp. 378-395

Skard, Sigmund (1980) *Classical Tradition in Norway*, Oslo: Universitetsforlaget

Skirbekk, Gunnar (1984) " 'I refleksjonens mangel ...': Om vekslande intellektuelle elitar i norsk etterkrigstid", in *Nytt Norsk Tidsskrift* 1/84, pp. 21-37, (reprinted in Skirbekk, Gunnar, *Til djevelens forsvar – og andre essays*, Oslo: Universitetsforlaget 1987, pp. 63-82)

Slagstad, Rune (1995) "Den annen front – i går og i dag", in *Nytt Norsk Tidsskrift* 1/1995 pp. 12-24, (reprinted in Kolstad, Hans & Aarnes, Asbjørn (eds.), *Stemmer i tiden: Humanistisk kollegium 1. årgang*, Oslo: Aschehoug, 1998)

---, (1998) *De nasjonale strateger*, Oslo: Pax

FUSING THE SACRED WITH TECHNOLOGY
The virtual basilica of St. Francis in Assisi

DANIEL T. MICHAELS

Modern computer technology now makes possible innovative research into the communication of medieval visual narratives (illuminations, paintings, glass, stone, etc.). Scholars today are increasingly sensitive to the symbolic methodology of medieval systems of interpretation, particularly as this methodology was employed in interpretations of Scripture. The power of computer assistance allows new analysis of the complex interconnections among text, image and architecture within medieval symbolism and biblical exegesis. With this in mind, the unfinished pilot project of my current research employs technology to digitally reconstruct the basilica of St. Francis in Assisi (hereafter basilica) with an eye toward identifying the copious interconnections between text, image and space. After a brief introduction, this essay will: describe the technology utilized in the project, outline how this technology can assist theological research, and indicate future applications of the technology.

My research adds three-dimensional analysis to the previous eighty years of art historical critique,[1] architectural analysis,[2] and comparative database collection,[3] which explore the basilica's elaborate theological, artistic and architectural richness. For example, digitally reconstructing the myriad of wall-to-wall frescoes (not to mention glass and stone) in three dimen-

FUSING THE SACRED WITH TECHNOLOGY

1   Upper Church main nave, basilica of St. Francis in Assisi

sions permits one to analyze and to appreciate the dizzy complexity and the simple beauty of the basilica's many interrelated narratives. Such a study interactively demonstrates how various forms of normative patterns and rules inform the medieval practice of communicating through visual narratives.[4]

These narrative patterns were developed for at least two reasons. On one level, the sophisticated symbolic associations – scriptural, historical, theological – present within the narratives cannot be adequately expressed by strictly linear patterns alone. That is, the space of the basilica, with its various walls, windows, and tiers of art, provide a means for different narratives to communicate with each other in any direction, thereby providing the fullest possible meaning (literal and symbolic). While on the more practical level, these patterns attempted to bring understanding of such complex theological concepts to an essentially non-literate public and to the lay and cleric followers of St. Francis, both of whom worshiped in the basilica. In short, the narrative patterns are twofold: their form allows for a non-linear communication of information, while their function provides religious formation. However, the dialectic between the form and the function in the basilica's sacred space assumes several layers of biblical, theological, historical and hagiographical elements that intersect with the goal of transforming the viewer into an experiential awareness of God's presence in salvation history. Interactive technology can provide the modern viewer, who may be alienated from the medieval symbolic mindset, a helpful portal into this multilayered process of transformation.

The technology

The virtual reconstruction of the basilica utilizes a variety of architectural, artistic, and three-dimensional software applications.[5] The digital process begins with the reproduction of the basilica's geometry. The computer based vectors, or measurements that maintain the integrity of the actual Assisi dimensions are taken from Giuseppe Rocchi's exhaustive study of the basilica's architecture.[6] These dimensions are entered directly into three dimensional render and animation software via Discreet's *3D Studio MAX* (*3DS MAX*). The various 3D objects of the basilica are created such that they form levels of geometry corresponding to the actual geometry of the church. These computer drawings are initially identical to computer based wire frame architecture drawings (e.g., CAD drawings), without any images or color.[7]

The next step involves the placement – or mapping – of images, known as textures, onto the level geometry.[8] The images are first edited in Adobe Photoshop and Macromedia Freehand,[9] in preparation for insertion onto the above mentioned wire frame in *3DS MAX*. Each individual image, down to the smallest detail of the basilica is meticulously plotted onto the surface of the geometry. From within *3DS MAX*, a series of lights and surface maps for reflection and detail are applied to the textures. A process in *3DS MAX* called "ray tracing" provides incredibly realistic lighting effects,

2   Northeast corner, Upper Church main nave, 3DS MAX screen shot. Areas in gray and black are not mapped with images.

and thereby completes a near perfect reproduction of the art and geometry of the basilica within *3DS MAX*.[10]

The extent of the reality and interactivity of the software is realized when the images and geometry from *3DS MAX* are exported to a real-time three-dimensional (RT3D) gaming engine, which ultimately allows viewers to navigate the virtual basilica as if they were in the actual space – similar to

3   *Northeast corner, Upper Church main nave, 3DS MAX screen shot. Areas in gray and black are not mapped with images.*

most real-time computer games. Transfer into the 3D engine begins in *3DS MAX* through a process known as "texture baking." The "baking" process essentially flattens every image in *3DS MAX*, sort of like unfolding a box with no overlapping surfaces. The baking process peels away and saves the images from the *3DS MAX* geometry, including all of the lighting information, leaving only the original wire frame geometry from the first portion

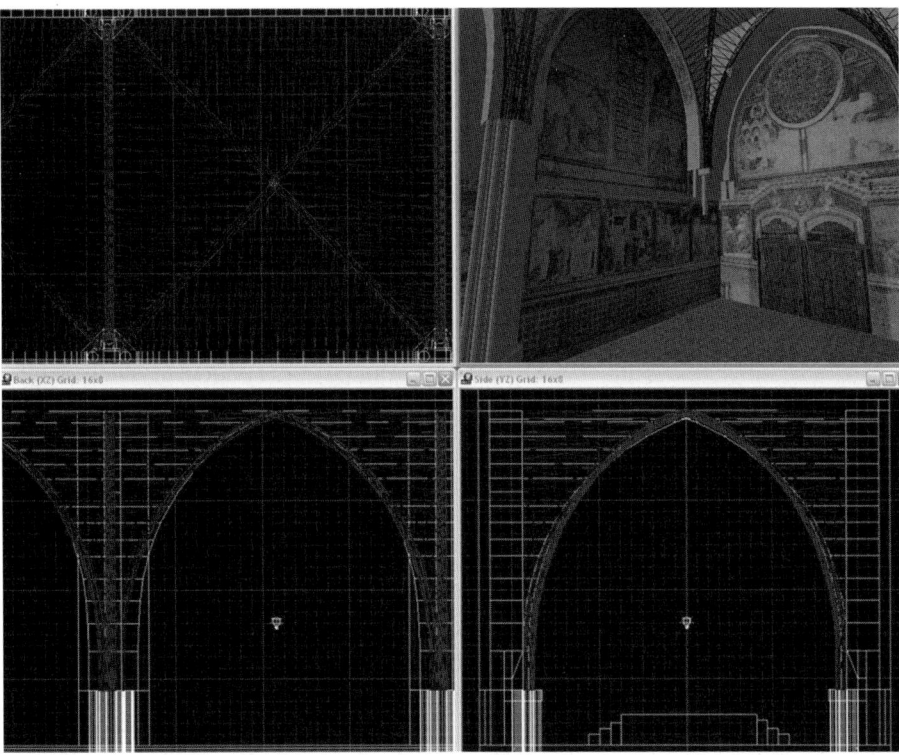

4   Northeast corner, Upper Church main nave, 3D Gamestudio 6 design screen shot

of the project. The bare geometry (wire frame) is then exported to the 3D engine, *3D Gamestudio 6* by Conitec Datasystems, California, U.S.A.[11]

The previously extracted texture baked images are then reapplied to the geometry in *3D Gamestudio* and the basilica is ready to be processed in the real-time engine. Because the images already contain lighting detail from *3DS MAX* there is no need to insert lights for the shadows and realistic effects, thereby eliminating memory intensive data from within the engine itself. Such a process drastically reduces file size and makes real time three dimensional projects of this magnitude possible, even when there are thousands of images such as with the basilica.[12]

Finally, the real time *3D Gamestudio* basilica is divided into four separate levels: exterior, crypt, lower church, and upper church. System memory is continually refreshed to allow space for more high quality textures and geometry as users moves from one level to another. In addition, hidden into each level is a series of "half levels", meaning that each level is divided into regions. As users move they encounter high resolution images within a virtual ten meter radius, and lower resolution images in the distance, thereby simulating human vision and continually reserving computer memory for the most important images – i.e., the images being viewed.

The result is a virtually exact and interactive experience of the basilica. Moreover, each sector of the basilica – every fresco and architectural segment (pillars, walls, windows, etc.) – provides access to pop-up 2D panels that provide textual analysis and virtual links to corresponding theological and architectural data and close-up images. The interaction between text and image offers viewers a guided experience of the complex theological structures that bind the frescoes and other artifacts together. Viewers may also choose to follow a preformatted tour of the narrative patterns of the basilica, or simply navigate the structure without assistance.

As mentioned above, the three-dimensional rendering of the basilica allows viewers to analyze otherwise extremely complex structures with greater ease. In fact, the digital program of the basilica actually permits examination of the interconnections and relationships among frescoes, stone and glass in ways that are physically not possible in the actual basilica. For example, objects (frescoes/glass) can be paired side by side, and/or selected segments of various structures can be processed through a numerical database applied in the system. This allows viewers to analyze the geometry of every part of the structure according to an architectural grid. Furthermore, viewers can actually float to any portion of the structure, providing otherwise impossible angles of view. A "ghost" mode also allows viewers to pass through windows, walls, and stone to discover hidden walkways, caverns, and explore every dimension of the basilica's Romanesque/Gothic structure. The result is a program that portrays a harmony of text and image, allowing a medieval artistic style to inform the intellectual tradition of today, and *vice versa*.

At present a preliminary demo of a section of the upper church of the basilica of Saint Francis in Assisi has been successfully tested. The expected completion date of the entire basilica, upper and lower churches, is August 2004.

Fusing the technology with theological research

That which makes the basilica of St. Francis unique is the most obvious, yet it is also very problematic: its form and function honor the life of its namesake. On the one hand, the basilica is covered with artistic narratives that portray and contextualize the life of St. Francis. Never before has a near contemporary been depicted in art and architecture on such a massive scale.

As such, the basilica is a visual documentary of Francis, displaying his role in the history and future of the Church. On the other hand, the portrayal of Francis in the basilica is not definitive. The artistic narratives, the earliest of which date to roughly forty years after Francis' death and the most recent completed and/or edited centuries later, are often compared to other literary and artistic sources inspired by the life of Francis: including sermons, legends, hagiographies, theological works, and in many cases, other works of the art. These writers and artists, including those of the basilica, continually articulated and rearticulated Francis' way of life, making it very difficult to single out one simple profile of Francis.[13] The basilica alone, with its two massive churches, one on top of the other, portrays Francis and his followers in a variety of historical and theological contexts through several artistic mediums, including wood, stone, glass, and paint. In addition to the explicit life of Francis, the art of the basilica was influenced by its patrons and artists such that Francis was placed within various historical and theological agendas, making his identification even more complex. Ultimately, the art of the basilica is an attempt to answer the basic questions, "who is Francis", and, "what role does Francis play in the Church."

A proper interpretation of the form and function of the basilica must critically engage historical, artistic, architectural, theological, and hagiographical evidence, the full extent of which is beyond the scope of this essay. Nevertheless, the virtual reproduction of the basilica rapidly provides access to all of these fields, allowing for some brief observations. Specifically, technology provides a lens through which I can analyze the many narrative images as part of one system.

I argue that the frescoes, stone, and glass of the basilica, both in their portrayal of Francis and the history of salvation, reveal a polyvalent image portraying a unified "text",[14] And that text, as suggested by the protocols of art and medieval exegesis, along with the Franciscan hagiographic tradition, reveals God's Word. In other words, the basilica displays the history and future of redemption – represented by Scripture – within the context of the Franciscan tradition.[15] For the medieval mind the Word of God, or Scripture, was the sole project of theology. Scripture was *the* source for understanding human sinfulness and the way to salvation. Life itself was defined by the Word. Therefore, it's not entirely surprising that Scripture played such a significant role in defining Francis and the church of his day.

The basilica's vast imagery of St. Francis, Scriptural scenes, saints, geometric and floral patterns, function as a single unit, or "unified text", composed of smaller units, that, overall, represent Scripture/Salvation history. As such these narratives should be "read" through a medieval Scriptural hermeneutic.[16] Such a hermeneutic approaches the basilica's "unified text" as a sequence of interrelated narratives that symbolically operate through four modes: literal (history), anagogical (desire/love), allegorical (faith/belief), and tropological (moral/action).[17] These medieval modes, known as the "senses" of Scripture, typically follow a complex pattern of rules which govern their application in text and art. It is beyond the scope of this essay to apply these rules in depth. The important point here is that Francis is placed into the basilica within the context of history and revelation – he joins the Scriptural narrative as a participant in the various modes, or senses of its interpretation. Francis' imitation of Christ is presented as a viable model of discipleship and the way to renewal in the Church. Ultimately, the paintings, glass and stone offer an interpretation that makes Francis and the Franciscan Order pivotal in salvation history, even ushering in a new age of peace.[18]

The resulting theological program invites the viewer, yesterday and today, to participate in salvation history through the reception of God's Word in the liturgy and the narrative artwork. In effect, this performative aspect of the sacred space has the potential to initiate the viewer to share in the mission of Francis of Assisi. The specific sequencing of narratives moves to display Francis' holiness up through the promise of salvation to all creatures that embrace God's Word.

The key then is to understand how the polyvalent sequencing of frescoes and its content mediates a specific theology rooted in the Word. It is with this complex task that technology offers great assistance in analyzing the numerous interconnecting levels of the basilica's symbolic, non-linear "visual text". To read the "visual text" three-dimensionally is to bring the text alive and glimpse its simple beauty within its sheer complexity. To read it otherwise is like trying to read a written, linear text without sequential page numbering. The technology facilitates the viewing of the basilica as a cohesive unit, or "unified text" as described above. This pictorial theology is critical for a better understanding of the medieval church in general and the Franciscan tradition in particular. When read properly, the hermeneutics of the basilica images facilitate new perspectives in the understanding of Scripture, the Order, and the craft of art in the Middle Ages.

The three-dimensional rendering of the basilica, in combination with such works as Marilyn Lavin's database analysis (see footnotes 3 and 4), New City Press' database of the new edition of the primary works in Franciscan hagiography,[19] and databases of the Vulgate and medieval theology and hagiography,[20] provides access to and analysis of a system of interpretation that until now has gone unrecognized. The utilization of technology highlights the Scriptural hermeneutic unifying the various levels of narratives (stone, fresco and stained glass) that comprise the basilica's many architectural elements.

The capstone of this project is the combination of theological research and interactive three-dimensional space into a fully integrated multimedia platform. The theological, artistic, historical and architectural information that would normally be published as a supplemental text will be embedded within the program's geometry and imagery. Scrolling over an object in the basilica will offer the option of accessing a cross-referenced database of textual information. As hinted above, this multimedia navigation will greatly assist in studying the hermeneutical method according to which medieval Franciscans framed their world in light of Scripture.[21] The investigation of visual exegesis, enhanced through computer analysis, will help demonstrate the unifying exegetical principles operative in the basilica's polymorphous organization of narratives, and ultimately help unveil the answer to the question: "who is Francis" according to the basilica?

Future application(s) of the technology

The application of this computer technology to theology and art has received national and international attention and, as such, was the inspiration for the start of a non-profit organization, the *Sacra Tech Foundation*,[22] which provides support for a combination of theological and technical tools for scholarly research in theology and its expression in visual terms. The motto of the foundation is *servare praeterita, servire futuris*, that is, "preserving the past, serving the future" by fusing the sacred (*Sacra*) with technology (*Tech*). The organization's vision is to utilize its interactive three-dimensional software to promote a deeper educational experience while also earning self-perpetuating revenue for the foundation which will disburse grants in support of Franciscan scholarship (theological, artistic, etc.). The virtual-interactive model of the Basilica of Saint Francis in Assisi is the foundation's maiden project. This pilot project forms the basis for future work on other religious centers (e.g., Assisi churches of San Rufino, Santa Chiara; the Bardi Chapel, Santa Croce, Florence; and Franciscan churches in Prato, Pisa, and Montefalco to name a few). The potential application of the software is expansive and not simply limited to architectural reproductions. All updates can be added as separate levels via Internet updates.

My hope in fusing the sacred and technology together is to reorient scholarly and popular reading of visual texts (frescoes, glass, statues, etc.) and written texts (Scriptural, theological, and hagiographical) in an effort to help articulate the rich dialogue that exists between the two. Indeed, it is my further hope that this new technological/theological approach will serve as a model for such interdisciplinary research in fields that incorporate a wider perspective than Franciscan hagiography and art alone.

Notes

[1] Major summaries of this tradition include, for example, Kleinschmidt and most recently Bonsanti.

[2] The most recent architectural description and measurements can be found in Rocchi (2002), and Bonsanti. These works are updates to Rocchi's earlier work, (1982).

[3] Lavin (1999).

[4] Lavin's groundbreaking *Place of Narrative* deals with the logic of narrative sequence in architectural space. She discusses in detail some 100 Italian religious narrative cycles, including the basilica in Assisi, beginning with the decoration of the great Constantinian churches in Rome in the Early Christian period and carrying through to the end of the 16th century. She collected the data by means of a computer database (268-89), arguing that "narrative disposition" carries a meaning of its own, intersecting with the meaning of individual narrative cycles. She identifies eight principle formats of narrative disposition (3-10).

[5] The basilica suffered a massive earthquake in 1997, destroying several of the larger frescoes in the vaults and many in the archways and walls. Many of the frescoes, while damaged, have been restored to their original location. The virtual 3D software of the basilica will offer views of the basilica before and after the earthquake.

[6] See note 2 above.

[7] It is also possible to import computer geometry directly into *3DS MAX* from architectural CAD software applications.

[8] The textures of the basilica, including all of the paintings and three dimensional structures (papal throne, pilasters, altar, etc.), frescoes and glass were provided in digital format by Fr. Gerhard Ruf, O.F.M., Conv. (*Sacro Convento*, Assisi, Italy), and Stefan Diller (Würzburg, Germany). Together, Diller and Ruf are responsible for some of the finest research and photography related to the basilica of St. Francis. Their image collection is available to the public through http://www.assisi.de .

9   *Adobe Photoshop* is an image editing program, while *Macromedia Freehand* is illustration software. Editing the static two dimensional images is critical for the success of the three dimensional process. Each image must be precisely color matched and aligned with other images. Images with curved surfaces must be distorted such that all edges are straight – upon reapplication into *3DS MAX* the images reappear curved and in perspective. Furthermore, all repeating patterns, including floor tiles, stone, etc., are carefully constructed for use in *3DS MAX*.

10 The lights and shadows created in *3DS MAX* can simulate reflections and high lights – such as one would see shining through a stained glass window – and they can be set to match specific times of the day or night. Furthermore, at this stage of the process virtual cameras can be added to *3DS MAX*, allowing for export into Apple's *Quicktime* movie format – which is a great way to deliver the medium to the Internet.

11 The geometry export is made possible through a special *3DS MAX* plug-in that translates the geometry from *3DS MAX* to *3D Gamestudio*. The plug-in is called "max2gs" and it is produced by Martin Malamud, www.malabar.tv . Martin has generously altered the plug-in to serve the complex needs of the basilica project.

12 The most common method for virtual reproductions of this magnitude uses a "module-based" system, where every segment of the space is rendered as a stand alone unit. This means that users skip from point to point with the ability to turn in any direction once they have landed. Module based programs achieve incredible resolution, but lack the interactivity of the real time environment. The virtual basilica of St. Francis preserves the look of module based programs, and adds interactivity. This innovative technique for the basilica of St. Francis was mastered by Dan Silverman, *3AM, 3PM,* Jerusalem, Israel (http://3am.web2d3.com) and George Pirvu, *Randombyte Software SRL*, Bucharest, Romania (http://www.randombyte.com). Dan Silverman and George Pirvu have also integrated a technique whereby screen resolution is toggled automatically through a series of half levels such that memory size is preserved and greater clarity achieved.

13 During the past one hundred years scholars have engaged various accounts for the life of Francis by analyzing date and authorship with respect to the earliest and most reliable sources. Commonly referred to as the "*question franciscaine*", or "Franciscan question", the debate over chronology of texts has been for the most part solved. See Solvi.

14 This is a break from the more common interpretation of the frescoes as individual segments of stories detailing the life and mission of Francis. For example, the Apse and nave are typically identified as separate units corresponding to related, but separate portrayals of the Church, Mary, the papacy and Francis.

15 For a complete analysis of this thesis see Michaels.

16 See, for example de Lubac. I propose that an understanding of medieval biblical hermeneutics, specifically as employed by Bonaventure in the *Life of St. Francis*, is a way to move forward toward greater understanding of the narrative sequence of images in the basilica of St. Francis.

17 In total these are the historical and spiritual senses of Scripture; see de Lubac.

[18] This becomes particularly evident in the theology of Bonaventure, who's *Life of St. Francis* heavily influenced the decoration of the basilica of St. Francis. Bonaventure does not explicitly use the term "salvation history", particularly as it came to be interpreted in the 19th century (*Heilsgeschichte*). Rather, he adopts an understanding of the division of time and redemption based on historical divisions of Old and New Testament. For Bonaventure, Francis was placed at the head of a new and final seventh age of beatitude. For an extensive discussion of Bonaventure's position, see Ratzinger.

[19] Francis of Assisi. New City Press will soon release a CD-ROM version of these same texts, along with a searchable Latin/English database.

[20] I refer here to the multitude of theological software applications available online and on CD-ROM (e.g., *Patrologia Latina,* Vulgate, etc.).

[21] The medieval Franciscan Scriptural worldview finds expression through a variety of sources: particularly text (hagiographical, commentary, liturgical) and image (illuminations, mural decoration, sculpture, architecture, and iconography). The basilica in Assisi represents a cross section of all these forms and, as such, serves as a model for understanding a comprehensive vision of a specific Scriptural hermeneutic overlaid with a particular Franciscan theology as especially expressed in the biographies of St. Francis by Thomas of Celano (1228-29) and Bonaventure of Bagnoregio (1257-63).

[22] For more information about the *SacraTech Foundation* visit http://www.sacratech.org .

Illustrations

1. Photo courtesy of Gerhard Ruf, O.F.M., Conv., and Stefan Diller, http://www.assisi.de
2. Photo courtesy of the SacraTech Foundation, http://www.sacratech.org
3. Photo courtesy of the SacraTech Foundation, http://www.sacratech.org
4. Photo courtesy of the SacraTech Foundation, http://www.sacratech.org

References

Belting, Hans (1977) *Die Oberkirche von San Francesco in Assisi: Ihre Dekoration als Aufgabe und die Genese einer neuen Wandmalerei,* Berlin: Gebr. Mann Verlag

Bonsanti, Giorgio (ed.) (2002) *La Basilica di San Francesco ad Assisi,* 4 vols. Modena: Franco Cosimo Panini

Francis of Assisi, (1999-2002) *Early Documents,* vols. I-IV, edited by Armstrong, Regis, Hellmann, J.A. Wayne and Short, William, New York: New City Press

Kleinschmidt, Beda (1915-28) *Die Basilika San Francesco in Assisi,* 3 vols. Berlin: Atlantis Verlag

Lavin, Marilyn Aronberg (1990) *The Place of Narrative: Mural Decoration in Italian Churches, 431-1600,* Chicago: University of Chicago Press

---, (1999) *Liturgia D'Amore: Immagini Dal Cantico Dei Cantici Nell'Arte Di Cimabue, Michelangelo e Rembrandt,* Modena: Franco Cosimo Panini Editore

de Lubac, Henri (1959) *Exégèse médiévale: Les quatre sens de l'écriture,* Paris: Éditions Montaigne

Michaels, Daniel T. (2004) *Imago ut verbum Dei: Applying Medieval Exegesis to the Façade and Counter Façade of the Basilica of St. Francis in Assisi,* Diss. Saint Louis University

Ratzinger, Joseph (1971) *The Theology of History in St. Bonaventure,* translated by Hayes, Zachary, Chicago: Franciscan Herald Press

Rocchi, Giuseppe (2002) *La Basilica di San Francesco ad Assisi: Prima, durante e dopo il 1997,* Firenze: Alinea

---, (1982) *La Basilica di San Francesco ad Assisi Interpretazione e Rilievo,* Firenze: Sansoni Editore Nuova

Solvi, Daniele (1995) "Lo 'Speculum Perfectionis' et le sue Fonti," in *Archivum Franciscanum Historicum* 88: 377-472

Used webpages

Dan Silverman, *3AM, 3PM,* Jerusalem, Israel, http://3am.web2d3.com

George Pirvu, *Randombyte Software SRL,* Bucharest, Romania, http://www.randombyte.com

SacraTech Foundation http://www.sacratech.org

PRAYERBALLS
Art objects for prayer and meditation in the dialogue between Christianity and Zen-Buddhism

1

Ball of Porphyry
2001
diameter 22-24 cm

GRETE REFSUM

Statement of problem

Dalai Lama says that to create peace it first has to be developed inside the individual human being and from the peaceful individual it may expand further to family, society and finally to the whole world.[1] All religions offer various meditative practices, techniques, or traditions of prayer that can help the individual to find her/his inner peace. After the Second World War interest in Japanese Zen-Buddhism has increased in the Western world[2] and an inter-religious dialogue between Christian and Zen-Buddhist thinking has been developed.[3] The meeting between the Christian tradition of prayer based on words with the Zen-Buddhist meditative tradition of za-zen focused on sitting posture and breathing may be enriching. In the Roman Catholic tradition of prayer the rosary and the Stations of the Cross have been central, but in our time and part of the world the practice of these prayers isdeclining. In the Lutheran tradition of Norway prayers are said or sung, but a silent meditative practice is lacking.[4] Instead Norwegians are known to "seek God in nature" rather than in church. The question is whether the Christian traditions of prayer may be developed and revitalized by Asian influence so as to fulfill the spiritual needs of people today.[5] If so, one would expect that the visual and tactile objects, such as beads, cross/crucifix and visual images used

Evolution exhibited 2003. A decade of the rosary reflecting the geological circuit and development of culture.

in the Christian tradition of prayer would change. To develop and produce such new objects intended for prayer/meditation is the challenge for artists and designers, and that is what this project is all about.

Aims of the project

By a documented production of new art objects this project aims at contributing to:
- a renewal of the Christian tradition of prayer;
- the development of Christian iconography;
- the ecumenical dialogues within Christianity;
- the inter-religious dialogue between Christianity and Zen; and
- the knowledge building and research community in the field of the visual arts and design.

Literary survey

Both Buddhist and Western Christian culture have many living artists and designers who work in their respective religious tradition.[6] There are also

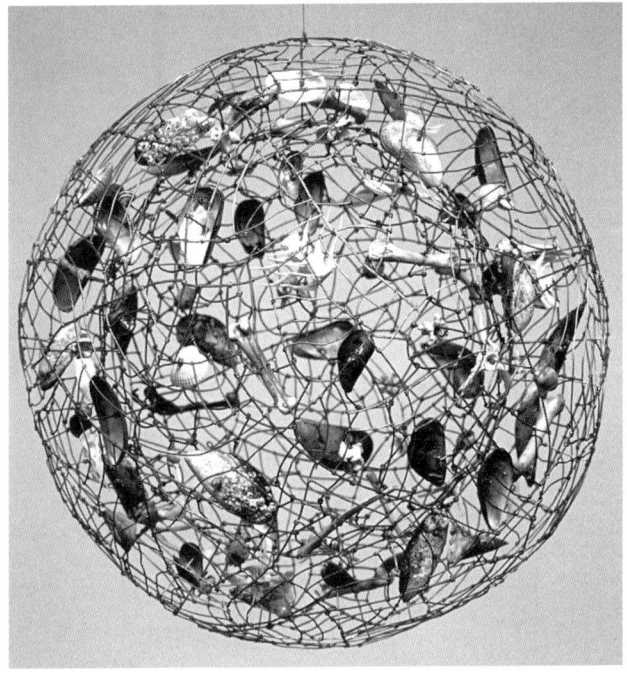

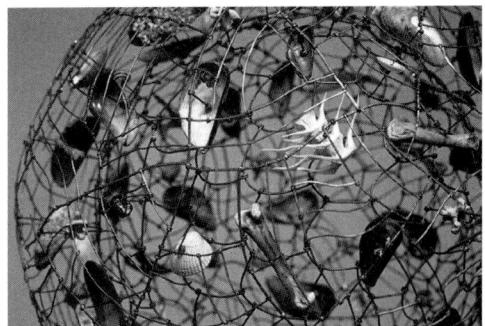

4   Detail

3

Animals 4. stage in Evolution.
Diameter ca 40 cm. metal thread,
animal remains, shells, bones etc.

numerous contemporary artists and designers who extend their culturally spiritual tradition into contemporary expressions.[7] Looking at visual images presented in literature on Christianity and Zen, however, two features are striking: first, traditional images are chosen;[8] secondly, images from the two traditions are placed side by side.[9] Images that reflect the dialogue between Christianity and Zen and new objects intended for prayer/meditation are difficult to find.

Context and ideas

In the tradition of prayer /meditation there are basically three elements:
- prayers;
- positions and methods; and
- praying objects.

In za-zen there is a sitting position, thumbs touching each other, and a focus on breathing; in the Christian tradition there are verbal prayers, standardized or personal, a lot of possible positions, as well as praying objects. However, in both Zen and Christian thinking everyday activities in

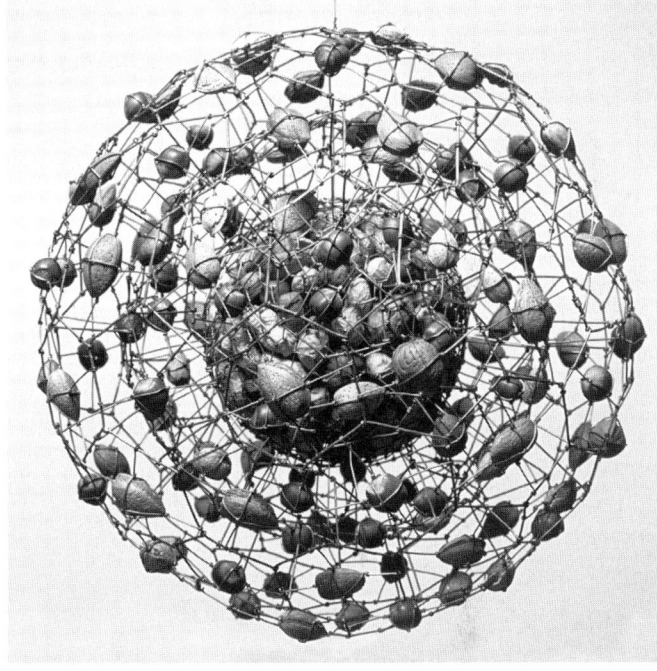

5 and 6

Stage 5. Store of food (Norwegian "forråd") various nuts, metal thread

themselves may be regarded as prayer/meditation. Since I am both culturally and spiritually Christian, the perspective in this study will be Christian. Personally, I enjoy the freedom to pray in various ways according to circumstances, and I experience my artistic work as a kind of meditation. This project adds to my previous work and continuous artistic process. I worked for seven years with the *Cross/Crucifix Series*, exploring cross/crucifix forms in order to understand more of the mystery of the cross; then another seven years on the *Small Altar Series*, sculptures made for private meditation and prayer that reflect the resurrection and the sacraments. Now, I enter a period in which I want to explore prayer and meditation by making objects that somehow reflect my meditative practice based on the Christian tradition and inspired by Zen. As a Roman Catholic, I would like to take the rosary as the point of departure. The structure of the rosary is to say a prayer while holding onto a bead, then moving on to another prayer and another bead.[10] Taken further, this structure of praying means that any prayer may be said while holding onto something.[11] By combining Christian and Zen-Buddhist traditions, I suggest that the merely holding or touching an object in silence may be a kind of prayer.

Artistic intention

The artistic intention is to produce art objects that reflect contemporary theology influenced by Zen-Buddhist thinking;[12] objects that can be seen, touched, held, or carried so that they visually and/or tactilely are an integrated part of the meditation/prayer.

Form, material, techniques

The bead, the circle, hemisphere, or ball, is taken as basis in the artistic process in combination with the dimensions of the body, particularly the hand.

The materials used will be found in nature, stone, vegetation, and traces of animals, in combination with metal wire.

Technically, my personally developed techniques of binding metal wire will be used.

Theory and method

This project is basically one of visual art, a developmental researchproject by producing art. It builds upon the theory and methodology developed in my Master and Doctoral theses. The inspirational sources will be given account for, the artistic process documented, and the results discussed.

Design of research

The project will be carried out in several phases. At the moment literary information is being collected, experiments of form, materials, and techniques are being carried out. Next, the new objects will be used in relevant milieus and the feedback will give rise to the improvement and production of new varieties.

The project resulted in *Evolution* finished 2003, see www.refsum.org.

Notes

1. Preface in Nhât Hanh.
2. The Christian monk and writer William Johnston S.J. says that: "Buddhism is going to make an enormous impact on Christianity of the coming century. If there has been a Hellenized Chritianity ... there is every likelihood that the future will see the rise of an Oriental Christianity." (Johnston, xiv).
3. See authors like Suzuki, Merton, Graham, Watts, Kennedy, Thelle, Nhât Hanh.
4. See Arvidsson.
5. See for instance Kennedy (2000) and Thelle (2001).
6. The English sculptor 20th century Jacob Epstein is a good example of the Christian tradition, the book *The Art of Twentieth-Century* Zen may represent the other tradition (Seo 2000).
7. See for instance Lin and Leung and Kaplan.
8. Kennedy (2000) uses twelfth century Chinese pictures as illustrations (5). The exception to the rule is the inclusion of a work by Jacob Epstein in his book *Buddha & Christ* (Elinor), otherwise Elinor deals with traditional artworks.
9. Typical is the frontpage of *Zen Spirit, Christian Spirit* (Kennedy 1999) that shows half Buddha and half Christ. The same is seen on the cover of the book by Elinor *Buddha & Christ* from 2000. In this connection the devotion to Holy Mary is of less importance. Cf. note 11.
10. In this connection the devotion to Holy Mary is of less importance.
11. In Orthodox Churches there are woollen prayer bands with knots on which the Jesus prayer may be said.
12. Including ecotheology (see Kristiansen) and theologies that explore spirituality as such regardless of confessional borders (as for instance Reat).

References

Arvidsson, B. (1987) *Bildstrid Bildbruk Bildlära: En idéhistorisk undersökning av bildfrågan inom den begynnande lutherska traditionen under 1500-talet*, Lund: Lund University Press

Elinor, R. (2000) *Buddha & Christ: Images of Wholeness*, New York & Tokyo: Wheaterhill

Graham, A. (1963) *Zen Catholicism: A Suggestion*, New York: Harcourt, Brace & World

Johnston, W. (1998) *The Still Point Reflections on Zen and Christian Mysticism*, New York: Fordham University Press

Kennedy, R. E. (1999) *Zen Spirit, Christian Spirit: The Palace of Zen in Christian Life*, New York: Continuum

---, (2000) *Zen Gifts to Christians*, New York: Continuum

Kristiansen, R. E. (1993) *Økoteologi*, Frederiksberg: Anis

Leung, S., Kaplan, J. A. (1999) "Pseudo-Languages: A Conversation with Wenda Gu, Xu Bing and Jonathan Hay" in *Art Journal Fall*, pp. 87-99

Lin, M. (2000) *Boundaries*, New York: Simon & Schuster

Merton, T. (1968) *Zen and the Birds of Appetite*, New York: New Directions

---, (1975) *The Asian Journal of Thomas Merton*, New York: New Directions

Nhât Hanh, Thích (1996) *Hvert skritt er fred: Kunsten å leve med oppmerksomhet og glede*, Oslo: Emilia

Reat, R. N., Perry, E. F. (1991) *A World Theology: The Central Spiritual Reality of Humankind*, Cambridge: Cambridge University Press

Refsum, G. (1991) *Kors/Krusifiks Kunsthistorisk oversikt over korsets/krusifiksets utvikling frem til reformasjonen og fremstillinger av kors/krusifiks for kirkelig bruk idag*, (Master thesis), Oslo: National College of Art and Design

---, (2001) *Genuine Christian Modern Art: Present Roman Catholic Directives on Visual Art Seen from an Artist's Persepective*, (diss.) Oslo: Oslo School of Architecture

Seo, A. Y., Addiss, S. (2000) *The Art of Twentieth-Century Zen: Paintings and Calligraphy by Japanese Masters*, Boston, London: Shambhala

Suzuki, D. T. (1973) *Zen and Japanese Culture*, Princeton N. J.: Princeton University Press

Thelle, N. (1991) *Hvem kan stoppe vinden? Vandringer i grenseland mellom øst og Vest*, Oslo: Universitetsforlaget

Thelle, N. (2001) *Zen: Lyden av en hånd*, Oslo: Gyldendal

Watts, A. W. (1973) *Zen-veien*, Oslo: Gyldendal

The Authors

Per Anders Aas
Dr., Associate Professor of Religion and Ethics, Faculty of Education, Oslo University College. He has published *Dannelse i krise: klassisk humanisme i møte med det moderne: Harry Fett, Charles Kent og A.H. Winsnes 1918-33*, Oslo 2003, and "Modernity vs. tradition – or other axes?" in *Nordisk arkitekturforskning*, 2003:4, pp. 57-62.

Gunilla Bandolin
Artist, Professor of Landscape Architecture at the Royal Institute of Technology, Stockholm, and Critic. She has arranged and participated in many Swedish, Nordic and international exhibitions, architectonic projects and manifestations; among these are *Potatodreams,* Forum, Stockholm/Museum of Jönköping, 1993, *Solomon's Well, For Frank Lloyd Wright,* outdoor earth-project at Socrates Sculpture Park, Queens, New York, 1994, *Imploded Architecture*, Forum, Stockholm, 1994, *Fluide Pheriperique,* Centre Culturel Suedois, Paris, 1997, *Artistic design of parts in a new traffic tunnel,* Södra Länken, Stockholm, competition, 2003, *Utposten,* Permanent landscape work, reclamation of granit quarry, Posten AB, Stockholm, 2004.

Sigurd Bergmann

Professor of Religious Studies (Theology, Ethics and Philosophy of Religion with Theory of Science) at the Department of Archaeology and Religious Studies, Norwegian University of Science and Technology, Trondheim. Editor of several Nordic anthologies on contextual theology and author of: *Geist, der Natur befreit: Die trinitarische Kosmologie Gregors von Nazianz im Horizont einer ökologischen Theologie der Befreiung,* Mainz: Grünewald 1995, (Russian edition Arkhangelsk 1999, rev. English edition *Creation Set Free: The Spirit as Liberator of Nature* forthcoming Grand Rapids MI: Eerdmans 2005), *Geist, der lebendig macht,* Frankfurt/M.: IKO 1997, *God in Context: A Survey of Contextual Theology,* Aldershot: Ashgate 2003, *I begynnelsen är bilden: en befriande bild-konst-kultur-teologi,* [In the Beginning Is the Icon: A liberative theology of images, arts and culture], Stockholm: Proprius 2003.

Gernot Böhme

Professor em. of Philosophy at the Technical University of Darmstadt. Gernot Böhme has lectured and published on ethics, aesthetics, the philosophy of nature, the theory of time and the theory of the technical civilisation, as well as on Kant, Plato and Goethe. Among his widely received publications are: *Alternativen der Wissenschaft* (1980), *Für eine ökologische Naturästhetik* (1989), *Atmosphäre* (1995), *Feuer, Wasser, Erde, Luft* (1996), *Ethik im Kontext* (1997) (*Ethics in Context,* 2001), *Die Natur vor uns* (2002) and *Leibsein als Aufgabe* (2003).

Pauline von Bonsdorff

Professor of Art Education at the University of Jyväskylä and Docent of Aesthetics at Helsinki University. She has published widely on aesthetics, environmental aesthetics, theory of architecture, art criticism and phenomenology. She is the author of *The Human Habitat: Aesthetic and Axiological Perspectives* (1998) and has edited and co-edited books on environmental aesthetics, everyday aesthetics and feminist aesthetics.

Birgit Cold

Professor of Architecture at the Faculty of Architecture and Fine Arts at The Norwegian University of Science and Technology, Trondheim. Lecturing and publishing within following topics: school environment; quality in architecture; sketching; the quality of research units; environmental evaluation and aesthetics, well-being and health. Birgit Cold is educated as an architect at The Royal Academy of Fine Arts in Copenhagen 1961. She has an architectural practice together with Professor T. Brantenberg and Professor E. Hiorthøy with social housing as the main field. The office has received several awards in architectural competitions. Her most recent publications are: (ed.), *Aesthetics, Well-being and Health: Essays within architecture and environmental aesthetics*, Aldershot: Ashgate 2001, *Skolemiljø – fire fortellinger,* Norsk Form, Oslo: Kommuneforlaget 2002.

Tim Gorringe
St Luke's Professor of Theological Studies at the University of Exeter, England. His two most recent publications are *Furthering Humanity: A Theology of Culture,* Aldershot: Ashgate, and *Crime,* London: SPCK, both 2004. He is also the author of *A Theology of the Built Environment: Justice, Empowerment, Redemption*, Cambridge University Press 2002.

Christiane Johannsen
DI, architect, Ph.D. student at the Department for Architectural Design, Form and Colour Studies, Faculty of Architecture and Fine Art, Norwegian University of Science and Technology, Trondheim.

Eivind Kasa
Architect, Ph.D., Associate Professor (Aesthetic Communication, Design History and Theory of Science) at the Department of Architectural Design, Form and Colour Studies, Faculty of Architecture and Fine Art, Norwegian University of Science and Technology, Trondheim. Eivind Kasa has published *Arkitekturen som kunst* [Architecture as Art] (2000), and co-edited *Forms of Knowledge and Sensibility: Ernst Cassirer and the Human Sciences* (2002).

Daniel T. Michaels
Ph.D., Saint Louis University; Executive Director, SacraTech Foundation. Daniel T. Michaels is a historical theologian with expertise in the medieval Franciscan tradition. His research explores the interaction and communication between medieval literature and artistic narrative cycles, with particular attention to the interpretation of Scripture. To understand better these narratives, he pioneered the development of a virtual three-dimensional rendering of the Basilica of St. Francis in Assisi. This innovative digital project provided the bases for an international organization, the SacraTech Foundation, which provides theological and technical tools for scholarly research.

Tom Nielsen

Architect, Ph.D., post.doc.-researcher at The Aarhus School of Architecture. He has published *Formløs* [Formless], Arkitektskolens forlag 2001, and co-edited *Urban Mutations,* Arkitektskolens forlag 2004.

Grete Refsum

Dr., sculptor, Associate Professor at the Department of Visual Arts, Oslo National College of the Arts. She works on the establishment of a contemporary Christian visual theology, and has recently edited *Forskning, utviklingsarbeid og fagutvikling i kunstfagene,* Oslo National College of the Arts Yearbook 2004.

Nancy M. Victorin-Vangerud

Rev. Dr., Executive Director at the ARC Retreat Community, Stanchfield, Minnesota, USA. She has published "Thinking Like Archipelago: Beyond Tehomophobic Theology" in *Pacifica: Australian Studies*, 16/2 (June 2003), pp. 153-172, "The Sacred Edge: Seascape as Spiritual Resource Towards an Australian Eco-eschatology", in *Ecotheology*, Vol. 6 (July 2001-January 2002), pp. 167-185, and *The Raging Heart: Spirit in the Household of God*, St. Louis, Missouri: Chalice Press 2000.

IKO - Verlag für Interkulturelle Kommunikation

Holger Ehling Publishing • Edition ZeitReise • Edition Hipparchia • Edition ÖKOglobal
Frankfurt am Main • London

Büro Frankfurt am Main
Postfach 90 04 21; D-60444 Frankfurt am Main
Assenheimerstr. 17, D–60489 Frankfurt
Tel.: +49-(0)69-78 48 08
Fax: +49-(0)69-78 96 575
e-mail: info@iko-verlag.de

Internet: www.iko-verlag.de
Verkehrs-Nr.: 10896
Auslieferung: info@suedost-verlags-service.de

Büro London
70 c, Wrentham Avenue
London NW10 3HG, UK
Phone: +44-(0)20-76881688
Fax: +44-(0)20-76881699

Aus dem Verlagsprogramm

Sigurd Bergmann
Geist, der lebendig macht
Lavierungen zur ökologischen
Befreiungstheologie
338 S., € 42,80, ISBN 3-88939-348-9

Franz Josef Stendebach
Wege der Menschen
Versuche zu einer Anthropologie des
Alten Testaments
Ethik – Gesellschaft – Wirtschaft, Band 11
346 S., € 22,80, ISBN 3-88939-558-9

Raúl Fornet-Betancourt (Hrsg.)
**Kapitalistische Globalisierung
und Befreiung**
Religiöse Erfahrungen und Option für
das Leben
Denktraditionen im Dialog, Band 9
506 S., € 39,80, ISBN 3-88939-543-0

Raúl Fornet-Betancourt (Hrsg.)
**Theologie im III. Millennium
– Quo vadis ?**
Antworten der Theologen
Dokumentation einer Weltumfrage
Im Auftrag des Missionswissenschaftlichen
Instituts Missio e.V., Aachen
Denktraditionen im Dialog, Band 7
Beiträge in Deutsch, Englisch, Spanisch
und Französisch
310 S., € 26,90, ISBN 3-88939-517-1

Norbert Arntz, Raúl Fornet-
Betancourt, Georg Wolter (Hrsg.)
Werkstatt „Reich Gottes"
Befreiungstheologische Impulse
in der Praxis
352 S., € 35,80, ISBN 3-88939- 638-0

Margarete Fujii-Zelenak
**Strukturen in den modernen
Architekturen**
Pier Luigi Nervi – Kenzo Tange
Ein Vergleich europäischer und
japanischer Architekturkultur
332 S., € 49,80, ISBN 3-88939-053-6

Sonja Nebel
**Habitat, Verstädterung und
kulturelle Identität**
Entwicklungsbedingungen kultur-
spezifischer Wohnformen in Ver-
städterungsräumen von Entwick-
lungsländern – dargestellt am Beispiel
Lusaka/Sambia
238 S., € 29,80, ISBN 3-88939-399-3

Eckhart Ribbeck
mit Sergio Padilla und Fatima Dahman
**Die informelle Moderne – Spontanes
Bauen in Mexiko-Stadt
Informal Modernism – Spontaneous
Building in Mexico-City**
356 S., € 30,00, ISBN 3-933093-25-2
Im Vertrieb bei IKO – Verlag

**Bestellen Sie bitte über den Buchhandel oder direkt beim Verlag.
Gerne senden wir Ihnen unser Titelverzeichnis zu.**